KING KONG COMETH!

Edited by Paul A. Woods

Plexus, London

All rights reserved including the right of
reproduction in whole or in part in any form
Copyright © 2005 by Plexus Publishing Limited
Published by Plexus Publishing Limited
25 Mallinson Road
London SW11 1BW
www.plexusbooks.com
First Printing

British Library Cataloguing in Publication Data

King Kong cometh! : the evolution of the great ape
    1.King Kong (Fictitious character) 2.Apes in motion picture
    3.Horror films – History and criticism
    I.Woods, Paul A.
    791.4'375

    ISBN 0 85965 362 5

Printed in Spain by Bookprint S.L., Barcelona
Cover and book design by Rebecca Martin

CONTENTS

INTRODUCTION

THE BEAUTY OF THE BEAST

By Paul A. Woods

All the little kids used to cry when the Great Ape died. For younger audience members, Kong's last stand atop the Empire State Building would be rivalled as a tearjerker only by the death of Bambi's mother.

Maybe it was a child's sense of identification with the simian behemoth. For Kong is Freud's innocent baby who would destroy the world if only he had the power, so much more sympathetic than his many nameless human victims that we hardly care about.

But it wasn't only the children. Adults in the Depression-era audience experienced vicarious joy through the Great Ape's onslaught on civilisation. However much they might have sympathised with the hapless New Yorkers whose lives were laid waste by Kong, they were more in thrall to the menacing charisma of a sixteen-inch doll.

'If Kong were purely a horrifying and horrible fellow,' reflected Fay Wray, the actress whose beauty drove the beast obsessively to his grave, many years later, 'the sympathy he evokes when finally, he is struck down, wouldn't exist . . . . Even I, seeing the film a year or so ago, felt a great lump in my throat on behalf of Kong.'

As Donald F. Glut, one of the central contributors to this book, asserts, Kong creator Merian C. Cooper 'insisted that the amount of sympathy aroused for the ape was in direct proportion to its degree of brutishness'.

Kong's creators director-producers Cooper and Ernest B. Schoedsack, were a rare breed of risk-takers who carved out a specialist niche for themselves in the formative era of documentary filmmaking. Cooper, the man who first conceived of Kong, was born in Florida in the late nineteenth century, and was akin to the last of the American frontiersmen: an explorer, soldier, journalist and opponent of Russian Bolshevism. 'Merian Cooper was a fascinating combination of high imagination, an implicitly rebellious nature, a political conservative, an intellect, an adventurer, and a visionary,' acclaimed Miss Wray, the woman he would make almost as iconic as her hirsute suitor.

(The hint of bestial miscegenation between the species is only ever alluded to, but it is the essence of Kong's quest for the unattainable. And Ann Darrow – as perfectly incarnated by curvaceous blonde/brunette Fay Wray, not yet surpassed by either Jessica Lange in the seventies or Naomi Watts today – is the essence of the unattainable. Every man/boy who ever met a woman/girl too beautiful, or delicate, or sophisticated for him, but whose dumb brute heart wouldn't stop yearning, knows what it is to be Beast to someone else's Beauty. When Miss Wray died at the grand old age of 96 – in the same month that preproduction began on Peter Jackson's *King Kong* remake – the lights that illuminate the Empire State Building at night were dimmed in her honour. For an old movie star whose screen myth has been absorbed into mainstream culture – and who never really cowered at the top of the Empire State – there was no finer tribute.)

RKO at first baulked at the oriental-sounding title *Kong*, until legendary producer David O. Selznick added the prefix *King*. While *Kong* was redolent of both *Chang* and *Rango*, it could also have been picked out of the cultural ether. *Kongo*, a 1932 African travelogue, had met with bad reviews under the impression that it was supposed to be a horror film; *Ingagi*, the notorious 1930 proto-mondo movie distributed by RKO, was produced by Congo Pictures.

By a poetic irony, Cooper and Schoedsack's most immortal creation would be born of a period when they turned their back on the diminishing little-explored regions of the globe, and even on location shooting. For *King Kong* is a monument to artifice, created almost entirely out of studio sets, miniature models and painted glass backdrops. It would come into existence as the type of film that had made a name for its creators collided with the birth of a prodigious new genre: the monster movie.

By the time Merian Cooper died in 1973, at the age of 79, his life had dovetailed with that of his fictional creation. 'I'm King Kong!' he told friend and interviewer Kevin Brownlow, one of this book's contributors. His friend Robert Armstrong, who played Denham, Cooper's alter ego on screen, had gone to his own grave only hours beforehand. And Kong had long since taken on a life of his own.

The power contained in that tiny stop-motion puppet, rendered larger than life against the artificial flora and fauna of Skull Island, was equal to that of the 1930s audience's dreams. The reverence in which stop-frame animation is held by many of the contributors to this book testifies to its primitive potency. Monsters and dinosaurs may be portrayed in more seamless movement by modern computer graphics, but there is an appositeness to the term 'animation' in the work of early special effects pioneer Willis O'Brien – who has an equal claim to Cooper to be the 'father of Kong', as stated in these pages by sci-fi/horror legend Forrest J Ackerman – his creatures were truly animated, as in imbued with life, with vitality, and personality.

The giant monster movie has long since become a stock pop-cultural cliché, something so familiar and reassuring that it's regarded as high camp. In an odd way, it's the 'second banana Kongs' (to quote Don Glut) that made the Great Ape into the cuddly pop-cultural icon he became. 'Kiko' (the son of Kong), Mighty Joe Young, even the Toho Kong in Japan, all shared much of the original Cooper/O'Brien Kong's stature but not his ferocity. The oddly docile giant ape we see parodied in countless newspaper cartoons owes more to these second-generation sons of Kong.

Though Kong never faced off against a giant Frankenstein's Monster, as announced in the early 1960s, he would make a grand sparring partner for Godzilla (though he had to grow several hundred feet to match the radioactive lizard's height) and Mechani-Kong, his own robot doppelganger. Purists sneered or cursed, and Merian C. Cooper threatened legal action (halted when it became clear there was already a done deal between RKO and Toho). Stop-motion animation was abandoned in favour of an outlandish ape suit that grew sillier with each film (*King Kong vs. Godzilla*, 1962; *King Kong Escapes*, 1967). It's hard to explain to cinematic sophisticates the appeal to a small child (as I then was) of the bug-eyed ape in *King Kong Escapes*. As absurd as he may appear in the few cinematic stills that survive, on the big screen he made an impact as a grotesque hero and a cartoon character (literally – the Toho movie was based on the Rankin-Bass Saturday morning animated show).

It's easy to mock the many cheap Kong rip-offs that emerged in later years: the Kongas, Gorgas, A*P*E*s and Mighty Peking Men you'll find in these pages also. But only someone too snobbish to ever be touched by grade-B (or grade-Z) monster movies doesn't know the strange, oneiric thrill of a bad actor hamming it up in a cheap creature costume. While none of the cheap rip-offs come within a million light years of the original *King Kong* – which is, as stop-motion expert Paul Mandell writes, 'a lavish exploita-

King and Queen of Skull Mountain: the miniature Kong atop his rocky model kingdom with a doll of Ann Darrow.

tion film which happened to work out splendidly' – there's still something about men in monkey masks that can reach a level of cheesy surrealism.

But remaking *King Kong* itself with a man in a gorilla suit was regarded as a heresy worthy of scourging by fire. The 1976 *Kong* remake is actually a piece of campy fun that functions on the level of pastiche, though the fact that it entered *Variety*'s list of the top ten box-office takers of all time, within weeks of its release, may well have convinced its producer that it worked well on every level. He would have been deluding himself.

With a post-*Jaws* eye for mainstream Hollywood spectacle, *King Kong* (1976) features a script by Lorenzo Semple, Jr. – then a scion of the screenwriting trade, now largely forgotten – that recalls his knowingly smartass take on *Batman* for the mid-sixties TV series. Almost painfully aware that, by the 1970s, everybody regarded themselves as more sophisticated than their grandparents' generation, Semple's screenplay might have worked better if it hadn't fought so shy of sincerity, of taking its premise seriously.

But instead it ensured that De Laurentiis' film would only ever be regarded as a take, a riff, a spoof on *King Kong*. The production garnered publicity by designing a vastly expensive Kong robot to scale, but only used it in one brief scene of the Great Ape standing upright and another where Kong is seen to clasp his hand. All other appearances by the title character featured makeup artist Rick Baker in the ape suit. De Laurentiis, an old-fashioned movie mogul, was conceited enough to believe he could make *his* Great Ape more sympathetic by eschewing stop-motion (a technique he found risible) and making him a besotted lover, *not* a monster. Any Kong fan could have told Dino he needed to be both.

(It's ironic that the King Kong attraction at the Universal Studios theme park in California for so many years was based not on the iconic '33 original but on the 'Dino Kong' model, neither of which was produced by Universal. The '86 sequel, *King Kong Lives* – which, like the second Toho film, was produced to the standard of a kids' TV sci-fi show – was promptly forgotten the moment it opened.)

As film historian William K. Everson, author of *Classics of the Horror Film*, complained of the Dino *Kong*'s faithfulness to its own era, 'in five years it'll be out of date . . . . The original – both in dialogue and especially in its fairy-tale-like visual design – was absolutely timeless . . . Much has been made . . . of the more sympathetic and tragic quality that Kong achieves in [the 1976] version . . . the original Kong, anti-social rascal that he was, had all of those qualities too. The old Kong was the ape world's own James Cagney . . .' All in all, a pretty radical stance for a respectable old gentleman to take – after all, the newly 'sympathetic' Kong only killed people inadvertently by stomping them underfoot, while the original model was a bloodthirsty miscreant who would literally bite your head off.

Kong is a reminder of the bestial side of ourselves. Neither good nor evil, but possessed of an indomitable will, his raw lifeforce may also be the better side of us. For Kong, whatever the privations experienced by this magnificent, lonely beast, never fails to act, to make an impact upon his environment.

'Most subsequent takes on the character emasculate Kong and plead for sympathy, but the original is stronger, taking rather than asking,' film critic and genre writer Kim Newman astutely noted. '. . . When Kong wrecks an elevated railway we cheer on that primal, fed-up-with-being-bullied part of ourselves.'

The appeal of mass destruction should not be underestimated. Long before Godzilla and his compatriots made a spectacle of stomping on toytown Tokyos and Yokohamas, Kong delighted the urban audience with an all-out assault on their environment. While his later incarnations were not as belligerent, the template for the giant monster movie was established. Read Forry Ackerman's joyful description of the abandoned Cooper-O'Brien project *War Eagles* and its 'flock of giant eagles, big as rocs, with fighting men astride their backs, attacking New York.' Most presciently, consider *Time* critic Richard Schickel's musing on the climactic scene in the '76 remake, where, instead of climbing the Empire State Building, Kong attacks the twin towers of the World Trade Centre: 'That final destructive binge could be seen and lines in the script lightly suggest it as a projection of Western fears of what might happen if the Third World should develop its potential power and strike back.' (The fact that those seemingly monolithic structures were obliterated not by a Kong-like force of nature, but by calculated malice, makes it seem all the more obscene.)

So New Zealand fantasy specialist Peter Jackson has taken on a big challenge in remaking his boyhood dream. In an age when young audiences have come to expect the impossible to be routinely performed with CGI, judged only in terms of whether space beasts and superheroes are *real* enough, he has to make an all-too-familiar pop-icon seem extraordinary again.

'Kong today is truly a loveable, nearly childlike icon who has, in many ways, become our favourite, most cherished pet,' agrees lifelong *Kong* enthusiast Steve Vertlieb. But still, after the screen fairytale has ended, the malevolence of its dark antihero remains. 'When I was a child,' Vertlieb continues, 'before I had ever seen the film, my vivid imagination painted a truly terrifying creature, stalking the streets of a great city, stimulating horror and revulsion in the hearts of its people. I can remember having nightmares of being stalked by the huge ape, and hiding in shadows to avoid my own murder and dismemberment. I'd like to see just some of that terror recreated in Jackson's film.' *King Kong* wasn't just a catalyst of dreams – as Ray Harryhausen and Danny Peary note in these pages, it *is* a dream.

Anticipation is high, but signals are mixed. 'Pete's not making a monster movie,' insists Andy Serkis, the actor who, in a complete break with precedent, has created the movements of Kong to be replicated by an entirely computer-generated image. 'He's making a character-driven story and Kong is one of those characters.'

More intriguingly, the special effects technician who has created Jackson's Kong, Richard Taylor, describes the great behemoth first encountered by Ann Darrow as 'a psychotic and lonely hobo, a street bum who is living in total seclusion . . . a tragic and broken character.' Director Jackson himself has stated his intention to 'start with the most terrifying, vicious-looking gorilla you can imagine and then start to reveal his heart, to peel the layers away.'

If Jackson is successful at revealing the lonely man inside the monster, his version of the screen dream may well have something to add. But he also needs to show us the beast inside every man. For *King Kong* is one of the few films to haunt this writer's dreams ever since I first saw it. Later cinema-infused nightmares had the advantage of full-colour violence in making their impact upon my adolescent imagination. But I had a dream that Kong had been sighted approaching the London skyline, towering above all the buildings, at least 400 feet tall, just like he loomed over NYC in the early promotional posters. While we all awaited our doom, it became clear that a primal destructive force had been released, like the sub-atomic energy that fuelled the nuclear bomb. Kong was the embodiment of all our rage and aggression – he was created by our anger, or, more specifically, he was feeding off the rage of myself, then just a boy. And, in my dream, there was nothing I could do to control him.

Kong remains king of a Darwinian universe, brought low in a world he never made. An immortal figure, a monster who was deified as a god not only by the fictional primitives of Skull Island, but by the pop culture that spawned him.

EVOLUTION

MISSING LINKS: THE JUNGLE ORIGINS OF *KING KONG*

By Gerald Peary

What strange beings inhabit the unexplored jungle regions of the earth? Carl Denham in *King Kong* was neither first nor alone in seeking answers to this alluring question. By the time Kong was tracked down and brought back alive in 1933, there had been a long tradition of sojourns into the depths in earlier 'jungle quest' movies.

A rather formalised narrative pattern was adhered to, regardless of whether the film was fictional or documentary. A party of explorers from 'civilisation' travel into the dark, foreboding tropics on some kind of scientific mission, typically aimed at challenging an ascribed-to biological theory about the area under surveillance. After the explorers have stood steadfast through a series of minor adventures and perils initiating them into the mysteries of the jungle, they are rewarded mightily for their perseverance. Before them appears some tremendous aberration of nature which undercuts the 'normal' conceptions of life on this earth.

At its simplest thematic level, the 'jungle quest' demonstrated vividly that the mysteries of the world can never be satiated; a supposedly extinct dinosaur or an unclassifiable variety of ape can storm out of the jungle growth, turning scientific belief on its head. It is this kind of inexplicable occurrence as payoff which flavours every 'jungle quest' movie, and endows this type of film (a genre?) with its inexhaustible vitality and appeal.

The lure of the jungle was felt early in the history of filmmaking, as turn-of-the-century documentarians employed by the Lumiere Brothers drifted away from well-travelled cities. Their aim was to capture on film those places where westerners never had travelled. *King Kong*'s Carl Denham echoed these early cameramen-adventurers in explaining his search for Kong: 'I'll tell you, there's something . . . that no white man has even seen. You bet I'll photograph it!'

Lumiere films were short-length 'actualities'. The world-wide favourable response to Robert Flaherty's *Nanook of the North* in 1922 made the full-length documentary a commercially viable product. *Nanook* prompted a series of expeditions to jungles and elsewhere with plans for ambitious films. Several of these projects are relevant to *King Kong*, not as direct influences but as demonstrations of *Kong*'s kinship with the more unorthodox topics of pioneering documentarians.

Bali, the Unknown: or Ape Island, made even before *Nanook* in 1921, concerned itself with the possibilities of a prehistoric 'ape man' civilisation in Bali. Even closer to *King Kong* was an untitled film much planned but never realised. In February 1925, a 29-person American crew arrived in Singapore with ambitions to capture on film a legendary 'ape man' periodically sighted in this area. Promised funding from California for the shooting never materialised. With unpaid hotel bills, the movie company was forced to give up and return home to Missoula, Montana. The 'ape man' eluded filming.

Closer to *King Kong* was *Man Hunt*, a 1926 release of FBO Studio (forerunner of *Kong*'s RKO), which followed the adventures of a real-life Carl Denham type named Ben Burbridge, who travels into Africa in search of gorillas to bring back alive in captivity. After thrilling encounters with various jungle inhabitants (elephants, pythons, crocodiles), Burbride accomplishes his task, catching six gorillas for his return to civilisation.

The thread between *King Kong* and 'jungle quest' documentaries is explained a bit by the knowledge that Merian C. Cooper and Ernest B. Schoedsack, co-directors of the movie, broke into film as part of the post-*Nanook* documentary rush. They were employed as cameramen and artistic advisors for Captain Edward Salisbury on his travelogue called *The Lost Empire*, adventures in the South Seas, Ceylon, and Arabia, and for *Gow, the Headhunter*, set in the Fiji Islands. Both were made circa 1924, though not placed in general release until five years later.

Far more significant as a career move was a decision by Cooper and Schoedsack to collaborate with famed newspaperwoman Marguerite Harrison on the film called *Grass*, which followed a tribe of Iranian nomads on a 48-day trek through the mountains. The object of this rugged journey, made annually by the tribe, was summer grassland for their flock, a more sober, pragmatic aspiration than that featured in most 'quest' pictures. *Grass* was released by Paramount in 1925, and widely praised for the anthropological seriousness of the filmmakers.

Paramount financed a second faraway filmic journey for Cooper-Schoedsack, to make *Chang* (1927) in the Siamese jungles. The somewhat parallel locales between *Chang* and *King Kong* was one shift by the two filmmakers, working without a third collaborator, toward future interests. More salient was their qualifying of the documentary with fictional elements. The cast and environment were authentic; the plot was pre-planned and fabricated. A third element to note: Cooper-Schoedsack used a member of the simian family as an essential ingredient in the narrative. Providing comic relief was a gibbon monkey, Bimbo.

Chang surpassed expectations by Paramount for profits from an esoteric semi-documentary. Cooper and Schoedsack were rehired immediately for an expensive fiction film, an adaptation of A. E. W. Mason's *The Four Feathers*, a Kiplingesque novel of betrayal and redemption in the British Foreign Service. The co-directors journeyed to Africa for authentic location photography, then returned to Hollywood to shoot the romantic story with Hollywood stars.

Cooper later claimed that he thought first of the giant gorilla that would evolve as Kong while shooting the African sequences of *The Four Feathers*. One scene of a jungle fire might have stuck in mind, in which flocks of adult baboons battled for safe spots high in the trees. In the Hollywood sections of *The Four Feathers* was a second link to what would be *Kong*. Appearing on camera thousands of miles from the baboons was a very young actress, Fay Wray. Was this budding starlet already envisioned by the filmmakers as the future object of Kong's desire?

Schoedsack, minus Cooper, made another semi-documentary of the *Chang* variety at Paramount, the all-silent *Rango* (1931), shot in the jungles of Sumatra with a native cast. Again, simians figured prominently in the tale. Rango, the titular hero, is an ourang-outang who is slain by a tiger, leaving his father, Tua, to mourn him up in the trees. The poignant moments of grief prefigured the melancholic demise of Kong several years after.

All these years, there was a simpler, less hazardous way to make 'jungle quest' movies than by travelling into the tropical wilds. That was the method of Georges Melies, who demonstrated early in cinema the almost limitless means of simulating reality without ever

Merian C. Cooper, creator of King Kong, *on location for* Chang *(1927), with co-star Bimbo the gibbon.*

leaving his Paris studio. It was Melies' development of the essential ingredients of trick photography – rear projection, single frame shooting, elaborate miniature models – which would become the basic tools of future 'jungle quest' fantasies. That King Kong, for one, moved at all, much less with animated grace and facial character, must be attributed ultimately to Melies' stop-action wizardry.

Melies' choice of Jules Verne-type narratives for his most popular narrative films (*Journey to the Centre of the Earth*, *A Trip to the Moon*, etc.) prefigured analogous 'jungle quest' movies, in which scientists went exploring and met with uncanny adventures. Finally, credit must go to Melies for his life-time insistence that the realm of the fantastic was appropriate subject matter for cinema.

Unlike Melies, the first 'jungle movie' cycle of narrative films in the USA, in 1913, relied on naturalistic elements to establish verisimilitude. *Beasts of the Jungle*, the three-reel Solax picture which spurred the cycle, mixed in with its actors an imported menagerie of two lions, a tiger, a monkey, and a parrot. Alice Guy Blache, who ran Solax, publicised the picture extensively, anxious to recoup an investment of $18,000 in the production. *Beasts of the Jungle* was 'the first picture in which as many different animals have been used . . .' and ' . . . in which the performers appear in the scenes with the wild beasts.' The publicity paid off, and other studios quickly made jungle films, a cycle capped at Famous Players by Adolph Zukor's extravaganza, *Captain Kearton's Wild Life and Big Game in the Jungles of India and Africa*.

In 1912, Edgar Rice Burroughs, who never had been to Africa, contributed to *All-Story* magazine an elaborate and brilliant jungle adventure story entitled *Tarzan and the Apes*, a literary work equivalent in imagination and in creative geography to Melies' films. Tarzan stories were sensationally popular, and, in 1918, the gargantuan D. W. Griffith muscleman, Elmo Lincoln, was called to the Louisiana location for the making of *Tarzan of the Apes*. Soon, Lincoln emerged as the first star of 'jungle quest' fantasies. Contemporaneous was the unveiling of the form's artistic genius, special effects expert Willis O'Brien.

In line with Melies, O'Brien constructed his own imaginary studio universe; his was a kind of magical Stone Age mixing of aboriginal men and prehistoric monsters. Designs for the Edison Company were prescient of his legendary conceptions for *King Kong*. Experimenting with clay models and stop-action photography, he masterminded a series of five-minute cavemen shorts featuring mobile, animated prehistoric animals in deadly combat. The first of these, *The Dinosaur and the Missing Link* (1914), offered a sneak preview of the battle far ahead of the fierce tyrannosaurus and Kong.

The apeman (Bull Montana) in The Lost World *(1925) – the film universally regarded by cinema historians as the prototype for* King Kong.

Also before *King Kong*, and essential to what *Kong* would be, was O'Brien's key silent-era designing assignment. He was hired for the Hollywood version of Sir Arthur Conan Doyle's novel, *The Lost World* (1925), which featured episodes in which the twentieth century explorers in South America rubbed against lost-tribe ape men and dinosaurs. O'Brien's inspired vision of this land-that-time-forgot, untapped Amazon would be reiterated in his conception of *King Kong*'s Skull Island, set in untracked waters of the South Seas. Not only do the two filmic locales share topography and inhabitants – primitive men and dinosaurs living in proximity – but the existences of these mutant environments can be explained by the elaborate *faux* scientific theory postulated in *The Lost World*, the novel.

Conan Doyle argued the possibility of a freakish land in which Darwinian processes had been so jolted that evolution moved forward and yet was suspended at the same time. There, creatures of various genetic evolutions and from various periods of the earth's life coexisted, including the ostensibly extinct: dinosaurs, 'ape men', long-disappeared Indian tribes. Survival of the species was the central issue of existence, occurring in many guises every tumultuous moment of the day. The Lost World was a land in upheaval, a shrill, screaming bloodbath answer to the prevailing romantic notion of a hidden, eternally tranquil sanctuary somewhere in nature. (Likewise, embattled Skull Island would prove the obverse of a Golden Age land.)

O'Brien's 'dinosaur-eat-dinosaur' jungle environment for *The Lost World* took its visual cues from the lucid, detailed descriptions of Conan Doyle. The final London sequences, in which the explorer party return home, found O'Brien expanding far beyond the brief paragraphs which abruptly halted the book. Doyle had offered up a single, tiny-sized pterodactyl, which flew about London for a bit before heading homeward to South America. O'Brien added to the British finale his most phenomenal animated creation to this point, a 120-foot brontosaurus, which escaped into the streets, created havoc among the populace, caused Tower Bridge quite literally to fall down under its weight, then swam up the Thames to disappear into the sea.

As noted earlier, Merian Cooper claimed conception of the creature, King Kong, while making *The Four Feathers* in 1927. But a better candidate for the inspiration comes through Willis O'Brien and *The Lost World* with its lost-in-time behemoth stumbling through the London streets, unleashing destruction with every step, so much like what Kong would do to New York. The brontosaurus even stuck its head through a third-storey window, an action so novel as to be repeated in *King Kong*, when the giant gorilla comes looking for Ann Darrow in the upper storeys of a hotel. And the brontosaurus's collapse through Tower Bridge, the city's most iconic public site? O'Brien brought the scene back, transformed into Kong's Empire State Building tumble.

An even more literal link in *The Lost World* to *Kong* was the 'ape man' of the movie, which chased the Londoners about the Amazonian jungle. Although played unconvincingly by an actor in painted makeup and furpiece attire, this character was at the centre of an episode so close to what occurs in *King Kong* that there can be no mistaking the *Lost World* source. When *Kong*'s Driscoll and Ann fled the mighty ape by climbing down a rope and dropping into the waters far below, they echoed Edward Malone's *The Lost World* escape by rope from the ape man down the side of a steep plateau. In both scenes, the excitement comes from the primate adversary taking hold of the rope and pulling it back, hand in hand, toward the top of the ravine. At the last moment, the dangling heroes in both films loosen their grasps and fall to safety, avoiding being mauled by the jungle beast at the top.

There is a far more obscure literary source than Conan Doyle which also affected the future shape of *King Kong*, a 1927 pulpish gothic mystery, *The Avenger*, one of the 173 novels of British author Edgar Wallace. He would go to Hollywood in 1931 and cooperate with Merian Cooper on the 'idea' of *King Kong*. Wallace also composed a completed early script version of *Kong* before dying suddenly in 1932, several months before the picture went into production. If not as essential a source as *The Lost World*, Wallace's *The Avenger* managed a modest influence on certain plot elements of *King Kong* and seems to have introduced sketchy versions of several of *Kong*'s characters.

In Wallace's novel, a movie company travels on location to the gloomy English provinces (Skull Island). Jack Knebworth, movie producer (Carl Denham), reaches among the anonymous extras on his movie and brings forward a new star, beautiful Adele Leamington (Ann Darrow, Denham's soupline discovery). Adele is plagued on the set by a mysterious ourang-outang named Bhag (Kong), who chases her across the provincial terrain.

And what of movies made without any of the *Kong* party? *Stark Mad* (Warner Brothers, 1929) was a 'jungle quest' fantasy which is lost today. That's unfortunate for film history, because descriptions suggest a genuine influence on *King Kong*. One scene from the plot summary sounds particularly relevant: an expedition into the South American jungles enters a Mayan jungle to find a gigantic ape chained to the floor. *Ourang* (Universal, 1930) was a film seemingly never released. If it followed true to its advertising campaign, *Ourang* would have been ahead of *King Kong* for its bestial sexual theme in its story of a woman carried off by ourang-outangs through the jungles of Borneo. A Universal ad in *Variety* showed an attractive female struggling in the arms of a large primate, three years prior to the subjugation of Ann Darrow.

About this time, Willis O'Brien teamed for the first time with Merian C. Cooper, working on a *Kong* prototype called *Creation*, about a shipwreck on a mysterious island filled with dinosaurs. A bit of this film was shot, then abandoned; Cooper wasn't happy yet with his story.

By 1930, the *King Kong* project was forming from at least three directions: from Willis O'Brien's *The Lost World* experience, from Cooper-Schoedsack's in-the-field documentary work, from Edgar Wallace's *The Avenger*. And jungle movies were suddenly so much in vogue that *Variety* commented in January, 1930, 'So many people are going into woolly Africa with cameras that the natives are not only losing their lens shyness but are rapidly nearing the stage where they will qualify for export to Hollywood.'

The cycle culminated with a tremendous box office hit, *Trader Horn* (MGM, 1931), shot in spectacular fashion, and with 92 tons of technical equipment, by W. S. Van Dyke on African location. The time was ripe for *King Kong*, though what was needed was an interested studio. The infamous *Ingagi* incident of 1930 served as catalyst for RKO's commitment to such a project.

In April, 1930, representatives of 'Congo Pictures, Ltd.' walked along Market Street in San Francisco offering the theatres purchase rights to a picture, *Ingagi*, said to show

The native jungle tribesmen of Skull Island line up behind Cooper, Fay Wray, Ernest B. Schoedsack and (foreground) stop-motion effects pioneer Willis O'Brien.

footage of Sir Hubert Winstead of London's sensationalist travels into the Belgian Congo. Every theatre but one turned down the film as a fake. The Orpheum decided not only to exhibit *Ingagi* but to promote it vigorously. A tabloid newspaper filled with stills from *Ingagi* was distributed door to door in the area of the theatre. A jungle exhibition was set up in the lobby. The Orpheum brought in $4,000 worth of business the opening day, an unprecedented $23,000 for the first week. RKO Studio, owner of the Orpheum, picked up national rights, and soon *Ingagi* was playing everywhere. It doubled house records in Seattle, was termed 'the talk of the town' in Chicago, and soon was among the highest grossing films in the USA.

'Photography is poor,' said *Variety*. 'Accompanying lectures, synchronised on the film, are supposed to have been done by Winstead, but the speaker uses a plain American accent.' None of this mattered to the public, nor the fact that three-fourths of the picture was taken up by tired stock shots of elephant herds, hippopotami, and sundry animals scurrying about the jungle. Real attention was directed to *Ingagi*'s last ten minutes, which showed an African tribe of completely naked 'ape women' (though obstructed from full view by strategic thickets) sacrificing one of their woman to a gorilla. *Ingagi* publicity centred on this final scene, shamelessly foregrounding the erotic aspects of the sacrifice, the perverse implied union of woman and jungle animal.

Audiences kept coming, prompting several Better Business Bureaus to appeal to the watchdog Hays Office to investigate the suspicious-looking documentary footage. In May, 1930, the Hays organisation announced its findings: 'Congo Pictures, Ltd.' never once stepped out of the West Coast in shooting the movie. 3,000 feet of the movie was duped from an ancient documentary of the Lady McKenzie expedition called *The Heart of Africa*. The sacrificial ending was filmed with Caucasian actresses in blackface at California's Selig Zoo. Following a conference at the Hays Office, RKO pulled *Ingagi* from all its houses, ending its brief but lucrative run.

Ingagi had done so well that promoters everywhere had scurried about for silent-era jungle documentaries to be dubbed with sound and re-released. But *Ingagi*'s withdrawal motivated filmmaking to go in other genre directions, to the 1930-31 gangster cycle, for example. Only RKO kept in mind the potential profits in combining gorillas, eroticised women, and the extra ingredient of ritualised sacrifice. In 1931, Willis O'Brien, Ernest Schoedsack, Merian Cooper, and Edgar Wallace were all busily employed at RKO. *The Four Feathers'* actress Fay Wray would join them in 1932, and also credited screenwriter, Ruth Rose. *King Kong*, at long last, was just around the corner.

CHANG

By Kevin Brownlow

The exception to every rule, *Chang* (1927) was no more a documentary than *King Kong*. It was conceived as a spellbinding 'natural drama', utilising the central family missing from *Grass* and depicting that family's struggle against the jungle.

Sequence by sequence, the picture was planned to seize an audience by the hair, to excite them as no ordinary film had ever excited them. And the magic works today. *Chang* is the audience picture supreme. Its slow start lulls them into condescension; its savagery takes them unawares. The rhythm builds, with sights unfamiliar despite the hundreds of wildlife pictures since, to a climax that belittles such publicity terms as 'stupendous'. As a piece of film craft, it is masterly and stands far beyond the other documentaries in that regard. But since it was not an unrehearsed record of real life, it was hard to categorise, harder still for historians to praise. *Chang*, overshadowed in Cooper and Shoedsack's career by *King Kong*, was cast aside, to join the ever-growing legion of lost films.

No script existed for *Chang* – and no title – when the two men set off for the jungles of Siam. They had the support of Jesse Lasky and some firm ideas about what they were going to shoot. When they arrived in Siam, they set out on location trips, each covering a separate area. Schoedsack went to Saigon, but reported little of interest apart from French professional hunters' camps. Back in Bangkok, they enquired about the most likely areas for tigers and elephants; they were told that tigers no longer existed in Siam. But some Presbyterian missionaries disagreed with the official view. 'Tigers?' they said. 'Plenty of tigers up at Nan. Last winter they killed nineteen people.'

Schoedsack set off for this location, while Cooper investigated South Siam. 'Without the missionaries we couldn't have done anything,' said Schoedsack. 'They supplied us with carriers and interpreters, and did everything for us. Of course, they were surrounded by nice Christians, but they were a good crowd.'[1]

Schoedsack's first encounter with the jungle was a route-march of a hundred miles along the trail to Nan. One night after he had shared dinner with an elderly missionary, there was a disturbance on the path in front of them. A leopard burst from the undergrowth and bounded away. 'Well,' said Schoedsack, 'this looks like a good place. What about tigers?' The missionary replied that several tigers had been reported in that area – all of them man-eaters. From a little one-wire government telegraph station, Schoedsack wired Cooper to come on up.

The missionaries provided the men with a deserted house, and helped them find local people to play in the film. The family was put together artificially: The mother, Chantui, was the wife of one of the carriers. The children, Nah and Ladah, came from other families. The husband, Kru, was the local carpenter. And there was a pet gibbon – Bimbo.

Cooper was kept occupied during these early days building traps for tigers. These were glorified rat traps, baited with live animals. One day a tiger was reported in a trap at the Kamuk village, and the villagers were afraid he might break out. While Schoedsack jumped to the task of getting the boats ready to send upriver with a cage, Cooper, Muang the interpreter, and Douglas Collier, a young missionary doctor, set off into the gathering darkness of the jungle on ponies.

'Neither Collier nor I had ever caught a tiger before,' wrote Cooper in *Asia* magazine. 'The few natives who had trapped tigers and leopards had always stabbed or shot them to death in the trap without attempting to remove them until they were dead. So we had to figure out our own method.'[2]

When the boats arrived with the cage, the villagers looked at it and laughed. 'The tiger will jump out of it,' they said. Cooper realised it was too weak and had it strengthened in a hurry. The next problem was how to persuade the tiger to leave the trap and enter the cage. The villagers tied trap and cage together. Anticipating that the cage would make the canoes top-heavy, Cooper had arranged for thick bamboo poles to be fastened to the sides to act as outriggers. The cage was lowered and the canoes cast off. Cooper and Collier, relaxing in folding chairs, congratulated each other. Ten minutes later, a tropical storm burst upon them – thunder, lightning, and torrents of wind-lashed rain.

Cooper wrote: 'Above the sound of the storm, a new noise struck my ear. Something gnawing wood, mixed with deep growls and grunts. A sound of something ripping. 'Now what in hell is that?' I grabbed Collier's flash light, jumped on the outrigger, almost knee-deep in water as it swung low with my weight, and hanging on the side of the cage, peered down. Then I jerked my head back like a shot. One log had been clear gnawed away or jerked out, another, half-way out. There, staring into my eyes through the ruin, were two big green eyes, and below them was a flash of red jaws filled with white teeth.'[3]

Collier and Cooper worked hard fastening logs into the gap. In five minutes the tiger had pulled them into the cage. They fastened more. Again the tiger destroyed their work. They could hardly hear each other above the roaring of thunder, rain, and water.

'Just as we began working the third time, the boat stopped with a shock and almost overturned. We were aground. The boatman had found it impossible to see the way, and the boat had run on a shallow near the middle of the river.'[4] Collier saved the day. He had brought a bottle of chloroform with him, 'just in case we might want to put the cat to sleep.' Cooper had ridiculed the idea, for in laboratory tests, feline animals had been set crazy by chloroform. But now he was ready to try anything. Climbing onto the outrigger, Cooper thrust a bamboo pole into the jaws of the tiger, while Collier poured down a shot of chloroform.

'The tiger gasped and coughed, but jerked the bamboo out of my hand and into the cage, where we could hear him chewing it to pieces in an excess of rage. Then he came back again, trying to tear his way out. We repeated the dose and the tiger repeated his performance. But the third time he didn't come back for more. He lay quiet, grunting and breathing hard, long enough for us to patch up the side of the cage again.'[5]

Cooper and Schoedsack gained their knowledge about tigers through such practical experience. They discovered that many of the facts in supposedly authoritative books were not correct at all. 'The books tell you no tiger jumps over eleven feet high,' said Schoedsack, 'so for the shot where the tiger leaps up the tree, I built my platform at thirteen feet. I think he jumped about twelve and a half.' The tiger literally nudged the lens, and since the Debrie was provided with a lever for such a purpose, Schoedsack calmly

The stalking tiger in Chang. *Like Denham in* King Kong, *Cooper felt no compunction about putting co-director/cameraman Ernest B. Schoedsack (or himself) in danger.*

pulled focus to ensure a crisp rendition of this magnificent close-up. 'There was nothing else I could do, so I figured I might as well keep on cranking.'

Cooper covered Schoedsack with a rifle whenever risk was involved. They began the expedition with a Springfield, which was not powerful enough to kill a tiger. Schoedsack acquired a heavier, Belgian-made gun during his trip to Saigon. It proved to be of limited value, for once fired it could not be used again until it had cooled.

'I knew nothing about tigers,' said Schoedsack. 'For the first tiger we beat out, I had the camera platform surrounded by barbed wire. I didn't know at the time, but any cat animal can go through anything that his skull can go through. This tiger saw me, rushed at me and got his head through the wire and his paws on the platform. I yelled at Coop – "Don't shoot . . . it's our only tiger!" Finally, the tiger ran away.'

They learned, too, that a tiger would not always follow through on a charge, unless the victim turned and ran. 'He stops about ten feet away, with a roar like a Ferrari racing car. That's his trick. We tried it with the dummy, and when the dummy didn't flinch, he'd generally turn away. Sometimes, when we yanked on the rope and the dummy moved, he would jump – and we could see how he attacks. A tiger holds and bites the head off. A lion strikes with his paws. A leopard is the worst of the lot. He doesn't stop for anything. In the shot of the dummy over the covered pit, you can see how they attack. They jump on the victim, and bite at the face while the hind feet are tearing the intestines out. I timed them with frames of film, and their take-off speed was 47 miles an hour. And they always seemed to go for a man with a gun.'

The approach for *Chang* was to achieve dramatic realism by observing how certain things happened and then causing them to occur again for the camera. Cooper separated a mother elephant from her baby and tied the baby to a house. With the camera ready, the mother was set free. 'She came like a bat out of hell. She just wanted to free her baby, and there's nothing staged about that. I knew she would get the baby loose – but I didn't know she was going to tear down the house.'

The actual method used to obtain the startling animal scenes remained a secret Cooper steadfastly refused to divulge. He came upon it, he said, in a book published in the early nineteenth century. This device, which he termed his invention, was tested first with the film's two children. 'I was practising running the children across, and releasing the leopard when they were in complete safety. Unfortunately, the native in control of the box must have released the leopard, being in a safe spot himself, not realising that I had given no signal. The leopard went right for the kids. For once I didn't kill with one shot – I wounded the leopard, and he crawled into the brush. The kids ran like hell. I followed him into the brush. I was on my belly, because you couldn't see much in there. I just saw his eyes as he jumped at me, and I shot him in mid-air, or mid-brush, and he landed with his paws either side of my head. I was very thankful the two kids weren't hurt. I don't think I ever told anyone about this. I was too ashamed.'

Schoedsack brought his Debrie camera, the veteran of *Grass*, and augmented it with a metal-cased Debrie purchased in Paris; in these tropical conditions, the metal-cased camera proved marginally superior. He had ordered panchromatic film especially wound for a Debrie, emulsion out, and packed for the tropics. The film was in 400-foot cans, sealed with adhesive tape, and placed in a 1,000-foot can, the edges of which were soldered. On location, the outer can was opened with a can opener, the smaller one placed in a changing bag. But Schoedsack received a shock when he ordered fresh stock from the United States. 'When I opened the first pack, do you know what those stinkers had done? They had electrically welded the 400-foot cans. The only way to get them open was with a can opener. That meant ruining the outer layer of film. And the only place to open

The elephant stampede in Chang. *The rescue of a villager's baby in this scene is the blueprint for the rescue of a Skull Island native's baby in* King Kong.

them was the changing bag. The bag never got dry between the perspiration and blood from my hands off the jagged edges of the can. You were lucky if you got 300 feet out of a 400-foot roll. Pull it out, and it stuck in the jagged tin. That's the way the picture was made.'

The all-pervading mildew threatened film and machinery; Schoedsack invented a tropical drying pack that worked well, using blotting paper soaked with calcium chlorate, baked crisp and placed between wax paper so that it would not come into contact with the film. This dried out each roll. The cameras and lenses were kept in boxes and the same technique used.

The major sequences with the elephants were shot at Chumphon, in the south. Cooper went ahead via Bangkok to handle the arrangements, and Schoedsack escorted their little family – Kru, Chantui, and the two children. 'It was the rainy season at Nan, and of course all the relatives wanted to come with us. They'd never been away from home. I had to march them a hundred miles in five days to the railway. They'd never seen a railway. The train ran alongside the ocean, and they'd never seen the ocean, so that was another big thrill. At Bangkok, the missionaries took care of them.'

No one was allowed to kill an elephant in Siam, although trapping was permitted. Thousands were in captivity, thousands more roamed the jungle in wild herds. Each area had its own method of trapping.

It was only through Prince Yugala of Lapburi, brother of the King of Siam, that Cooper and Schoedsack were able to secure the elephant sequences at all. The authority of the royal family was absolute; the King was supreme law and could make and unmake laws at will. The King had his own private herd – it could trample fields and villages with impunity. Nobody could interfere. This is what gave Cooper the idea for the climax of *Chang* (the title itself means 'elephant'), when a herd of 300 elephants destroys a village.

A pit was dug in the soft sand, and covered with logs, level with the earth. A heavy stone was placed on top. 'I should have had a still of that place,' said Schoedsack. 'It looked like a grave. We camouflaged the pit with brush. I'm cranking away through the little hole, and the elephants are coming, and I'm hoping they'll step around the pit. Just a few of them get over, and they start kicking the camouflage all over the thing, and they cut off the view. I think they did a war dance on top. The pit only sank a couple of inches. I didn't know what I had, but it was enough. The worst part was the heat and the stench – swimming in my own sweat and smelling 300 elephants at close range.'

During this period, Schoedsack was suffering from malaria. It was the hottest part of the year, and they had a very crude, rough camp. To make things worse, a cholera epidemic broke out among 700 men invited to round up the elephants.

Having observed the elephant drive, they decided to use native labour to construct a kraal for the film, somewhat larger than the one they had seen, and built in the open. Schoedsack had a platform built in a high tree, and he photographed much of the scene from this vertigo-inducing height, while still suffering from malaria. (He suffered sunstroke no less than five times, and has been allergic to sun and heat ever since.)

One method of hunting elephants used in the film came from *Macbeth* (via *The Covered Wagon*), rather than reality. The Siamese concealed themselves behind bushes, and advanced like Birnam Wood. Cooper said they liked the idea so well they adopted it, and it thus became authentic.

Despite all their experiences, Cooper and Schoedsack were high in their praise for the Siamese. 'The Siamese and the country Turks are my two favourite people,' said Schoedsack. 'It was such a calm, peaceful place in those days. What it's like now, I hate to think.'

Schoedsack with tribesman Kru, his wife Chantui and child. None of the 'cast members' were really related, as Chang *was as contrived as any Third World mondo movie.*

Disaster was narrowly averted during the developing of the film. In a normal climate a photographer would stop down and use the smallest diaphragm in bright sunlight. But Schoedsack found that the contrast was too high. He discovered that the best results were obtained by working wide open – overexposing the film, but using a soft developer.

An American living in Bangkok operated a local newsreel and had a small laboratory. He showed some of his work, and it seemed to be good, so Cooper and Schoedsack entrusted him with the precious negative of the elephant stampede. Their film was normally sent back, undeveloped, to Paramount, but before they themselves left for the United States, they wanted to ensure that the big scene was all right. It would have been, if they had not taken this precaution. 'The newsreel man proudly sent me back in an envelope some samples,' said Schoedsack. 'I held them up to the sun. I could hardly see through them. I'm afraid he ran out of ice, went out for a drink, and the stuff boiled. A lot of it was so heavy that a copper sheen had developed on one side.'

The chances of a successful retake were slim. Schoedsack realised he would have to take the negative back with him, and step-print it, giving a long exposure to each frame. This method saved the scene, but much of it still appears grainy.

When the material from Siam filtered through to Paramount, newsreel head Emmanuel Cohen wanted it for his department. Jesse Lasky had delegated responsibility for the project and was involved elsewhere. Sensing these warning signals, Cooper and Schoedsack quietly proceeded with the editing of the film, and as soon as they had cut it to their satisfaction they burned every foot of unused negative and positive. They remembered Paramount's infuriating habit of tampering with pictures – they had tried to inflate *Grass*, and sure enough Sidney Kent, head of the sales department, wanted to add another 1500 feet.

'He nearly had a fit,' said Cooper, 'when I told him there was no more film to add!'

One shot – just one shot – was taken at the Central Park Zoo. The monkey dropping coconuts on the elephants during the stampede, a characteristic Cooper-Schoedsack touch, had not registered satisfactorily. 'So we went out and bounced coconuts off the tame, mangy elephant they had in Central Park.'

A novelist with the picturesque name of Captain Achmed Abdullah was hired to add an oriental flavour to the titles. He did an abominable job, and his cute, wisecracking titles are an affront to the picture. (Ramsaye's were not much better on *Grass*.) Yet Cooper and Schoedsack passed them, and Cooper wrote some of them himself. If the flowery style of the Victorian lecturer survived into the era of FitzPatrick Travel Talks, the comedy titles of *Grass* and *Chang* were perpetuated in scores of American documentaries – including the Disney True-Life Adventure Films.

Chang provided an opportunity for a new process called Magnascope. Lorenzo del Riccio had developed it from a Bausch and Lomb wide-angle lens for outdoor projection; the idea of using it as a dramatic device was Glendon Ailvine's. The idea was simple; a second projector, with the sequence to be magnified, was equipped with the wide-angle lens. On cue, the screen cutouts pulled back, and the sequence was thrown on a new, gigantic screen. Magnascope had been introduced with the James Cruze sea epic *Old Ironsides*. Cooper and Schoedsack had experimented with anamorphic lenses, but they decided in favour of Magnascope. They secretly arranged for a special score from Dr. Hugo Riesenfeld, and a special preview for the Paramount people was held at the Criterion Theatre.

'It was a terrific score,' said Schoedsack, 'and a great orchestra, with lots of brass – and six-foot thunderdrums back of the screen. They went into action as the screen opened up on the elephant stampede. You never heard a sound-track like it. Coop and I were waiting in the lobby as the big boys came out. Lasky was smiling from ear to ear.

Walter Wanger and Adolph Zukor were smiling, too. Zukor said to Lasky: "How much did the boys get?" Lasky said, "40 percent." Zukor's smile disappeared.'

The picture had been budgeted at $60,000. By the time the stampede was ready for shooting, they were down to $20,000. Prince Yugala charged them $30,000, a figure which appalled them both. They decided to take the risk and went $10,000 into the red. Wrote Jesse Lasky: 'I was delighted with the picture and impatient to congratulate them. I expected them to come right to my office as soon as they docked, but instead they disappeared for several days. When they did put in a nervous appearance, they handed me a cheque for $10,000, mumbling apologies for running over their budget and the delay in raising money to pay me back what they "owed" me. They had been ashamed to face me until they could make it good. You would have thought they were confessing to embezzlement.

'I laughed with relief and tore up the cheque. I hadn't restricted their budget . . . they were actually working on an unlimited expense account but didn't know it.'[6]

Chang received critical acclaim from all over the world and was one of the first Academy Award nominations. Richard Watts, in the New York *Herald Tribune*, wrote: 'Messrs. Cooper and Schoedsack have incorporated into their work some of the most thrilling moments any dramatic form has been able to encompass. For they are, above all things, shrewd showmen, who have not been content to rely merely on the bald camera record of a journey through the Siamese jungle. *Grass*, the earlier picture made by Cooper and Schoedsack, fell, for example, considerably short of the marvellous show provided by the Siamese film, but it had a stark, heartbreaking sincerity that must of necessity be lacking from a production in which comedy and drama are mingled with a showman's conscious skill. It was a happy alliance of virtues that the producers, in addition to the ability to get out and get the sort of picture they wanted, were possessors of a high technical skill. The film has many of the admirable uses of tempo that *Potemkin* and *The Big Parade* employed to such effect. In addition, it is filled with pictorial beauty and photographed superbly."[7]

After *Chang*, Cooper and Schoedsack wanted to make a picture about starvation among the American Indians – similar to *The Silent Enemy*. The project came to nothing, as did Cooper's attempt to persuade the Rockefeller Foundation to finance him at $10,000 a year to develop the story-telling teaching film.

Their next collaboration was *The Four Feathers*, which involved an expedition to Africa, where they shot spectacular location footage of bush fire, stampeding hippos, and battling tribesmen, to be intercut with the studio-shot narrative.[8] Schoedsack then went to Sumatra, with Ruth Rose, and made *Rango*, an exquisitely photographed, extremely funny picture about an orangutan.

Ruth Rose, in her script for *King Kong*, wrote Cooper into the character of Denham (Robert Armstrong) and Schoedsack into Driscoll (Bruce Cabot). The story is woven around a documentary film-maker and his journey to a mysterious island. He takes a young girl, Ann (Fay Wray), along, to give his film some chance at the box office. Aboard ship, he makes a test.

DENHAM That was fine. I'm going to try a filter on this one.

ANN Do you always take the pictures yourself?

DENHAM Ever since a trip I made to Africa. I'd have got a swell picture of a charging rhino, but the cameraman got scared. The darned fool. I was right there with a rifle. Seemed he didn't trust me to get the rhino before it got him. I haven't fooled with cameramen since. Do the trick myself.

Ruth Rose looks up to husband 'Shorty' Schoedsack on location for Rango *(1931). She would co-write* King Kong *with James Creelman, from the story by Cooper and Edgar Wallace*

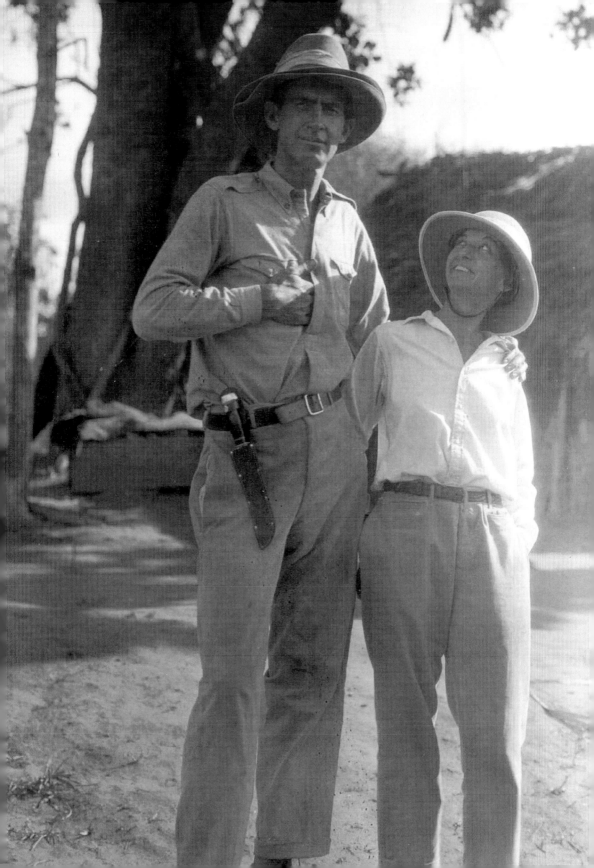

Cut to bridge. Captain Englehorn (Frank Reicher) and Driscoll leaning over, watching Denham and Ann.
DRISCOLL Think he's crazy, Skipper?
ENGLEHORN Just enthusiastic.

1. Interviews conducted with Merian Cooper and Ernest Schoedack, as well as tapes and letters. *2. Asia* magazine, June 1927, p.507. *3. Ibid.*, p.508. *4. Ibid.*, p51 *5. Ibid.* 6. Jesse Lasky and Don Weldon, *I Blow My Own Horn* (London: Gollancz, 1957), p.189. 7. Quoted in Rudy Behlmer, 'Merian C. Cooper', *Films in Review*, January 1966, p22. 8. For an account of the filming of *The Four Feathers*, see A. J. Siggins, *Shooting with Rifle and Camera*, (London, Wright & Brown, 1929), and Orville Goldner and George G. Turner; *The Making of King Kong* (New York: A.S. Barnes, 1976).

HIS MAJESTY, *KING KONG* – I
By Donald F. Glut

No icon in the history of monster films has proved as famous or durable as King Kong perched on the summit of the Empire State Building. The monster gorilla, a survivor from prehistoric times, clutches a screaming blonde woman in one massive paw. Then after setting her down, he lashes out at the swarm of biplanes that blast him with barrages of machine-gun fire.

This screen image, since it was first viewed by the public in 1933, has passed into the category of the popular myth. The huge ape's confrontation with the seemingly almost as primitive airplanes has been spoofed more times than any other single sequence from a fantasy motion picture. Immediately a giant gorilla atop any building brings to mind the classic and original *King Kong,* considered by most aficionados as the greatest single monster film ever made.

Basically, five men were responsible for the creation of *King Kong* – producer Merian C. Cooper, writer Edgar Wallace, director Ernest B. Schoedsack, sculptor Marcel Delgado, and special effects maestro Willis O'Brien.

Known as the Sphinx of Hollywood (and to his friends as simply 'OBie'), Willis O'Brien (1886-1962) had perfected the art of puppet animation or, as he put it, 'animation in depth'. Simply stated, the process, also known as stop motion, involves the movement of an inanimate object on the screen. A model or puppet is moved a fraction of an inch, after which the camera clicks off a single frame of motion picture film. The procedure is then repeated, with countless movements and single frame exposures. The end result of this process is a strip of film, each frame having recorded another succeeding increment of movement. When projected, our persistence of vision interprets the footage as if the inanimate object were moving. This process can be incredibly time consuming but the miracles that may be achieved through skilful puppet animation can certainly be worth the effort.

O'Brien did not invent the process. It had been utilised in films during the very early part of the century. But he did perfect the art to the extent that dimensional animation made the transition from the simple trick photography of the short novelty films to one of the important processes used in the production of feature-length motion pictures.

He discovered animation after a varied career during which he worked as a prizefighter, factory worker, wilderness guide and fur trapper, sports cartoonist (for the San Francisco *Daily World*), cowboy, railroad brakeman and surveyor. In 1915, O'Brien was sculpting models in clay for an exhibit at the San Francisco World's Fair. He and his brother were modelling miniature clay boxers and soon were pitting one fighter against the

Willis O'Brien, Kong's second 'father'. He may not have invented stop motion, but his prehistoric beasts and giant monsters made the process an integral part of the cinema.

other by bending them into various positions. When O'Brien saw the possibilities in applying such manipulations to the still new motion picture medium, he brought the tiny boxers to the screen in an experimental and crudely executed short. This was the beginning of Willis O'Brien's motion picture career.

O'Brien began to experiment. He had a fondness for prehistoric life and had even served as a guide for a group of University of Southern California scientists brought to unearth a fossil sabre-tooth cat in the Crater Lake region. Besides, puppet animation seemed to be designed for bringing to life dinosaurs and other extinct beasts which had few other opportunities for resuscitation. Animating a clay model apatosaurus (commonly known as brontosaurus) and caveman, O'Brien produced 75 feet of film comedy – the first of his many prehistoric animal films.

In 1917, Willis O'Brien made a one-reel comedy short, *The Dinosaur and the Missing Link*, which was later bought for $525 by the Thomas A. Edison Company and theatrically released. The entire cast for this film consisted of animated models constructed of wooden 'skeletons' over which the likenesses were sculpted in clay. Working from the basement of San Francisco's Imperial Theatre, O'Brien manipulated his cave people and prehistoric animals over a period of two months.

The Dinosaur and the Missing Link was indeed prophetic. The picture involved prehistoric human beings in an anachronistic adventure with creatures that should have been extinct for some 70 million years.* The real star of the picture was the Missing Link himself, a mischievous ape who eventually battles and is killed by a brontosaur. O'Brien later referred to the prehistoric simian as 'Kong's ancestor'. Fortunately this and other early O'Brien efforts are extant and we can make the comparisons between the Missing Link and King Kong ourselves.

Following *The Dinosaur and the Missing Link*, Willis O'Brien shot a number of animated shorts. Three of these, *Morpheus Mike*, *R.F.D. 10,000 B.C* (or *Rural Delivery, Ten Thousand B.C.*) and *Prehistoric Poultry* were made for Edison in 1917 and featured all-puppet casts of cave people and prehistoric animals. Seen today, the films are crude yet imaginative and enchanting. O'Brien was not striving for realism in these early pictures. That came a scant two years later.

The Ghost of Slumber Mountain was made in 1919 for World Cinema Distributing Company. Major Herbert M. Dawley produced, wrote and directed the picture and later, as we shall see, claimed credit for work he had not even performed. Under the guidance of Dr. Barnum Brown, the famed American Museum of Natural History palaeontologist, O'Brien constructed his first realistic prehistoric animals (as opposed to the caricatures of the 1917 productions), fashioned from clay and cloth. Brown also made suggestions as to the behaviour of the creatures and O'Brien followed them quite closely.

O'Brien's dinosaurs do not appear until the final minutes of *The Ghost of Slumber Mountain*. Under the provocation of his young nephews, Uncle Jack tells of his adventure on Slumber Mountain and Dream Valley, where the River of Peace flows. The mountain is the site of the supposedly haunted cabin of Mad Dick, a hermit who also happened to be a palaeontology buff. In the cabin the ghost of Mad Dick (allegedly played by O'Brien himself) appears to Uncle Jack and points out a strange instrument. When Uncle Jack peers through the instrument toward the valley, he beholds the region as it existed millions of years ago. Uncle Jack watches as various prehistoric monsters feed and battle to the death. A carnivorous allosaurus vanquishes a three-horned triceratops, after which the towering predator turns on Uncle Jack. But before the bipedal dinosaur can feast on human flesh, Uncle Jack awakens from a dream. This most convenient of all silent movie denouements suited the storytelling frame of *The Ghost of Slumber Mountain.*

Once *The Ghost* was released, Dawley assumed full credit for the apparent miracles audiences had seen on the screen. Dawley went so far as to claim that one of O'Brien's miniature monsters was actually his own 'seventeen-foot high' creation. Since the film was cut down to nearly half its original length before release, Dawley found himself with a considerable surplus of O'Brien's animation footage. This he edited into his own 1920 film *Along the Moonbeam Trail,* but as O'Brien's talents continued to mature there was little doubting who accomplished the special effects in *The Ghost of Slumber Mountain.* The dinosaur scenes from *The Ghost,* along with footage of Carl Hagenbeck's life-sized dinosaur models in Hamburg, Germany's Zoological Park, were later incorporated into the documentary film *Evolution,* produced by Max Fleischer in 1923 for Red Seal and released in 1925. All of the *Evolution* dinosaur scenes were then used in *Mystery of Life* (Universal Pictures, 1931), a sound documentary directed by George Cocharne. Later yet, in the early 1960s, the allosaurus vs. triceratops battle from *The Ghost of Slumber Mountain* became part of a television commercial for a candy company.

One of the persons to become suitably impressed by O'Brien's work in *The Ghost of Slumber Mountain* was Watterson Rothacker who, with Earl Hudson, had purchased the motion picture rights to *The Lost World,* a novel by Sir Arthur Conan Doyle, published in 1912. Doyle's fantastic adventure opens with a dying man staggering into an Indian village in the Amazon jungle, his possessions including drawings of a plateau inhabited by dinosaurs. Professor Challenger, a boisterous explorer (who appeared in other Doyle novels and later pastiches), organises an expedition to this 'lost world', discovering living counterparts of such extinct saurians as the flesh-eating megalosaurus and the herbivorous iguanodon, the latter having been domesticated by primitive man. After a number of perilous incidents, the explorers return to civilisation. In Challenger's possession is a living pterosaur, a winged reptile which he exhibits to a packed audience at Queen's Hall in London. The animal flies over the audience, creating some panic before escaping through an open window.

The Lost World was scheduled for shooting in 1925 by First National, with Harry O. Hoyt directing. Two years earlier O'Brien, who was then attending Otis Art Institute in Los Angeles, was considering the elaborate special effects required by a project like *The Lost World.* The cruder models animated in *The Ghost of Slumber Mountain* simply would not suffice and O'Brien realised his need for an assistant.

It was during O'Brien's attendance at art school that his historic meeting came with Marcel Delgado, a fellow student who had been earning his tuition by doubling as a school monitor. Delgado was a sculptor and it was shortly after the meeting that O'Brien suggested that they join forces on *The Lost World.* O'Brien offered his new friend an impressive $75 a week but Delgado declined, afraid that taking the job would take precious time away from his art studies and eventually forestall his hopeful art career. Delgado had come from an impoverished family in Mexico and considered a career in art to be more secure than a job in the motion picture industry.

Delgado did, however, accept O'Brien's invitation to visit the First National studios. O'Brien personally guided the sculptor's tour of the studio and finally brought him into a workshop with numerous dinosaur models and reproductions of Charles R. Knight's famous paintings of prehistoric animals. (Knight's paintings of extinct life have graced such institutions as Chicago's Field Museum of Natural History, New York's American Museum of Natural History and the Los Angeles County Museum of Natural History. Reproductions of his restorations of prehistoric animals have appeared in countless books and articles on palaeontology.) Over four decades later, Marcel Delgado recalled it this way:

'"Well, Marcel [said O'Brien], how do you like your new studio?" Stupefied as I was, I said, "What studio?" He said, "The one you are standing in. It is all yours. That is, if you want it." I really didn't know what to say. I had been taken completely by surprise. O'Brien had finally won. So he said, "Well, when are you going to start?" "Right now," I replied. He took me to the office and signed me up, and I started to work that day.'

Basing his models on the Charles R. Knight restorations, Marcel Delgado constructed them roughly eighteen inches in length. Over ball-and-socket-jointed 'skeletons' Delgado built up the musculature from sponge rubber, over which he added the animals' latex skins and finally all external protuberances. For added realism Delgado built an airbladder apparatus into some of the models which could simulate breathing. O'Brien was pleased with the monster menagerie created by Delgado; for sheer realism they surpassed any prehistoric animals as yet created especially for the motion pictures.

Using Delgado's creations, Willis O'Brien finished a short piece of film showing the dinosaurs in action. Doyle, who was in New York on a lecture tour, approved of the footage in which various genera of dinosaurs battled one another. An audience of professional magicians, including the incomparable Harry Houdini, marvelled at what they saw on the screen and were unable to discover O'Brien's secret.

Herbert M. Dawley, however, did know how the effects were done and used that knowledge to threaten Rothacker and Doyle with a $100,000 law suit. Dawley claimed that he had invented the puppet animation process, completely ignoring the fact that such effects were pioneered on the screen long before the making of his *Ghost of Slumber Mountain*. Furthermore he stated that his former employee had stolen the process for use in *The Lost World*. But Dawley's case did not halt production on the new First National motion picture.

The Lost World was almost a blueprint for the later masterpiece *King Kong*. Not only were both films enhanced by Willis O'Brien's animated effects, they were also similar in story structure, so much, in fact, that *King Kong* is often regarded by film historians as an unauthorised remake of *The Lost World*. The film opens with newspaper reporter Ed Malone (Lloyd Hughes) unable to marry his fiancée until, on her insistence, he first accomplishes an act of heroism. Meanwhile, the boisterous and bearded Professor Challenger (Wallace Beery) is derided for his theory that explorer Maple White had discovered a plateau teeming with prehistoric life. Challenger detests reporters and fights Malone from his house and into the street before accepting him as a member of his expedition to the 'Lost World'. Soon Challenger, Malone, Maple White's daughter Paula (Bessie Love) and Sir John Roxton (Lewis Stone), a big game hunter, number among the professor's expedition into the unexplored Amazon jungle.

From the base of the plateau, the group sees a living pteranodon, a giant winged reptile. Perhaps prophetically the group is watched by a beastlike apeman, or another Missing Link (played by Bull Montana), and his pet chimpanzee. (This was Montana's second foray into an apeman role. In the 1920 silent film *Go and Get It*, directed by M. Neilan and Henry R. Symonds, he played the monstrous result of the transplantation of a dead criminal's brain into the skull of a gorilla.) Scaling the towering walls of the plateau, the explorers encounter a number of supposedly extinct prehistoric creatures – including a massive,

WILKES THE LEADING THEATRE
PROSPECT 525 GEARY & MASON

TWICE DAILY AFTER
TONIGHT at 2:30 and 8:30
NIGHT, 50c-$1.50; MAT., 50c-$1

BEGINS TONIGHT
—PACIFIC COAST PREMIERE—

It Will Astound You and Enthrall You!

PREHISTORIC
MONSTERS
CLASH WITH
MODERN
LOVERS

MOST
AMAZING
PICTURE
EVER
MADE

A First National Picture

The LOST WORLD

Sir A. Conan Doyle's
Stupendous Story
—with—
BESSIE LOVE,
LEWIS STONE, LLOYD
HUGHES, WALLACE BEERY

The Lost World was the first feature-length prehistoric monster movie – the progenitor not only of King Kong, but of Jurassic Park (1993) and its sophisticated special effects.

snaky-necked apatosaurus. After a battle with a carnivorous allosaurus, the herbivorous giant plunges from the cliff side to land in a mud-pool below.

In *The Lost World* live actors and dinosaurs appeared simultaneously on screen, which was certainly a startling image to behold in 1925. To achieve this effect O'Brien animated his dinosaurs on a miniature set with flora made of sheet metal to insure against unnecessary movement. The scenes of the live actors were photographed separately. By masking off portions of the animation and live action footage, O'Brien was able to combine the two, arriving at such impressive composites as Challenger and his colleague Professor Summerlee (Arthur Hoyt) crouching behind a tree to observe a passing apatosaurus.

After the group finds the skeletal remains of Maple White, a natural phenomenon occurs which, over the following years, would become a cliché of the 'dinosaur' film. The volcano, which had apparently been content to merely belch smoke for millions of years *until* the arrival of the explorers, erupts. In an incredibly spectacular sequence (tinted red) virtually the entire cast of O'Brien's animated characters flee the descending fire and lava, often many of them in a single shot. At last the human band manage to climb down the cliffside via a rope. The apeman grabs the rope (another prophecy of *King Kong*, while Malone is descending but Roxton shoots the monster, saving the life of his rival for the love of Paula.

The final sequences of *The Lost World* set down the rules for the *King Kong*-style film. Professor Challenger, aided by the Brazilian government, returns the trapped 'brontosaur' to London where he plans to exhibit the animal. But the monster breaks free of its cage and soon the streets of London are in panic as a frightened and rampaging apatosaurus charges through the streets. The dinosaur, seen in more of O'Brien's composites and also thundering through a miniature representation of London, destroys some of the city's landmarks. Finally the creature steps onto Tower Bridge which, quite literally and perhaps traditionally, starts falling down beneath the monster's 30-ton weight. The dinosaur splashes into the Thames River, presumably to return to the Lost World. Paula and Malone go off to be married, though audiences quickly forgot the film's romantic sequences; what stayed in people's memories were the dinosaurs of Delgado and O'Brien.

*The erroneous combination of cavemen and dinosaurs in motion pictures, while ridiculed by the scientists, has become a convention in motion pictures since the silent era. D. W. Griffith made *Man's Genesis* in 1912 for the Biograph Company and one year later filmed a sequel under the title *War of the Primal Tribes,* which was copyrighted as *The Primitive Man*. The film, which was officially released as *Brute Force*, brought cavemen up against prehistoric reptiles. An alligator and a snake were given horns and other attachments to make them appear to be prehistoric monsters. But the real saurian star of the production was a life-sized moving mock-up of the horned flesh-eating dinosaur ceratosaurus.

THE LOST WORLD

By Denis Gifford

The star of the most sensational American silent film of them all was less than human, less even than animal. It was a toy, a thing of rubbery stuff moulded around a jointed wire skeleton, all of twelve inches high. But when shown on the cinema screen, it became a monstrous brontosaurus that made Tower Bridge come falling down. The fair lady was Bessie Love, a box-office attraction not found in Sir Arthur Conan Doyle's original novel of *The Lost World* (1925).

Wallace Beery played Professor Challenger, leader of an expedition up the Amazon to find prehistoric life. Among the flora and fauna was Bull Montana, the well-known apeman. This time he was in the full, hirsute suit, as created by First National's wizard of the whiskers, Cecil Holland. Acting and direction (Harry O. Hoyt) were no great shakes, but the camerawork and effects were the best the Hollywood movie had yet produced. A team of three photographed: Arthur Edeson, Fred Jackman and Homer Scott used masking and double-exposure to combine men with models that had to be shot in stop-motion, two frames at a time.

The man behind the models was an ex-cartoonist from Oakland named Willis O'Brien. He became the special effects king of Hollywood horrors and as such finally won an Academy Award in 1949 (for, curiously, his worst work, *Mighty Joe Young*). Yet always his horror was diluted by the light touch inherited from his previous profession. It showed in his first film, *The Dinosaur and the Baboon* (1917). This told the 500-foot tale of Stonejaw Steve and Theophilus Ivoryhead who try to catch a pterodactyl for lunch. Wild Willie, the missing link, encounters a monster. 'The dinosaur is some battler and Wild Willie meets his Waterloo and is sent on his way to baboon heaven.' Ivoryhead chances upon the body and claims it as his own, planting his foot upon the baboon's chest in a gesture of triumph that would become an O'Brien trademark. In this little puppet comedy can be found elements that O'Brien and his disciples would use through half a century of spectacular cinema. Two years later he made a slightly more serious single-reel dinosaur fantasy, *The Ghost of Slumber Mountain* (1919). This caught the interest of the other missing link in the *Lost World* story, Watterson R. Rothacker.

Rothacker, West Coast manager of *Billboard*, saw the potential in films for publicity as early as 1911. Forming the Industrial Motion Picture Company he evolved many specialised techniques: he used animation to make movies of Gus Edson's newspaper comic strip, *Old Doc Yak*. O'Brien joined Rothacker and together they created the monsters of *The Lost World*. Although the flickery dinosaur was outclassed by the dragon Fritz Lang built in Germany for *Siegfried* (1924), the American epic had the showman's touch. The erupting volcanoes, stampeding monsters, and destruction of London thrilled a vast audience which would have been bored by the turgid Teuton legend. The film still thrills as Professor Challenger lowers his binoculars and mouths the immortal subtititles 'This is the greatest moment of my life. I have seen a living pterodactyl!'

THE LOST WORLD: MERELY MISPLACED?

By Scott MacQueen

On the evening of June 2, 1922, the American Society of Magicians held a dinner at the Hotel McAlpin in New York City. Along with the coffee, brandy and cigars, the conjurers took turns demonstrating their mystifying art.

It was one o'clock in the morning when a motion picture screen and projector were brought into the banquet room. Chairman Houdini, an avid debunker of the supernatural, turned the dais over to Conan Doyle, a true believer and active promoter of Spiritualism since the death of his son in World War One. Conan Doyle spoke briefly and soberly. 'If I brought here in real existence what I show in these pictures it would be a great catastrophe. These pictures are not occult. This is psychic because everything that emanates from the human spirit or human brain is psychic. It is not supernatural. It is the effect of the joining on the one hand of imagination and on the other hand of some power of materialisation. The imagination, I may say, comes from me. The materialising power comes from elsewhere.' Sir Arthur cautioned his audience that he would answer no questions, and the lights were dimmed. What happened next was reported the following morning on the front page of the *New York Times*:

DINOSAURS CAVORT IN FILM FOR DOYLE
Spiritist Mystifies World-Famed Magicians
With Pictures of Prehistoric Beasts
'Monsters of several million years ago, mostly of the dinosaur species, made love and killed each other in Sir Arthur's pictures,' ran the breathless report. 'In living pictures, a family of dinosaurs was seen nuzzling affectionately, only to be attacked by a group of tyrannosaurs. The tyrannosaurs then fought among themselves until one broke the other's back and was prevented from devouring his kill by the arrival of a triceratops, which drove away the predator. A late arrival, a stegosaurus, remained impervious to attack by nature of his natural armour-plates.

'His monsters of the ancient world, or of the new world which he has discovered in the ether, were extraordinarily lifelike. If fakes, they were masterpieces.'

Conan Doyle made a clean breast of things the same day in a letter to Houdini: a motion picture was to be made of his novel *The Lost World* by Watterson Rothaker. 'The dinosaurs and other monsters have been constructed by pure cinema, but of the highest kind,' he wrote, explaining that his purpose in showing them was simply 'to provide a little mystification to those who have so often and so successfully mystified others.'

There had been plans to film *The Lost World* since 1919, when Conan Doyle sold a five-year option to London producer J. G. Wainwright of Cineproductions, Ltd. for £500. Wainwright's option was bought out by the Chicago promoter Watterson R. Rothacker in September of 1922, and a new eight-year arrangement was made with Conan Doyle. Rothacker produced advertising films and owned film laboratories. A feature film of the proportions of *The Lost World* was feasible only because of Rothacker's association with Willis O'Brien.

O'Brien had independently pioneered stop-motion puppet animation of cavemen and dinosaurs. His first film came to the attention of the Edison Company. After a brief association with Herbert Dawley for the dinosaur fantasy *The Ghost of Slumber Mountain* in 1918, O'Brien signed with Rothacker (who had been impressed with O'Brien's work as early as 1914) to make animated novelty films.

No sooner had Conan Doyle revealed the purpose of his animated dinosaurs than litigants jumped in with claims to the film rights and patents on the processes used in the demonstration. After these claims were proven false, Rothacker signed an agreement with Associated First National Pictures on December 14, 1923.

The story of the movie is familiar to many. Professor George Challenger (Wallace Beery) organises an expedition to the uncharted jungles of South America to prove his claim that living dinosaurs still roam a remote plateau. He is accompanied by newspaperman Ed Malone (Lloyd Hughes); Paula White (Bessie Love), the daughter of an explorer lost on the plateau; Sir John Roxton (Lewis Stone), a sportsman; Professor Summerlee (Arthur Hoyt), Challenger's critic and an eccentric specialist in beetles; Challenger's manservant, Austin (Finch Smiles); and Zambo (Jules Cowles), a black American jack-of-all-trades. Challenger's claims prove true, but the party becomes marooned on the plateau, where they are constantly threatened by the battling dinosaurs and a ferocious ape-man (Bull Montana). After many adventures, they escape, returning to London with a captive brontosaurus. The creature escapes, however, and wrecks half of London before paddling up the Thames to open sea.

At First National the project was put under the supervision of Earl Hudson with a scenario written by Marion Fairfax. Many wonderful passages from the original story were omitted out of necessity.

The major changes were in the interest of showmanship. The invention of Paula White added a feminine presence conspicuously absent from the book, generating an effortless love triangle as Paula's affections hovered between the courtly, more mature Sir John Roxton and the youthful reporter Ed Malone. More sex appeal was provided by Marquette, a flirtatious half-caste girl whom the adventurers encounter at a trading post.

A much grander ending was also conceived. In Conan Doyle's story, it is a young pterodactyl that Professor Challenger smuggles back to London; the flying dinosaur escapes from Queens Hall with minor incidence. In the film, the captured brontosaurus plunges all of London into a state of fear and confusion.

Arthur Edeson, ASC, the great cameraman who shot Douglas Fairbanks's *Robin Hood* and *The Thief of Bagdad*, was in charge of live-action photography. As shooting became protracted, a second unit was established under director William Dowling to accelerate the schedule until the final weeks of production, when the two companies were merged. Filming was accomplished at First National's Brunton Studio in Burbank, with the prosaic Los Angeles River suitably camouflaged in tropical trappings.

Ralph Hammeras had been operating his own motion picture special effects company on the Brunton lot when Earl Hudson persuaded him to join the staff at First National. As Hammeras recalled in correspondence with Don Shay, the security afforded by so large a company was not the only enticement for joining the studio. 'Another reason I signed the contract was because Mr. Hudson told me that he had a man by the name of Willis O'Brien, who did the most unusual things like making prehistoric animals come to life on the screen.'

49 new, larger models, based on Charles R. Knight's paintings, were built by Marcel Delgado. Delgado's dinosaurs averaged eighteen inches in length. The skeletons were made of tempered dural and steel with articulated backbones and ball-and-socket joints for all movable digits and appendages. Sponge rubber muscles were applied and made to flex and stretch as real muscles do. The armature was then shaped out into the basic form of the animal. The skins were made of latex and rubber sheeting. All spines, plates, and other protuberances were made separately and applied to the textured skins. Football bladders in the bellies, inflated with an air compressor, allowed the models'

diaphragms to rise and fall as they 'breathed'.

O'Brien was impressed by Hammeras' development of glass painting (which Hammeras patented in 1925), whereby elaborate vistas and architecture, painted on glass, could be combined with live photography. This technique allowed the exotic locales necessary for *The Lost World* to be created affordably and believably at the studio. Hammeras and his crew of 125 technicians also developed the miniature sets in which O'Brien's creatures lived. They typically measured six feet wide by four feet deep and were elevated on platforms three feet off the floor, though for a sequence involving a fire and a dinosaur stampede, a special 75' X 150' stage was constructed.

Battling dinosaurs created by Willis O'Brien and modelmaker Marcel Delgado for The Lost World. *Similar techniques were used for creatures like the apatosaurus (right) in* King Kong.

Once the technicians had lined up the camera and lit the set with flickerless Cooper-Hewitt mercury vapour units, O'Brien was boxed into the miniature set so that nothing and no one could disturb his concentration. Except for the complex stampede sequence, which required assistants due to the sheer number of creatures in motion, O'Brien performed all of the animation himself. Typically, a day's work yielded 35 feet of film – 560 frames of movement for less than 30 seconds of screen time. After a year of work on the animation, First National relocated studio operations to New York and O'Brien's crew completed *The Lost World* at the old Biograph Studio in The Bronx.

The in-camera mattes, by which live actors and real lakes and rivers are interposed with the dinosaurs, seem rudimentary today but were ingeniously conceived and executed for their time. During the London climax in particular, there is one superb and startling early travelling matte shot of the brontosaurus. The battle between the allosaurus and monoclonius is moodier for clouds drifting across the night sky as the monsters battle; in but a few years, such a shot would be easily handled by rear-screen projection, but in 1925 it could only have been achieved by animating the background. Such attention to detail made O'Brien's lost world a real place, just as his concern for the interior lives of his beasts endowed them with personalities and characteristics that made them seem believably alive. *The Lost World* was the wonder picture of 1925 when it opened at New York City's Astor Theatre in early February on a limited, twice-a-day basis. The picture went into general release in early summer and was a tremendous hit. Quite simply, nothing like it had ever been seen before, nor would anything like it be seen until *King Kong* in 1933. (*Kong* was so closely modelled on the structure of *The Lost*

World that RKO took the precaution of purchasing the story rights and the 1925 film for $10,000 in May of 1932.)

In 1929, Aileen Rothacker (as successor to her husband's rights) and First National reached an agreement to withdraw *The Lost World* from distribution. Mrs. Rothacker was paid $1,225 as a final settlement on all outstanding profits. She also retained remake rights in the story. The supposition is that the decks were being cleared for a sound remake. First National could junk and destroy all positive prints and the foreign negative, though the domestic negative was to remain stored. The fate of the domestic negative is unknown. According to the terms of the RKO sale, Warner Bros. (which by then had absorbed First National) and Aileen Rothacker were to retain possesion of the negative. It has not survived at Warner Bros., though, and can be presumed to have been junked or to have decomposed long ago.

On July 8, 1929, First National contracted *The Lost World* to Kodascope Libraries, Inc., which, beginning in 1930, made the film available non-theatrically in an abridged 16mm version. A 35mm lavender positive printed from the camera negative was edited to five reels. From that, a 35mm nitrate dupe negative was made for reduction printing 16mm safety film release prints.

The Lost World has survived only in its Kodascope edition. The editing is seamless and well executed, betraying few obvious gaps in continuity. Virtually all shots were trimmed to a bare minimum. Judging from contemporary reviews which mention more frequent close-ups and more carnage, some of the more graphic shots of the beasts have been removed to meet the sensibilities of the Kodascope Library's major customers: schools and church groups.

Editorially, the overall effect is to accelerate the pacing of the film far beyond what its makers intended. In its ten-reel form, *The Lost World* followed the precise pattern repeated by *King Kong* – slowly developing its characters and anticipating the terrors to come in its relaxed first half, then shifting into high gear for the non-stop monster show of the last half. Even in this second half, however, the monster battles did not take place in the frenetic, non-stop fashion in which they now appear.

In its original theatrical release, *The Lost World* consisted of 9,209 feet of 35mm film. (Its premiere engagement at the Astor Theatre, as reported by *Variety*, was 104 minutes.) Musical cue sheets compiled by James Bradford for the 1925 general release are annotated with timings which total 106 minutes. This would indicate a projection speed of 87 feet per minute, or 23 frames per second – virtually 'sound speed'. (The projection speed of silent films was not necessarily the same as the speed at which they were photographed, and the quickening of action achieved by slightly faster projection was an accepted convention of the period.) The animation of *The Lost World* has been said to have been photographed at 16fps. The live-action photography appears to have been closer to 20fps, with deliberate undercranking to 16fps for much of the London climax.

In preparing an archival laserdisc presentation of *The Lost World* for Lunuvision Corporation of Denver, Colorado, I became interested in learning exactly what the film had looked like in its original release.

Most useful were the brief descriptions and scene timings of the 1925 music cue sheets. These were compared with a timed continuity of the five-reel version adjusted for 23fps, and the missing action determined from Marion Fairfax's original scenario. (Incidentally, the film boasted an original theme song by Rudolf Friml – a waltz that was used as Paula White's theme. It was issued as sheet music with loony lyrics by Harry B. Smith: 'Oh! the world was lost I knew/On the day that I lost you/And the stars will guide us beaming above/Till we find our lost world of love.')

KING KONG COMETH!

One of the biggest revelations regarded sequences shot for *The Lost World* that never made the final cut. Enough footage for two movies had apparently been shot. When Ray Harryhausen was working with O'Brien on *Mighty Joe Young* in 1945, 'OBie' recounted to him how First National had reservations that the animated beasts would work. Marion Fairfax earned O'Brien's undying enmity by reassuring him that she had constructed the scenario in such a way that, if the animation was a failure, the dinosaurs could easily be left out! In this no-faith scenario, *The Lost World* would become a straightforward jungle adventure, with cannibals, the missing link and a mutiny being the only dangers encountered on the plateau. The action is as follows:

True to Conan Doyle's book, the expedition party prepares to leave by steamship from the Liverpool docks. Challenger becomes annoyed at Summerlee's insistence that Roxton lead the group, and quietly leaves the ship with Austin after posting a mysterious letter for his associates in the ship's mail. The letter allegedly contains his secret maps and is to be opened on December 12th at 6 a.m., in a trading hut on the Branco River. The nervous party forges ahead to the trading post, where, at the appointed hour, the envelope's secret contents prove to be blank paper. As despair grips the expeditioners, a grinning Challenger appears, having amply demonstrated that he alone is master of the expedition.

An inhabitant of the rough-hewn, mud-infested trading post is the owner's daughter, Marquette, a pretty Portuguese half-caste who sings love songs and plays a guitar, flirting with Ed Malone while he types his dispatches to London.

The expedition heads down the river with hunting dogs and local bearers, supervised by the villainous Gomez, a thieving half-breed. Bull Montana, who portrayed the ape-man, doubled in the straight role of Gomez, with Chris-Pin Martin as his partner in

This brontosaurus, in The Lost World, *is trapped and taken from its isolated Amazon home to London – where it escapes and wreaks havoc on civilisation, just like Kong.*

crime; Martin also doubled as one of the cannibals!

Challenger reveals a glade of green rushes that mask the tributary leading to his lost world. Eerie drums follow the explorers' progress down the river. When one of the bearers is killed by a poison arrow they realise they are stalked by Nhambiquara cannibals. Roxton, Challenger and Malone scout the vicinity and observe the Nhambiquara performing a savage dance under the full moon. Deciding to push on down the river that night, they quickly return to camp only to find that Gomez has led a mutiny. The bearers have absconded with most of the canoes, the dogs and supplies. Paula is discovered, bound and gagged but otherwise unharmed, while the faithful Zambo has had his arm nearly amputated by a machete (which explains why he appears with his arm in a sling for the balance of the movie!).

This superfluous half-hour of additional material, though filmed, was removed even before the Astor Theatre opening in New York and was never seen by the public.

Major deletions from the ten-reel version include the following:
- The main titles, played over Ralph Hammeras' matte painting of the plateau, originally included a vignette where an expeditioner encountered a trachedon in the glass-painted jungle (3:00).
- The main titles were followed by an on-camera endorsement by Sir Arthur Conan Doyle seated at a desk as he penned the inscription that opens his novel (:45).
- Establishing shots of London on a foggy day, with Malone arriving at the home of his fiancée, Gladys Hungerford. As she toys with her pet kitten, she makes it clear that she will marry Ed only if he does something outstanding to make a name for himself (2:30).
- The newspaper office sequence has been trimmed in half. Missing is a look at the newspaper's report of Challenger's outrageous dinosaur claims. The editor discusses a lawsuit threatened by Challenger and proposes a countersuit for the beatings Challenger has given his reporters, three of whom are seen bruised, bandaged and crippled.

The 'Zoological Hall' sequence is missing about two minutes, mostly in pacing and characterisation. Ed's escape from the lecture hall originally had him climbing over a dinosaur skeleton to outdistance the Professor.
- When Ed bursts in on Challenger at his home, tiny Mrs. Challenger berates her husband for his brutish behaviour, only to be hoisted onto a high pedestal by the Professor. After Sir John's arrival, more time was spent developing his romantic interest in Paula White.
- Kodascope prints removed eleven more minutes from the first portion of the expedition. Much of this comprised comedy scenes that built character, spotlighting the eccentric clash of egos between Challenger and Summerlee.
- The sighting of the pterodactyl appears to be briefer ('The greatest moment of my life!' exclaims Challenger) and the felling of the great tree and the subsequent ravine crossing are shortened.
- Following the allosaurus attack, Ed climbs the gingko tree to scout around and sights the caves where they will take refuge. Unbeknownst to Ed, he is tracked through the tree by the ape-man. The party below observes his peril, and Roxton fires at the ape.
- The passing of another day has been deleted, and we discover Challenger preparing a 'dinosaur weapon' by bending liana trees into catapults. Summerlee offers his unwanted advice, and sits on the bent-over tree. The end of this sequence is missing in the Kodascope version: the two argue whether a rock released by the liana will describe a curve or a parabola as it soars through the air. The ropes part, and Summerlee becomes airborne and is pitched into the lake. 'I was right!' shouts Challenger gleefully. 'You described a curve!'
- The eruption of the volcano and the ensuing dinosaur stampede was originally a five-

minute sequence which now plays in less than 90 seconds. This is most unfortunate, as some of the most ambitious animation sequences in history may have been tossed away. Marcel Delgado indicated that all 49 of his models made the mad dash; a maximum of ten are on view in existing prints.

- All of the action following the fire, and the party's escape from the plateau, has been halved. Missing is the last half of the sequence where Roxton reveals to Paula her father's remains and she prays by candlelight at the makeshift grave ('. . . as fine a piece of photographic art as has been seen in a long, long while,' wrote *Variety*). Missing entirely is a long exchange where Roxton, Cyrano-like, goes to Paula on Ed's behalf.

- Challenger's triumphant address back in London has been trimmed by a minute and a half. The audience turns hostile with disbelief when Challenger announces that his beast has escaped, and they block him from leaving the hall. Zambo, Austin and the Major help him break through the mob. As they arrive on the steps outside, the brontosaurus ambles into view. Challenger prances madly around it, trying to shepherd it. Roxton and Paula pursue in a motorcar.

- A full minute and a half has been removed from the brontosaurus' stampede in London. The scenario was not followed to the letter, so we can't be certain of the action. For example, the sequence where the creature topples a building and nearly crushes a woman and her child is not in the script, nor is a comic sequence which was reported by the reviewer for the *New York Times*: '. . . a man the worse for drink staggers out of a public house, suddenly sees the brontosaurus, and beats a hasty retreat, emerging a few moments later with milk for the "kitty" which he imagines has grown to unbelievable proportions merely in his mind.' The reviewer reported this brought a roar of laughter from the audience, as did a sequence where the monster smashed its head through a third-storey window, terrorising a poker game. Others found this sequence nightmarish – Ray Harryhausen has never forgotten this moment seen in childhood. In addition, a machine-gun battery is set up by the military at the Tower Bridge to head off the creature, while Challenger intercedes and begs them not to shoot.

- As the brontosaurus swims down the Thames to open sea, Challenger watches with tears streaming down his face. Professor Summerlee, however, loses all interest in the retreating behemoth when he spies an insect flitting past, and squats on the sidewalk to examine his new specimen. In the crowd thronging the waterfront, Ed stumbles on his betrothed Gladys and her lecture companion: her new husband, an effete, overdressed ribbon counter clerk named Percy Bumberry. 'I hope you'll forgive me for not waiting,' she whines coquettishly. Ed is delighted, as he now has a clear path to Paula.

The scenario has a wonderful tag shot: on the open, a sea steamship passes the brontosaurus as it swims happily back to South America. A feature article on the film's production in the May, 1925 issue of *Science and Invention* magazine rather conclusively indicates that this coda was filmed.

The Lost World has invariably been seen in murky, tattered dupes of the abbreviated Kodascope edition. But superior elements of this short version have been preserved at George Eastman House and were utilised by Lumivision Corporation for laserdisc release.

The 35mm nitrate Kodascope negative was acquired by James Card for the International Museum of Photography at George Eastman House in April of 1949. With the limited funds then available for archival work, Eastman House struck an excellent 16mm reduction safety film master positive of all five reels. In 1970, with funding from the National Endowment for the Arts, Eastman House printed reels one, two and five to 35mm Fine Grain Masters (unfortunately, reels three and four had decomposed by then).

This vintage 1920s lobby card for The Lost World *contrasts the matinee idol looks of the romantic leads against Willis O'Brien's reptiles.*

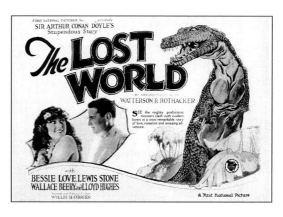

With the cooperation of Dr. Jan-Christopher Horak, curator of the Eastman House film archive, Lumivision utilised the 35mm Fine Grain for telecine of Kodascope reel numbers one, two and five. Reels three and four were drawn from the 16mm master positive. The 1925 projection speed of 23fps was deemed unacceptable for modern presentation. The film was obviously shot at a slower rate, and today's audiences don't easily adapt to the silent convention of a pace faster than nature. The radical trimming of individual shots in the Kodascope negative – some as brief as sixteen or 30 frames – alone necessitated slower treatment.

As telecine approached, no records could be found of authentic theatrical tinting. We knew that original 16mm Kodascope prints were amber, with red for the fire scene, but this didn't seem to do justice to the drama of the story. Based on toning and tinting practices of the period, a new palette of conjectural colours was created during transfer. Several gentle colour transitions were justified after carefully verifying that such effects were accomplished with chemical tints in the 1920s.

A worldwide search of archives uncovered little else. The UCLA Film and Television Archive has preserved an original, three-minute 35mm trailer which contains five shots not found in the Kodascope. Additionally, 365 feet of nitrate fragments were identified at the Library of Congress too late to negotiate their use in Lumivision's presentation.

A recent examination of the still-viable nitrate roll in the LOC's vaults shows it to contain a dozen unique shots culled from the full body of the narrative. The hoped-for sequence of the brontosaurus interrupting the poker game is sadly not there. Its absence is almost compensated for by another in-camera travelling matte shot that combines animation, glass painting and live action – the brontosaurus ambling up to Zoological Hall as the terrified audience flees the lecture hall. These new fragments, along with the relevant shots held by UCLA, will hopefully be incorporated into an archival film restoration of *The Lost World* currently proposed by George Eastman House.

Most satisfying was the fact that the LOC roll proved *The Lost World* to have been elaborately tinted (rather than toned), just as we had suspected. No fewer than ten base tints are employed and, four out of five times, they match precisely the educated guesses made in telecine.

With a newly created score by R. J. Miller (performed and recorded in the digital domain), Lumivsion's laserdisc edition of *The Lost World* is the finest showcase the film has had since 1925. Though no additional footage has been recovered, what is there looks magnificent, and the missing five reels are thoroughly represented in the laserdisc's still-frame library.

A remarkable achievement in 1925 and often imitated since, *The Lost World* is no less remarkable today.

RESTORATION: *THE LOST WORLD**

By Lokke Heiss

Each year, film enthusiasts gather in Pordenone, Italy (a small town near Venice), to watch a programme of silent films gathered from collections and archives around the world. Past festivals have shown the silent live-action version of *Pinocchio*, an early rendition of *Peter Pan*, and even a Soviet adaptation of Poe's *The Masque of the Red Death*.

One of the joys of this festival is the screening of rediscovered or restored films. The highlight of this year's festival was the premiere of an essentially full-length version of *The Lost World* (1925), the grand-daddy of all rampaging dinosaur movies. Based on a novel by Sir Arthur Conan Doyle (creator of Sherlock Holmes), this film had its running time cut in half after its initial release, severely affecting the story, characters, and special effects. For years the only copies available were taken from poorly duped 16mm prints. In 1991, Lumivision produced a laser disc edition (with tints and a musical score) that came much closer to the experience of watching the original film. But what could be done about the missing half of the footage?

In an effort requiring cooperation from film archives around the globe, *The Lost World* was painstakingly reassembled. The biggest help was the discovery of a European release version held by the Filmovy Archive of the Czech Republic. This enabled the archivists to restore most of the lost running time.

After all this time and care, what is the verdict? Happily, the restored film is immensely better. The human characters (featuring Wallace Beery as Professor Challenger) have more time to develop relationships that make the story far more interesting. The dinosaurs (courtesy of stop-motion pioneer Willis O'Brien) also fare better, with some beautiful, tinted shots of herds roaming on the plateau. The crucial last segment of the brontosaur's London rampage is still missing a few shots, but it is almost complete. (O'Brien more or less recreated this sequence decades later for 1958's *The Giant Behemoth*.) A restored scene shows the brontosaurus poking his head in a hotel window, making the precedents for O'Brien's future work on *King Kong* even more obvious.

My favourite scene in this restored version comes at the very end. There is a brief, stop-motion animated sequence of the escaped brontosaurus swimming away to safety in the Atlantic. He lifts up his head to see a steam ship cross by, then swims on. The Ancient World and the Modern World pass each other in the night, irreconcilable, capable only of destroying each other if forced to live together.

*This 1997 review was written after the premiere of George Eastman House's restored version of *The Lost World*.

HIS MAJESTY, *KING KONG* — II

By Donald F. Glut

A sequel to *The Lost World*, again to be directed by Hoyt and animated by O'Brien, was planned well into 1928, but this followup was never filmed. Still there was considerable mileage to be derived from the original film and the story on which it was based.

Encyclopedia Britannica Films issued a short subject in 1948 under the title *A Lost World*, using footage from the 1925 production enhanced by a soundtrack. *Magic*

Memories, a compilation film of various trick scenes, included a battle between a tyran-nosaurus and triceratops, purporting to be from O'Brien's *Lost World*. But the scene does not appear to be O'Brien's work. The dinosaur models seem almost comical, the animation is crude and jerky and there is considerable blood flowing when the flesh-eater bites into the neck frill of its horned adversary. The origin of this sequence remains a mystery unless it is actually part of the test reel screened in the presence of Sir Arthur Conan Doyle. Scenes from the real *Lost World* (in addition to scenes from *Brute Force* and other movies) appeared in Blackhawk Films' *Film Firsts, Chapter II.*

Buddy's Lost World was a cartoon spoof of *The Lost World* made in 1935 by Warner Brothers (the company which owned the 1925 movie) and released the next year. Jack King directed and Bob Clampett wrote this animated short in which the character Buddy sails to a prehistoric island where he mistakes the legs of a huge apatosaurus for trees. The brontosaur gives Buddy a wet 'slurp kiss'.

When a child, Clampett had seen *The Lost World* in its original release. Marvelling at the dinosaur effects, he quickly began work on his own epilogue to the film using a com-ical version of Professor Challenger and a sea serpent counterpart to the movie's apatosaurus. Soon, using hand-puppet versions of the characters and a 'Jocko' monkey puppet that reminded him of *The Lost World*'s Missing Link, Clampett staged his own amateur productions. His sea serpent character (who frequently made use of the 'slurp kiss') eventually evolved into Cecil the Sea Sick Sea Serpent who starred in the television puppet serial *Time for Beany* during the early 1950s. Among the show's regular cast was Captain Horatio Huffenpuff who was based directly upon Wallace Beery's Professor Challenger. In 1962 the characters from *Time for Beany* became animated cartoon fig-ures in the *Beany and Cecil* television series.

Every film in which a party of explorers discovers a land inhabited by prehistoric beasts owes its very existence to *The Lost World,* some more so than others in plot or title. *Two Lost Worlds* (United Artists, 1950), directed by Norman Dawn, was a tale of piracy and kidnapping during the nineteenth century, concluding on a prehistoric vol-canic island. But, like seemingly countless other films of this type, all the monster scenes came from an earlier epic, *One Million B.C.* (Hal Roach, 1940). More obvious in story was *Lost Continent* (Lippert, 1951), directed by Samuel Newfield. A group of scientists tracks an atomic rocket to a mountain-top where prehistoric life yet flourishes. As in *The Lost World,* an apatosaurus figures prominently and, as in *King Kong*, traps one of the explor-ers in a tree and kills him. The dinosaurs of *Lost Continent* appeared in crude model ani-mation with all the scenes set in that prehistoric world tinted green. Dinosaur footage from *Lost Continent* later reappeared in the unbelievably cheap *Robot Monster* (Astor, 1953), a 3-D movie that also used extensive regular footage from *One Million B.C.*, and in the television series *The Adventures of Rin-Tin-Tin*. Both *Two Lost Worlds* and *Lost Continent* climaxed with that convenient plot device introduced in *The Lost World,* the erupting volcano. A Japanese film *Daitozoku* ('Samurai Pirate'), made by Toho International in 1963, was a colour fantasy having nothing to do with *The Lost World*. But when it was released two years later in the United States, American International Pictures called it *The Lost World of Sinbad.*

An actual remake of the Doyle story came out of Twentieth Century-Fox in 1960, pro-duced and directed by Irwin Allen. Much excitement was generated among movie enthu-siasts when it was announced that the film would not only be made in colour but also feature special effects by the great Willis O'Brien. To everyone's utter disappointment – most of all O'Brien's – the remake utilised live lizards instead of puppet animation, sure-ly a waste of the master's abilities. The new version of *The Lost World* starred Claude

Rains as a less boisterous Professor Challenger, who discovers atop the prehistoric plateau man-eating plants, a giant spider, headhunters and modern-day lizards unconvincingly adorned with shields, horns, spines and nodes to represent dinosaurs. Even the youngest members of the audience chuckled when Challenger points to an overblown iguana and stakes his reputation on its being a living 'brontosaurus!'

The Missing Link of the first version was now a beautiful female savage. Added to the plot were such elements as Poxton's (Michael Rennie) financing the expedition because he believes the Lost World to hold a treasure in diamonds. The ending of the new *Lost World* was most disappointing to those who fondly recalled the 1925 picture. After leading his crew to safety through a graveyard of dinosaur bones and following an encounter with a 'fire monster' (actually a tegu lizard decorated with fake horns and other unconvincing attachments) that lives in a stream of hot lava, Challenger shows them what he plans to bring back to civilisation – the 'fire monster's' egg. The group watches the egg hatch into a junior version of its parent. And when Challenger identifies this mythical creature as 'tyrannosaurus rex!' the audience has even more reason to laugh. The film ends with the hint of a sequel, which was announced in 1964 as *Return to the Lost World*, but, perhaps fortunately, the picture was never made. The movie's 'dinosaur' footage, however, was used again and again in Irwin Allen's various television series, including *Voyage to the Bottom of the Sea* and *The Time Tunnel*. Several shots from the picture even made an unwelcomed appearance in *When Dinosaurs Ruled the Earth* (Hammer Films, 1970), which otherwise featured the superb model animation of Jim Danforth.

To publicise *The Lost World*, Twentieth Century-Fox issued a one-page newspaper comic strip. In 1960, Dell Comics (Western Publishing Company) presented a comic book of *The Lost World* based on the remake film. During the 1940s, Planet Comics (Fiction House) ran a series called *The Lost World* about Earth's future take-over by conquerors from another planet. During the early 1940s there was also a radio drama of *The Lost World*, written by John Dickson Carr and serialised by the BBC.*

In 1930, Marcel Delgado was telephoned by Willis O'Brien. Following the completion of *The Lost World*, Delgado had lost his prestige at the studio. 'Only the "top" stars and officials were allowed to visit our department,' Delgado wrote. 'Among the "Greats" was Milton Sills, who had formerly been a college professor. He talked to me for hours about dinosaurs and prehistoric animals, which helped me a great deal in my work. I also had the great privilege of meeting Greta Nisson, Nita Naldi, Colleen Moore, Bessie Love, Rudolph Valentino, Lewis Stone, Wallace Beery, and many others. These people were all very gracious to me, but I was to find that after *The Lost World* was finished and I had to seek employment in the regular miniature department of the studio, I was treated with disrespect and discriminated against because of my Mexican heritage. I realise now that it was a mistake for me to have taken work in the regular department but I felt it was necessary in order for me to continue my work along that line.' O'Brien told Delgado that he and director Harry Hoyt were about to embark on another dinosaur project, this time for RKO-Radio Pictures. The film was to be called *Creation* with special effects to make *The Lost World* appear crude by comparison. Naturally, Delgado joined the team.

Creation was to be an adventuresome story of a group of people who journey by submarine to an enormous promontory that rises to the surface of the sea during an earthquake. Stranded on this body of land, the party encounters more brontosaurs, a pair of battling triceratops and other prehistoric animals. Later, one of the crew members (played by Ralf Harolde) kills a baby triceratops, after which its mother pursues and gores him to death (this sequence being the only extant footage from *Creation*). The action continues as the group is pursued by a plated stegosaurus to the ruins of an ancient temple, after

Concept art for the triceratops attack in Creation*, one of the few surviving scenes of the film. Denham and the* Venture *crew are subject to a similar attack in* King Kong*.*

which the dinosaur fights and is killed by a hungry tyrannosaurus. It is during another volcanic eruption that the group is finally rescued by two Chilean airplanes.

Delgado, O'Brien and Hoyt worked on *Creation* in 1930 and 1931. Had the picture been completed it would have exceeded the million-dollar price range. But except for some impressive test scenes, it was never finished, though Harry Hoyt was determined to keep the project alive. Revamping the *Creation* storyline, Hoyt planned to make *Lost Atlantis* in 1938, utilising the talents of Fred Jackman, one of the special effects technicians on *The Lost World,* who built 25 new dinosaurs for the upcoming production. The picture was halted prematurely but was revised in 1940, with Walter Lantz and Edward Nassour intended to create the dinosaur effects. But Hoyt's *Lost Atlantis* project, like its namesake, perished, never to resurface again.

Even so, the *Creation* project was not entirely dead. Elements from it would merely be shifted to a new home, the stunning special effects designed for a film that brought to life the prehistoric denizens of the unmapped Skull Island. This was the domain of Kong.

* The Canadian remake of *The Lost World* (1992) was screenwritten by exploitation veteran Harry Alan Towers, featuring John Rhys-Davies (Gimli in *The Lord of the Rings*) as Challenger and some underwhelming rubber dinosaur suits. It made few waves but garnered a sequel (*Return to the Lost World*, 1993). Much more impressive was BBC TV's Christmas 2001 version, starring Bob Hoskins as the professor and computer-animated primordial beasts created by the team behind the award-winning *Walking with Dinosaurs* series. With obvious technical advantages over the O'Brien classic, it has some claim to being the definitive film version of Conan Doyle's fantasy adventure.

HIS MAJESTY, *KING KONG* — III
EIGHTH WONDER OF THE WORLD

By Donald F. Glut

Merian C. Cooper and Ernest B. Schoedsack had been prominent military figures during the second decade of the twentieth century. Their exploits in foreign lands were heroic and colourful enough to rival those of their imaginary counterparts, Carl Denham and Jack Driscoll, the two heroes of *King Kong*. In 1923 the two men formed Cooper-Schoedsack Productions, a company to specialise in documentaries on such subjects as wild animals and savage tribes. But their first movie venture, capturing native Africans on film, ended in disaster, as a ship explosion destroyed all of the team's precious footage.

Grass (1925), a film made by Cooper, Schoedsack and author Marguerite Harrison, followed Mrs. Harrison into Asia in search of a lost tribe. She was shown accompanying the forgotten Baba Ahmedi tribe in search of grasslands in the valleys near Persia's central plateau. Following her filmed adventure, Mrs. Harrison left Cooper and Schoedsack who went ahead with another motion picture two years later.

It was with this 1927 production, *Chang*, that Cooper and Schoedsack were planting the seed which would eventually mature into the classic *King Kong*. Set in a Thailand jungle, *Chang* is a man-vs.-beasts story in which a Lao tribe is in conflict with the predacious cats of the jungle. Yet the people's most dangerous threat is the dreaded *chang* which is finally caught in a trap and exposed as a baby elephant, a creature that had ruined the rice patch necessary for their survival. The high point of the films was an elephant stampede that destroys the village before the *chang* monsters can be rounded up and dominated. Insofar as the film's advertising was concerned, *chang* was a word enveloped in mystery and with an obvious similarity to the name Kong. The animal footage from *Chang* was later incorporated into a good number of films including *The Last Outpost* (1935) and *The Jungle Princess* (1937), both made by Paramount.

But Cooper wanted to film 'the ultimate in adventure', something to thrill not only the demanding public but himself as well. He was thinking in terms of a fantasy as opposed to the *Chang* style of dramatic documentary. In Cooper's mind was the image of an enormous gorilla battling a fleet of fighter planes from its perch atop the Empire State Building. (In 1962 French writer Jean Boullet suggested that *King Kong* might have been strongly influenced by Jonathan Swift's 1726 novel of *Gulliver's Travels*. Illustrations from various editions of *Gulliver's Travels* depicting an enormous monkey or ape tenderly caressing Gulliver, reaching for him through a window, carrying him across the rooftops and finally holding him while surmounting a tall tower-like building, though published long before *King Kong*, bear striking resemblances to scenes in Cooper's motion picture.)

Escape from Skull Mountain: Ann (Fay Wray) is lowered from the cliff on the back of her rescuer, Jack Driscoll (Bruce Cabot). But Kong will follow her to the ends of the earth.

KING KONG COMETH!

Cooper's friend W. Douglas Burden had related his adventures on the Malaysian island of Komodo, inhabited by the giant Komodo dragons (*varanus komodoensis*), the largest existing lizards, some weighing 250 pounds and attaining lengths of ten feet. Knowledge of these formidable reptiles fed the plot hatching in Cooper's brain. He envisioned a prehistoric island where a primitive people gave worship to ancient gods, where saurians from the dinosaur era roamed and hunted at will, and all under the domination of his original conception of a gigantic gorilla. Then Cooper began to backtrack, considering the expedition that would discover the great anthropoid monster and bring him to Man's world. Gunfire would prove useless against the huge creature, yet there would be one weapon against which not even he could survive. Cooper recalled the fairy tale of 'Beauty and the Beast'.

Cooper's original idea was to feature an actor in a gorilla suit for the proposed film while the prehistoric reptiles would be played by live Komodo dragon lizards. But the project would have been a time-consuming and expensive one which neither Paramount nor Metro-Goldwyn-Mayer cared to undertake. For a while Cooper abandoned the motion picture medium altogether to pursue a new career in the aviation industry.

In 1931, Merian C. Cooper was commissioned by RKO-Radio Pictures producer David O. Selznick to salvage a number of unfinished movie projects including the scrapped *Creation*. Cooper did more than merely salvage the footage. He felt that *Creation* was not viable in its present form of 'just a lot of animals walking around', but he recognised O'Brien's prehistoric world as the perfect setting for his monster gorilla.

Both Willis O'Brien and Marcel Delgado were soon working again on what was developing from their aborted *Creation* project. After Selznick gave Cooper the go-ahead to produce a reel of test footage, O'Brien instructed Delgado as to the design of Kong, Cooper's gorilla. Following the animator's description, Delgado created a combination gorilla and human being, which Cooper dismissed as resembling a 'monkey and a man with long hair'. When Delgado's second attempt at creating a suitable ape monster still retained certain human characteristics, Cooper roared that he wanted the most brutal and monstrous gorilla that anyone had ever seen. O'Brien argued that human qualities were necessary in order for the public to sympathise with the beast, but General Cooper, accustomed to giving commands, insisted that the amount of sympathy aroused for the ape was in direct proportion to its degree of brutishness. For the final word in the monster's design and proportions, Cooper received the cooperation of Harry C. Raven, curator of zoology at the American Museum of Natural History in New York.

For the present, Cooper's project was entitled *The Beast* and O'Brien commenced to shoot a test reel. Delgado constructed the eighteen-inch-tall ape's body from a metal, ball-and-socket-jointed 'skeleton' and padded him with realistic cotton muscles. The outer covering was made from rabbit fur.

Meanwhile mystery writer Edgar Wallace was assigned to write the script for *The Beast*. Actually, Wallace's work on the production was minimal insofar as the final product was concerned. He prepared a 110-page scenario titled *Kong* which he admitted was mostly Cooper's story. In the Wallace version of the plot, Carl Denham, an explorer, circus man and once friend of P. T. Barnum, is aboard a tramp steamer when he rescues the survivor of a shipwreck on an uncharted island. Denham laughs at the man's tale of sea serpents. Meanwhile, Shirley and John, the heroine and hero of the story, and a crew of ex-convicts are in a lifeboat which is overturned by an apatosaurus. The survivors reach the island where prehistoric monsters abound. Shirley becomes the intended rape victim of the crew when Kong appears, rescuing her from one 'fate worse than death' and carrying her through the jungle to one considerably worse. In his cave Kong displays his affections for Shirley by gently caressing her cheek and offering her a pterodactyl egg. Later a drugged Kong is exhibited to the public in Madison Square Garden. But when the giant ape sees his beloved Shirley menaced by Denham's circus tigers, he escapes his cage and kills them. His final stand atop the Empire State Building occurs during a storm. After being riddled with bullets fired by airborne policemen, Kong is electrocuted by a bolt of lightning.

Left: Merian C. Cooper peruses Kong's *magazine serialisation with leading lady Fay Wray. Right: Cooper follows in the Great Ape's footsteps, courtesy of Miss Wray.*

When RKO disdained the *Kong* title because of its Oriental sound and its similarity to *Chang*, Wallace suggested that the project be renamed *King Ape.* The title was considered; but that change proved to be the end of Wallace's involvement with the picture. Early in February of 1932 he was stricken with pneumonia and on the tenth of that month, his condition further complicated by diabetes, Edgar Wallace died. Schoedsack's wife Ruth Rose (whose daring and loyalty to her husband's adventurous career were the inspirations for *King Kong*'s heroine Ann Darrow) wrote the final version of the film which went into production as *The Eighth Wonder of the World.*

Using the woodcut illustrations of Gustave Doré (*The Divine Comedy, Paradise Lost,* and *The Bible*) for a basis, O'Brien's craftsmen created an atmospheric nightmare realm in miniature, with added detail and depth achieved by painting scenery on sheets of glass. For economy some of the prehistoric creatures left over from *Creation* were taken out of storage. With the Kong model completed, the test reel for the film was ready to be shot.

The utmost secrecy was maintained as O'Brien shot his creatures frame by frame. Meanwhile, Cooper and Schoedsack had joined forces in 1932 for *The Most Dangerous Game*, a movie based on Richard Connell's famous short story about a big game hunter who stalks human beings. A moody jungle set was erected for the movie, with dense foliage, rocks and even a ravine bridged by a fallen tree. Starring in *The Most Dangerous Game* were Robert Armstrong and Fay Wray. Cooper lured Miss Wray to the *Kong* project by promising that she would star opposite 'the tallest, darkest leading man in Hollywood'. While Schoedsack directed *The Most Dangerous Game*, Cooper managed to borrow both Armstrong and Wray between takes, using their talents in the *Kong* live-action footage. He also utilised the ravine and its log, shooting scenes to match what O'Brien was creating on his animation tables. The result was a remarkable ten minutes of action-jammed footage.

The test reel of *Kong* opened with the *Creation* scene of the man being slain by the irate triceratops. Meanwhile, Kong is carrying Ann Darrow (Fay Wray) across the log bridge. Denham (Robert Armstrong) and his crew members are charged by an arsinoitherium, a fantastic, extinct horned mammal. When the men are forced onto the log, Kong shakes them off and into the ravine, where they become food for an enormous spider, octopus and various lizards seemingly born in Doré's engravings. The sequence climaxes with Kong's battling a huge tyrannosaurus to protect Ann, after which a monstrous vulture (teratornis) flies away from its scaly corpse.

The test reel, most of which would inevitably be used in the finished production, was received with general enthusiasm. *Kong*, or *King Kong* as it was later rechristened to make the title sound less Oriental, was given the official RKO go-ahead. Delgado promptly constructed an additional five Kong models. For shots in which human beings and Kong were shown in close proximity, the RKO propmen built an enormous paw (that could grasp and release Miss Wray and whomever else it held), a foot and a full-sized bust of the King. This latter contrivance had a face six and one half feet wide, ears twelve inches long and ten-inch fangs. 85 motors permitted the eyes and face to move realistically, all operated by six men crowded together inside the chest. The whole affair was covered with the skins of 30 bears. Brow furrowing, eyes rolling, nostrils flaring and mouth opening to reveal the white teeth, this apparatus provided some terrifying close-ups of an angry or curious Kong.

In animating the miniature figure of King Kong, Willis O'Brien infused much of his own personality into the giant ape. Darleen O'Brien, his widow, has been reported as stating that Kong's mannerisms were her husband's, and that is yet another reason for the durability of the mighty anthropoid. Kong, though usually a mere miniature puppet brought to life by the animation process, had personality, a quality that is sorely lacking in most film behemoths. For the story that Merian C. Cooper had in mind, the film required a monster for whom his audience would care.

THE KING OF KONGS

By Denis Gifford

Fay Wray was at RKO-Radio as the title role in *The Most Dangerous Game* (1932): pursued through a foggy, boggy jungle by a Russian Count with a Tartar bow and *The Hounds of Zaroff* – which was the British title for this exciting expansion of Richard Connell's award-winning short story. Leslie Banks played the twisted sadistic aristocrat, a Hollywood debut for the British actor continuing the sinister tradition. Zaroff gave his pretty prey a head start in more ways than one. His trophy room was hung with stuffed souvenirs of similar hunts. This scene was too much for Britain: the censor, Zaroff-like, chopped it off. Fay Wray learned it had all been a dummy run when she was summoned by the producer.

'Mr. Cooper said to me that he had an idea for a film in mind. The only thing he'd tell me was that I was going to have the tallest, darkest leading man in Hollywood. Naturally, I thought of Clark Gable.' What she got was King Kong.

Merian Coldwell Cooper, a Florida-born flier, soldier of fortune and journalist, had joined forces with an ex-Keystone Comedy cameraman named Ernest B. Schoedsack to create the American documentary. Their *Grass* (1925) and *Chang* (1927) are classics of authentic adventure – yet it is through their fantastic fiction of *King Kong* (1933) that they will be ever remembered in cinema history.

> 'Out of an uncharted, forgotten corner of the world, a monster . . . surviving seven million years of evolution . . . crashes into the haunts of civilisation . . . on to the talking screen . . . to stagger the imagination of man!'

Those words in the Souvenir Programme hardly prepared audiences for the film that was about to unreel. 'The Strangest Story Ever Conceived by Man!'. . . 'The Greatest Film the World Will Ever See!' For once the catchlines were right. In the history of horror movies, indeed of movies, *King Kong* still towers above them all.

Kong, the fifty-foot King of Skull Island, somewhere south-west of Sumatra, had in reality a bigger build-up than even the 50 mist-wreathed minutes that precede the shock of his first in-film appearance. The movie was three years in the making, more if you include a pilot piece of prehistoric monster animation made for Harry O. Hoyt's abandoned project, *Creation*. This model work had been done by Willis O'Brien, man of *The Lost World*, and it caught the eye of David O. Selznick, newly arrived at RKO as vice-president in charge of production. He showed the reel to Merian C. Cooper, who had already come up with an idea about an outsize ape. Instead of expensive location shooting, could Cooper construct his giant gorilla idea entirely in the studio, using animation?

Edgar Wallace, whose play *The Terror* had been the first horror talkie, arrived from London on 5 December 1931. He had an eight-week contract with RKO to script a horror film. Three days later he wrote to his wife, 'I am also doing a story of prehistoric life!' For inspiration they ran him *Dracula* ('Crude horror stuff, but I must say it raised my hair a little bit') and *Murder by the Clock* ('The actor was the very man I want for my horror story'*), and on the 12th Cooper took him to see O'Brien making another test, a process shot.

> 'The camera shoots against a blue background lit up by about 50 orange arc lamps. It was two men making an attack upon a prehistoric beast. The beast, of course, was not there: he is put in afterwards, and every movement of the men is controlled by a man who is seeing the beast through a moviola, and signals by means of a bell every movement that the men make.'

KING KONG COMETH!

Pre-release publicity for Kong, *January 1933, before his royal title was added. The Great Ape peels away Ann's clothes in a scene later censored by the new Hollywood Production Code.*

This was the Dunning Process in action. On 30 December, Wallace saw the finished scenes: 'They were not particularly good, though there was one sequence where a man is chased by a dinosaurus.' Wallace went into the animation room, a projection room converted into a workshop. O'Brien had completed the skeleton and framework of 'the giant monkey which appears in this play' (the King was as yet unchristened).

'I saw a woodcarver fashioning the skull on which the actual figure will be built. In another place was a great scale model of a gigantic gorilla, which had been made specially. One of the gorilla figures will be nearly 30 feet high. All round the walls are wooden models of prehistoric beasts. There are two miniature sets with real miniature trees, on which the prehistoric animals are made to gambol. Only 50 feet can be taken a day of the animating part. Every move of the animal had to be fixed by the artist, including the ripples of his muscles. Of course it is a tedious job.'

To anyone but a man of Willis O'Brien's devotion. Kong and the other models had to be separately photographed every time their position was changed a sixteenth of an inch. Said O'Brien, 'We worked ten hours a day – the fight between Kong and the pterodactyl took seven weeks to film!'

O'Brien had his work on *The Lost World* to guide him, but this time there was a brand-new problem. Since 1925 the movies had learned to talk: what did a prehistoric monster sound like? Murray Spivak of RKO's sound department built 40 noisemaking instruments in all. To vocalise an arsinoitherium he blew a column of air through a vox humana pipe from an old organ. He next rerecorded this hiss at a subnormal speed: lowering it an octave added a note of terror. Then he reversed the soundtrack and slowed that down yet another octave. For other monsters he recorded the growls of cougars, leopards and lions, reversing them to obtain previously unknown noises. His biggest problem, of course, was Kong. The type of sound made by a prehistoric ape would naturally relate to its present-day descendant, but a gorilla's growl was less than effective: Kong was 50 feet tall. Recording gorilla cries backwards at a slow speed was part of the answer, the rest was a specially built sound-box 25 feet square. This came in handy for hollow thumps when the great ape beat his chest.

Cooper had key scenes sketched in detail before the film went on the floor, and no fewer than 27 models of Kong were made, in different sizes but all to scale with the ape's official vital statistics:

Height	50 ft
Face	Seven ft from hairline to chin
Nose	Two ft
Lips	Six ft from corner to corner
Brows	Four ft three in
Mouth	Six ft when stretched as in a smile
Eyes	Each ten in long
Ears	One ft long
Eye-teeth	ten in high, seven in at base
Molars	Fourteen in round, four in high
Chest	60 ft in repose
Legs	Fifteen ft
Arms	23 ft
Reach	75 ft

When Kong reached for Fay Wray and examined her curiously, peeling off what was left of her clothes, the half-minute scene took 23 hours to film.

'They had a huge rubber arm with a steel cable inside large enough to hold me. The fingers were pressed around my waist and then, by leverage, they lifted me up into the air. All the close-ups were done that way. There was a tiny little doll model used for when King Kong was holding me. It was about three inches long. I couldn't tell the difference when I would go to see the day's work, it was blended that well.'

Kong's name came from Cooper's fondness for mysterious monosyllables. Selznick liked the title, but the New York office objected: they thought it too much like his *Chang* and *Rango*. They publicised it as *The Beast*. Wallace suggested *King Ape* in January 1931, and although the complete picture was actually advertised as simply *Kong* in January 1933, it was finally combined with Wallace's title for copyright registration on February 1933 as *King Kong*: exactly one year after Wallace's death.

King Kong had a monster premiere: it opened at the world's two largest theatres, the Radio City Music Hall and the Roxy in New York, simultaneously: the only picture ever to do so. 10,000 seats packed for ten shows a day: for escapist entertainment there was clearly no Depression. *King Kong* came in at $650,000: it is still making money. When unloosed on television for the first time, one New York station ran it sixteen times in seven days.

* Irving Pichel. He did not, in the end, act in it; he directed it! (*Before Dawn*, 1933.)

THE MEN WHO SAVED *KING KONG*

By Steve Vertlieb

King Kong had his Hollywood premiere at Grauman's Chinese Theatre on Friday evening, March 24th, 1933. The souvenir-programme book contained the following publicity blurb: 'Out of an uncharted, forgotten corner of the world, a monster surviving seven million years of evolution . . . crashes into the haunts of civilisation . . . onto the talking screen . . . to stagger the imagination of man.' *Mystery* magazine celebrated the event by beginning a serialisation of the story in their February, 1933 issue. Bruce Cabot and Fay Wray were on the cover, and the cover blurb billed the tale as 'The last and the greatest creation of Edgar Wallace.'

On opening night in Hollywood the premiere jitters were building and managed to leave practically no one untouched. But this night was not the beginning of the suspense, only the climax, for rumours had been circulating for months as to who and what King Kong was to be. RKO Radio pictures purchased one of the longest commercials in advertising history when, on February tenth, 1933, the National Broadcasting Company aired a 30-minute radio programme to let America know of the impending birth of King Kong. It was a show within a show; a sort of coming attraction, complete with specially tailored script and realistic sound effects. Reaction to the broadcast was exactly as hoped for – merely tremendous!

Original publicity releases and newspaper ads gave out verbal previews of what was to come: 'Monsters of Creation's Dawn Break Loose in Our World Today' . . . 'Never before had human eyes beheld an ape the size of a battleship' . . . 'They saw the flying lizard, the fierce brontosaurus, big as twenty elephants . . . and all the living, fighting creatures of the infant world.' . . . 'The giant ape leaped at the throat of the dinosaur and the death fight was on. A frightened girl, in 1933, witnessed the most amazing combat since the world began.'

Trailers (Coming Attractions) at the time, normally accustomed to previewing the most exciting scenes in a picture in order to entice a given audience, were deliberately secretive and non-committal. Only a huge, frightening shadow was seen by theatregoers, accompanied by warnings like 'This is only the shadow of King Kong . . . See the greatest sight that your eyes have ever beheld at this theatre – beginning Sunday!'

Sid Grauman was a showman and had earned his reputation from years of inventive staging. On this night of all nights he wasn't going to be caught with his curtains down. Grauman arranged for a very special seventeen-act extravaganza to precede the first showing of *King Kong*. He hired dancers, singers and musicians for the gala evening. To be sure, it was a night that no one who was there would ever forget. Recreated in these pages is the original program produced for that memorable evening over 70 years ago. Outside Grauman's Chinese Theatre, that opening night was a life-size replica of Kong's head!

Finally, the moment that the huge audience in Hollywood had waited for was at hand. The house lights dimmed, the projectionist started his machine and a hush fell over the crowd. On screen, the mammoth Radio Pictures tower beeped excitedly atop a spinning globe. It faded out and into a *Radio Pictures Presents* plaque. Finally, the logo faded out and onto the waiting screen came the title in great block lettering, 'KING KONG'. And did it come? From the background, the title suddenly zoomed up front to take its rightful place, prominently, in the foreground. It might have almost been an early form of 3-D!

Joel McCrea, Fay Wray's co-star in The Most Dangerous Game *(1932), was Master of Ceremonies for the elaborate premiere of* King Kong *at Graumans' Chinese Theatre*

KING KONG COMETH!

It was rumoured several years ago that a special fifteen-minute, introductory film was made for the premiere showing of the feature in Hollywood that explained, basically, how the technical wizardry in *King Kong* was accomplished. Supposedly, the prologue was never again seen outside of the 'Official' premiere.

Yet, according to the man behind the ape, Merian Cooper, no such film was ever made. Your author spoke to Mr. Cooper about this, and 'Coop' emphatically states that the film in question does not now, and never has existed. The studio wanted to keep their new discoveries private. After all the work and risks involved in the making this revolutionary film, *no one* at RKO (least of all General Cooper) , was about to advertise their secrets.

It has been said that newly rediscovered 'censored' scenes from *Kong* were snipped by censors' scissors in time for the big theatrical reissue in 1952 because they were too brutal and . . . well . . . sexy. Scenes were of King Kong playfully and naively inspecting the torn dress worn by Fay Wray, and then removing parts of it, lifting them to his nose and sniffing the strange scent; holding a villager between his teeth; smashing down violently a structure upon which natives were standing and hurling spears; grinding the head of a writhing native into the mud on the ground with his foot; climbing the outer wall of a New York hotel at which Ann Darrow (Fay Wray) was staying, in search of his captive at large, and finding the first woman he sees asleep in her bed, then drawing her to him out through the window, examining her in mid-air and, realising that he has picked the wrong girl, callously allowing her to slip through his fingers and fall to the ground below; and, lastly, chewing casually on a native New Yorker. It's surprising he didn't break his teeth!

It may now be wondered, however, if those sequences weren't actually discarded in 1933 *after the first run engagements*, and when the film went into general release, for the recorded 'running time' listed in the original studio press book is 100 minutes some five minutes less than the film would last with the additional 'censored' scenes left intact. In 1952 it was still 100 minutes.

As big and exciting as the Hollywood premier was, *King Kong* really gave its world premiere some three weeks earlier to the city that graciously destroyed itself for movie history. It was fitting and proper that New York City host the unveiling of Carl Denham's Monster, King Kong, the eighth wonder of the world!

King Kong *impacts upon civilisation. This classic poster emphasises Kong's assault upon Manhattan.*

Kong premiered simultaneously at the Radio City Music Hall and New Roxy in New York. In Hollywood, Grauman's Chinese Theatre featured a jungle cabaret with 'Voo-doo dancers' attended by celebrities like Chaplin and Dietrich.

And so it was that on March 2nd, 1933, *King Kong* created almost as much chaos for real as he did in the film. This was no ordinary premiere for, so great was the demand to see the new film that, in the midst of America's worst and most tragic Depression, *two enormous theatres* were required to play the film simultaneously in order to fill the public's demand for seats. Both the Radio City Music Hall and the Roxy Theatre, *with a combined seating capacity of 10,000 people*, were filled for every performance of the film from the moment when the doors opened at 10:30a.m. on Thursday, March 2nd. Both theatres took out combined ads in the *New York Times* the day preceding the opening. Kong, himself, was pictured atop the Empire State Building holding Fay Wray in one paw, and crushing a bi-plane in the other. The caption next to the ape and atop the title read: 'KONG THE MONSTER!'

Huge as a skyscraper . . .crashed into our city! See him wreck man's proudest works while millions flee in horror! See him atop the Empire State Tower! Battling planes for the woman in his ponderous paw! *King Kong* outleaps the maddest imagination!'

As in Hollywood there were stage shows here also. 'Stage Shows as Amazing as These Mighty Theatres', proclaimed the advertisement. "Jungle Rythms" – brilliant musical production! Entire singing and dancing ensemble of Music Hall and New Roxy!

Kong towers above the urban skyline, with a gigantic Fay Wray in his paw. This publicity still communicates the nightmarishly surreal tone of King Kong.

Spectacular dance rhythms by ballet corps and Roxyettes! Soloists, Chorus, Symphony, Orchestras, Company of 500!' 'Big enough for the Two Greatest Theatres at the same time!'

Kong played to standing crowds for ten complete performances daily. On the day of the opening a second ad appeared in New York's entertainment pages. The publicity blurbs read, in part, 'Shuddering terror grips a city . . . Shrieks of fleeing millions rise to the ears of a towering monster . . . Kong, king of an ancient world, comes to destroy our world – all but that soft, white female thing he holds like a fluttering bird . . . The arch-wonder of modern times.'

When, in 1933, President Roosevelt declared a moratorium and closed the banks, the following ad appeared in New York's papers: 'No Money . . . yet New York dug up $89,931.00 in four days (March 2, 3, 4, 5) to see '*King Kong*' at Radio City setting a new all-time world's record for attendance of any indoor attraction.' This is all the more startling considering that general admission prices were far less expensive (10c to 50c) than they are today. Full page ads in the trade journals were headed by the impressive lead-in, 'The Answer To Every Showman's Prayer.' And it was. This was no case of attempting to sell a loser, for *Kong* was surely a box office bonanza for all film exhibitors sharing in the feast.

Fay Wray's awesome scream is equalled in its popularity only by Johnny Weissmuller's well known cry as Tarzan, the Ape Man. No one has ever attempted a guess at why Fay's screaming should have so completely overshadowed the tries of all other actresses through-out the 70-odd years since *Kong*'s first release but few would doubt her right

This 1933 poster shows the beginning of Kong's rampage in New York. The 2005 Peter Jackson remake will stay faithful to the events depicted by Cooper and O'Brien.

to the title of the world's most celebrated screamer. So, it is not surprising to learn that RKO used that contract scream in the voices of countless other actresses who were not as healthily endowed. When Helen Mack opened her fragile lips to cry out in *The Son of Kong* it was not her voice audiences heard but that of Fay Wray. As late as 1945 Fay's scream could be heard for Audrey Long in the remake of *The Most Dangerous Game*, *Game of Death*.

But of all of the memorable sounds to come from *King Kong*, the immortal music score by Max Steiner has been heard the most. *Kong*'s thrilling and intricate themes have been played in such later films as *The Son of Kong*, *The Last Days of Pompeii*, *Becky Sharpe*, (the first *full* Technicolor feature), *The Last of the Mohicans*, *The Soldier and the Lady* (from Jules Verne's *Michael Strogoff*), and John Wayne's *Back to Bataan*. Sets and props used in *Kong* also had ways of turning up before the cameras of other pictures. The huge log that Kong hurled furiously into the spider pit was seen in the very same jungle in *The Most Dangerous Game*.

The doors that Cooper had built into the heart of DeMille's Roman wall were transposed two years later from the tropical heat of Skull Island in the East Indies to the Artic wastelands for duty in the second filmed version of H. Rider Haggard's classic fantasy, *She*.

Kong, unlike many other elder film favourites, seems to grow in stature with the passing years and is more cherished today than when it was first released back in the midst of the Depression. At the box office *King Kong* grew more financially rewarding with every new release and must come second to *Gone with the Wind* in its number of new re-releases. It continued to come back to first-run theatres in 1938, 1942, 1947, 1952, 1956 and finally in 1970 for a limited engagement at art theatres across the country. Today's film fans and critics have begun noticing all manner of subtle sophistications that totally escaped the more naive film-goers of the thirties.

In 1932 the cast and crew of *King Kong* sent a Christmas card to Merian Coldwell Cooper that portrayed him, in caricature, shouting, 'Make it bigger. Make it bigger.' Well, the prophecy was realised and Coop got his wish. Carl Denham, a thinly disguised replica of Cooper himself, said on the eve of their coming adventure, 'I'm going out and make the greatest picture in the world, something that nobody's ever seen or heard of. They'll have to think up a lot of new adjectives when I come back!' Denham kept his work, and so did Cooper. He gave the world the finest, best loved and remembered fantasy in the history of motion pictures. And they did have to think up a lot of new adjectives when he came back.

Were it not for Cooper and his deeply rooted faith in *Kong* the movie might never have been made . . . or, worse, it would have been made without its gifted creator continually at the helm. Without his belief in animator Willis O'Brien's stop motion; his insistence that Max Steiner create an original music score for the film when the 'money men' were against the idea; his feeling for authentic, far-off adventure, *Kong* would have turned out quite a different film indeed and, quite probably, would be long forgotten by this time.

However, Merian C. Cooper was very much behind the making of the movie and he, more than Willis O'Brien and Max Steiner, was responsible for saving *King Kong*.

HIS MAJESTY, *KING KONG* – IV

By Donald F. Glut

King Kong unreels with a title card quoting a seemingly authentic 'Old Arabian Proverb' which states: 'And the Prophet Said – And lo, the Beast looked upon the face of Beauty. And it stayed its hand from killing. And from that day, it was as one dead.' In truth the proverb was penned by Cooper himself, though, like the often quoted poem from *The Wolf Man*, it has become assimilated into the canon of popular mythology. Cooper's proverb established the Beauty and the Beast theme right from the outset, though audiences were about to watch the strangest variation on that theme ever filmed.

Aboard the *Venture*, a steamer docked outside New York, Carl Denham, a disgruntled motion picture producer specialising in films about animal life, informs a theatrical agent that his next movie needs a woman to meet the public's demand for a love interest. The agent has not supplied Denham with an actress because the producer has planned a voyage to some unknown destination aboard a ship harbouring a large supply of ammunition and several boxes of gas bombs. Actually, Denham represented Cooper, who was often cruising to savage lands to photograph the unknown. (Denham's stated disdain for cameramen, one of whom panicked at the sight of a charging rhinoceros even though Denham was standing nearby with a rifle, paralleled an actual and

Kong advances on the great doors that separate the village from his primordial domain, like a monster burst forth from the subconscious.

quite similar incident experienced years earlier by Cooper.) Denham is forced to hunt the streets of New York for an actress, finally coming upon an attractive (and hungry) blonde named Ann Darrow who was in the process of stealing an apple from a fruit vender. After Denham offers her a chance at movie stardom, she agrees to go on his mysterious voyage. First mate Jack Driscoll (Bruce Cabot) complains about having a woman aboard ship, but the *Venture* begins its voyage on schedule.

With the *Venture* somewhere in the Indian Ocean 'way west of Sumatra', Denham at last reveals their destination to Captain Englehorn (Frank Reicher), who claims that there is nothing out there for thousands of miles. But Denham's map was drawn by the captain of a Norwegian barque who had sketched an uncharted island. 'And across the base of that peninsula,' says Denham, 'cutting it off from the rest of the island, is a wall . . . built so long ago that the people who live there now have slipped back, forgotten the higher culture that built it. But it's as strong today as it was centuries ago. The natives keep that wall in repair. They need it. There's something on the other side . . . something they fear.'

When Englehorn suggests a hostile tribe, Denham returns with the name of Kong, which the captain believes refers to a Malay superstition.

'Anyway,' Denham replies, 'neither beast nor man. Something monstrous, all-powerful . . . still living, still holding that island in the grip of deadly fear.'

Driscoll gradually becomes infatuated by Ann and worries for her safety as Denham shoots her screen test. Ann is dressed in a filmy 'Beauty' costume ('Beauty and the Beast' the basis for Denham's film as it is Cooper's). Denham directs her to scream, which Ann does thereby continuing Fay Wray's reputation of the screen's champion screamer. (Fay Wray had given out comparable screams in the earlier horror films *The Mystery of the Wax Museum*, *The Most Dangerous Game*, *Dr. X* [all 1932] and *The Vampire Bat* [1933].)

When the *Venture* finally hoves to at their destination, Skull Island (so named for a mountain suggesting a human skull), Denham goes ashore, taking Driscoll, Englehorn, some of the crewmen, and of course the star of his intended motion picture, Ann Darrow. In his direction of the island scenes, Schoedsack was careful to photograph his human actors with as few close-ups as possible. Most of these scenes were taken in full or long shots and often from a high angle, as if to imply right from the beginning the presence of something huge dominating the island.

The rest of Denham's cast is already involved in a show all their own. Dwarfing the village of Skull Islanders is an expansive wall with two enormous wooden gates and surmounted by a tocsin gong. (Actually this magnificent set was not built for *King Kong*. The wall was standing on the lot of the RKO-Pathé Studio in Culver City and was originally constructed for Cecil B. DeMille's 1927 biblical epic, *The King of Kings*. After its appearance in *King Kong*, the wall with its gong became part of the lost island of Lemuria in the serial *The Return of Chandu* [Principal, 1934], starring Bela Lugosi as the famed magician. The serial was later re-cut into a feature-length movie, *Chandu on the Magic Island*, in 1935, while scenes from the chapterplay were included in the compilation feature *Dr. Terror's House of Horrors*, released by National Roadshow in 1943. The wall made its final stand in the Selznick epic *Gone with the Wind* [MGM, 1939] during the spectacular burning of Atlanta sequence, staged by special effects expert Lee Zavitz. Few people in the audience recognised the camouflaged structure that blazed in the background as the wall from King Kong's island.)

There is never any explanation given as to *why* the wall would be equipped with the gates. Certainly whoever built the wall would not have provided an easy entrance for whatever titanic being lived on the apposite side. A native ceremony is in progress in front of the wall, with a young native girl adorned by flowers and several warriors dancing about clad in the skins of gorillas. The savages are shouting, 'Kong! Kong!' to the thunderous sound of drums.

The scene was augmented by the powerful strains of Max Steiner's music score. Steiner, whose distinguished career would eventually include scoring more than 300 motion pictures, had watched the *King Kong* footage *sans* music and wrote what he felt, resulting in an impassioned masterpiece that perfectly conveyed the power and raw savagery of the King and his primitive world. Using a stopwatch, he timed his music so that it coincided perfectly with the visuals. (When the tribal chieftain, played by Noble Johnson, notices the presence of the Caucasian intruders, his every step matches a beat of Steiner's music.) *King Kong* proved to be one of the earliest fully-orchestrated motion pictures with an extensive score and its music was later recycled for a number of films. (Steiner's musical score for *King Kong* included the following selections: 'King Kong', 'Jungle Dance', 'The Forgotten Island', 'A Boat in the Fog', 'The Railing', 'Aboriginal Sacrifice Dance', 'Meeting with the Black Men', 'Sea at Night', 'Stolen Love', 'The Sailors', 'The Bronte', 'Cryptic Shadows', 'The Cave', 'The Snake', 'Humorous Ape', 'The Pen', 'Furioso', 'The Swimmers', 'The Escape', 'Return of Kong', 'King Kong March', 'Fanfare No. 1', 'Fanfare No. 2', 'Fanfare No. 3', 'Agitato', 'Elevated Sequence', ' The Train', 'The Aeroplane' and 'Dance of Kong'.)

The chief and the witch doctor want to replace the native girl with the golden-haired Ann for the 'Bride of Kong'. Naturally Denham refuses, quietly ushering his group back to the ship. That night Ann is kidnapped by the natives and forced back to the island. By the time that Denham and Driscoll realise she is missing, Skull island is already alive with flickering torches and rhythmic drum beats.

The gates of the great wall are opened and Ann, screaming desperately, is dragged through them and up to a raised altar, where she is bound between two pillars. The chief, standing at the top of the wall, invokes the name of Kong while his men sound the ritual gong. Ann writhes as she hears the sounds of ponderous footsteps and bestial grunts (all timed with Steiner's music). Then, as the trees are torn aside, she stares into the leering face of Kong, a monster gorilla about 50 feet high. Kong releases her from bondage and, fascinated by her beauty, carries her into his jungle kingdom. Peering through a window at the bottom of the wall, Driscoll briefly glimpses the hairy abductor of the woman he loves.

Never is it explained just what Kong does with his human 'brides'. Nor is it ever revealed just what his fascination is for the yellow-haired Ann Darrow unless it is her uniqueness on this island. Whatever his attraction to her, it is enough for him to be virtually tame when alone with her and a raging monster when her life is threatened. Biologically there can be no real sexual attraction by a gorilla for a female *homo sapiens* – especially when the ape is some 50 feet tall. Surely the relationship between King Kong and his blonde captive remains one of the most bizarre 'love affairs' ever photographed by motion picture cameras. Somehow audiences accepted it.

Denham, Driscoll and a rescue party, leaving a number of sailors with the natives, pursue Kong on the other side of the wall, guided by a trail of giant footprints, broken foliage and the sounds made by the giant ape. Yet there are horrors besides Kong in this prehistoric jungle. The party is attacked by the plated dinosaur stegosaurus which Denham fells with his gas bombs. (The *King Kong* stegosaurus, showing the dorsal plates paired and with eight deadly spikes on the tail, was actually in error, apparently based upon restorations of the animal by E. Ray Lankester in 1905 and Richard Swann Lull in 1910. A more correct restoration of the animal, with alternating plates, four tail spikes and a less 'squarish' body shape was made by Charles R. Knight as early as 1903.*)

The chase continues as the rescue group comes upon a misty swamp. But as they traverse the water in a hastily constructed raft, their craft is overturned by an angry

Mis-match of the twentieth century: with his fluidly changing scale placing him at his greatest height, Kong growls with excitement at his prize, the terrified Ann.

apatosaurus which snaps some of the men up in its powerful jaws and charges the rest of the group onto the beach. One crew member is trapped in a treetop by the roaring saurian and meets a gruesome end in the monster's teeth.

Hearing the approach of his human pursuers, Kong places Ann in the fork of a gnarled tree, then confronts them in an edited version of the *King Kong* test reel. Six sailors are trapped by Kong on the log bridge (the arsinoitherium footage having been excised) and shaken off to perish in the pit below. Driscoll, who has managed to climb down a liana, watches in horror from a shallow cave in the cliffside. Originally Driscoll beheld the devouring of the men by a giant spider and other nightmarish creatures of the pit, but that footage never survived into the theatres.

(A popular legend insists that the spider sequence was censored for its being overly gruesome. But actually Merian C. Cooper snipped it out of the work print before the film's initial release because, 'It slowed down the action,' as he said to me in 1966. Following its deleted performance in *King Kong*, the giant spider enjoyed a brief motion picture career. In *Genius at Work* [called *Master Minds* before its completion], an RKO movie directed by Leslie Goodwins in 1946, the spider model and other creatures from *King Kong* and *The Son of Kong* can be identified on a background shelf of a movie studio set. The spider later returned in full animation in *The Black Scorpion* [Warner Brothers, 1957], directed by Edward Ludwig, with special visual effects by Willis O'Brien and Pete Peterson. In many ways this film about giant scorpions emerging from underground to menace civilisation is similar to *King Kong*. A scorpion is shown in its underground domain where it battles and kills such monstrous enemies as the spider and a number of oversized worms. Later the scorpions attack mankind and are finally destroyed. The last appearance of the *King Kong* spider was in the science fiction picture

61

KING KONG COMETH!

Women of the Prehistoric Planet, which went into filming as *Prehistoric Planet Women* in 1965 and was released the next year by Realart. Arthur C. Pierce both produced and directed the colour low-budget picture. The spider was not animated, however. It simply 'jumped' when a technician manipulated an unfortunately obvious 'invisible' wire.)

Having dispatched the sailors, Kong attempts to snatch up Driscoll in his huge paw. The first mate slashes Kong's fingers with his knife, then cuts down a weird reptilian creature (with two claws on each hand yet lacking any hind limbs) which had been climbing the vine. Driscoll is saved when Ann's screams and the roars of a tyrannosaurus attract the ape's attention. (During the 1960s, Merian C. Cooper referred to this theropod dinosaur as an allosaurus. But the animal was clearly modelled after a painting of tyrannosaurus in the American Museum of Natural History by Charles R. Knight. Tyrannosaurus rex translates as 'King Tyrant Lizard' and it is only fitting that 'King' Kong should confront the so-called 'king' of the dinosaurs.)

The battle between Kong and the tyrannosaurus re-mains one of the most memorable scenes from *King Kong*. Kong fights his scaly adversary with near-human cunning, leaping on the dinosaur's back, punching it with prize-fighter expertise, using a crude judo throw on it. During the struggle, the tree in which Ann had been placed crashes to the jungle floor. But at last Kong manages to tear open the tyrannosaur's jaws and kill the monster. (This entire sequence was devoid of music, the only sounds being those made by the two battling creatures.)

Carl Denham returns to the great wall while Jack Driscoll resumes his trailing of Kong. Within Skull Mountain, Ann is menaced once again, this time by an elasmosaurus, a reptile with a squat body, serpentine neck and four paddle-like appendages (and somehow remembered by most viewers as simply a colossal snake, the flippers being forgotten). With O'Brien's attention to detail we literally see the tiny figure of Driscoll swimming through the cavern lake from which the saurian had emerged. Kong battles the plesiosaur which coils about him like a prehistoric boa constrictor. Using the reptile's neck like a whip, Kong dashes its head against the rocks until the neck dangles lifelessly in his paws. The ape roars triumphantly and beats his chest, then carries Ann to a ledge which overlooks the island and the docked *Venture*.

Outside the cave, Kong sits with his golden prize, gently touching her, sniffing her and tearing away her clothing like the petals of a flower. But Kong's idyllic moments are interrupted once again, this time by a bat-winged pteranodon which swoops down and attempts to fly off with the woman in its hind claws. While Kong tears the pterodactyl to death (in a battle that required some seven weeks of animation), Driscoll and Ann attempt an escape on a vine hanging down from the cliffside. Kong begins to pull up on the vine when Driscoll and Ann drop down into the lake below.

Breathless, Driscoll and Ann return to the safety of the wall, when Denham's mind begins to work. 'We came here to make a moving picture,' he shouts, 'but we've got something worth more than all the movies in the world!' From Kong's point of view, that something is Ann and soon he is at the gates, then breaking through the massive doors despite the huge bolts. When he does burst through, he unleashes his full wrath against the villagers in an attempt to retrieve his 'bride'. Natives flee in terror as their god grinds them between his jaws and stomps them beneath his feet. Only the gas bombs hurled by Denham and his men eventually bring down the mighty Kong so that he lies unconscious on the beach. 'We'll give him more than chains,' promises Denham. 'He's always been king of his world. But we'll teach him fear. Why, the whole world will pay to see this! We're millionaires, boys! I'll share it with all of you! In a few months it'll be up in lights . . . "Kong, the Eighth Wonder of the World!"'

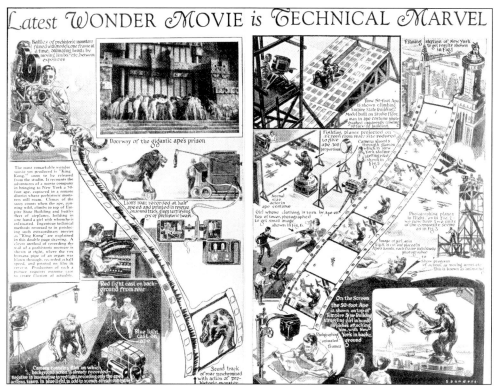

Rare pages from the April 1933 edition of Modern Mechanix and Inventions. *This comic- style production report created the myth that a man in an ape suit appears in* King Kong.

Denham's prediction proves entirely true. Though we are never actually shown just *how* the bulk of Kong was shipped to the city of New York, his mysterious name is soon luring in the patrons at $10 per ticket. The live action for this sequence was shot in Los Angeles, at the Shrine Auditorium. (Originally, Kong was intended to break loose at Yankee Stadium.) Denham, wearing a tuxedo, proudly steps upon the stage to address the crowd: 'Ladies and gentlemen, I'm here tonight to tell you a very strange story, a story so strange that no one will believe it. But ladies and gentlemen, seeing is believing. And we – my partners and I – have brought back the living proof of our adventure, an adventure in which twelve of our party met horrible deaths. But first I want you to see the greatest thing your eyes have ever beheld. He was a king and a god in the world he knew. But now he comes to civilisation merely a captive, a show to gratify your curiosity. Look at Kong, the Eighth Wonder of the World!'

When the curtain rises the crowd gasps, for upon the stage, strapped to a crosslike structure by chrome steel bands, is the helpless Kong. Denham brings Ann and her fiancé John Driscoll onto the stage, then summons the news photographers to snap the first pictures of Kong in captivity. Kong, however, believes that the flashbulbs are harming Ann. With a mighty burst of strength, the ape frees himself from the steel manacles and shackles. Moments later he is loose in the streets of New York.

As in the village, Kong is on a destructive rampage. Driscoll, meanwhile, has led Ann to the safety of a hotel room. Hearing a scream from an upstairs window, Kong ascends the wall of a building, seizing a woman thinking her to be Ann. Realising his mistake, Kong lets her drop to the pavement head-first. Continuing his search, Kong peers through another window and perceives Ann. There is a crash of shattering window glass and Ann is again in the hand of Kong. Just as Kong once confronted the elasmosaurus on Skull Island, he now becomes intrigued by an approaching snakelike object which glows bright in the darkness. Kong's head emerges through the elevated tracks to see the train approaching (its cars boasting advertisements for Cooper and Schoedsack's earlier film *Chang*). Again the ape is the victor as he smashes the tram with his fists while the tiny human beings inside drop to the street.

The climax of *King Kong* is the most famous sequence of all. Just as Kong once roared his defiance from the highest point of Skull Island, now he seeks the tallest peak on his second island home of Manhattan. With the Empire State Building standing out against the dawning sky, the distant figure of King Kong can be seen scaling the towering walls.

The long shot in which King Kong scaled the Empire State Building has long been a source of controversy. The story has persisted through the years that this scene employed an actor in a gorilla costume. The logic behind it was sound enough: Why bother to use the time-consuming animation process for a shot in which the ape could hardly be seen? The story was reinforced by a feature in the April 1933 issue of *Modern Mechanix and Invention* magazine. The article depicted an actor in an ape suit scaling a replica of one side of the Empire State Building which had been built along the studio floor. Furthermore the 'normal size actor in ape costume' was shown atop the Empire State Building's dirigible mooring mast, recreated in miniature, swatting at a scene of attacking airplanes on a rear projection screen.

The myth was given more credence by a number of actors who claimed to have essayed the part of King Kong. Charles Gemora, a Filipino actor who specialised in portraying motion picture apes, was reputed to have played the title character in *King Kong*. His *New York Times* obituary was headlined, '"King Kong" is Dead at 58' and declared, most likely wrongly, that he had played that role. (Gemora did, it is certain, spoof Kong on two occasions.) Ken Roady was given the same credit in the December 21, 1969, issue of the *Chicago Sun-Times* and claimed to have shared animosities with Robert Armstrong and Fay Wray during production of *King Kong*. Later he identified himself as Carmen Nigro, whose story was published in the March 4, 1976, edition of the same Chicago newspaper when both Paramount and Universal were battling for the remake rights to *King Kong*. Nigro claimed to have stood atop a model of the Empire State Building while the photograph accompanying the write-up clearly showed the miniature animation model battling the planes. His description of the sequence was the same as that in *Modern Mechanix and Invention*. 'The way it worked,' he added, 'I had this little doll in my hand that was supposed to be Fay Wray. I put the doll down on the ledge, and then I had to catch one of them little planes. I was wearing ballet shoes covered with fur, and I had rubber suction cups on the bottoms so I could stay balanced on top of the building. It took about four hours to shoot it.' Nigro also claimed to have portrayed the gorillas in *Tarzan of the Apes*, *Tarzan and His Mate* and *Mighty Joe Young*, the third of these actually featuring another ape animated by O'Brien. A later newspaper article published a photograph of Nigro in his gorilla suit which, after being examined by several authorities on motion pictures, make-up and ape costumes, was said to depict a completely unfamiliar ape; Nigro's claims are unable to be substantiated.

Cooper denied any performance by an actor in a gorilla costume in *King Kong*. A good photograph does exist of animator Buz Gibson manipulating a Kong model up the side of a miniature Empire State Building. Perhaps a human actor was used in a bit of forgotten test footage before the film went into production, but thus far the matter remains a mystery.

At the top of the old dirigible mooring mast of the Empire State Building, King Kong

'He was a king and a god in the world he knew. But now he comes to civilisation merely a captive . . .' Crucified before a Broadway audience, this Christ figure won't turn the other cheek.

seems impervious to all harm. It is Driscoll who suggests, 'There's one thing we haven't thought of – airplanes! If he puts Ann down and they can pick him off without hurting her . . .' Soon four Navy biplanes are circling the hairy giant like four mechanical pteranodons. But these winged attackers are equipped with machine guns that blast into his hide, confusing as well as hurting him. Kong grabs one of the planes and sends it crashing down to the street, but his victory is short-lived. A final volley of machine gun fire (the two pilots in this death ship being played by Cooper and Schoedsack in an unbilled cameo) tears into Kong's throat. Dying, a saddened Kong looks toward Ann then topples off the mooring mast. (A high angle shot of a superimposed Kong falling to the street was photographed but never used, as the ape appeared transparent.) As King Kong lies dead in the street, a police officer says to Carl Denham that the airplanes got him. 'Oh, no,' says Denham shaking his head while speaking the classic lines, 'it wasn't the airplanes. It was Beauty killed the Beast.'

King Kong cost a total of $430,000 (or $650,000 including the money spent on *Creation*). What Cooper had was an economically produced epic that ran a total of fourteen reels. In his opinion, however, the picture ran too long. Cooper cut the film down to a more commercially viable length, snipping out some of O'Brien's animation footage including scenes of the arsinoitherium, styracosaurus and triceratops, along with a shot of Kong descending Skull Mountain in pursuit of Driscoll and Ann. The final cut of the picture was ready for public screening by March of 1933. (Scenes from *King Kong* later appeared in the movie *Morgan, A Suitable Case for Treatment* [seen in the United States as

Kong's last stand: one of the greatest moments of the commercial cinema, as the Great Ape snarls defiance at civilisation's pesky little birds that spit lead.

Morgan!] from Cinema V in 1966, in *Rendezvous* [1973], and *Revenge of Rendezvous* [1975]. *King Kong* footage was also incorporated into the television special, *Hollywood: The Selznick Years*. A strange piece of film purporting to be from *King Kong* was included in the 'Monsters We've Known and Loved' segment of the *Hollywood and the Stars* television series in 1964. The scene, showing an unconvincing giant gorilla exhibited on an auditorium stage, was obviously not from this movie.)

The picture premiered at both the New Roxy and Radio City Music Hall on March 2, 1933, the only film ever to play simultaneously at New York's two largest theatres. Accompanying the film was a spectacular stage musical, *Jungle Rhythms*, which helped to pack in the crowds. When the picture opened in Hollywood at Sid Grauman's Chinese Theatre, patrons were greeted by the actual mechanical bust of Kong in the forecourt. Before the film flashed upon Grauman's screen for the first time, Jimmy Savo's chorus line of 50 black dancing girls performed a spectacular number called 'The Dance of the Sacred Ape.' The picture had been brought to the public with a ballyhoo worthy of a real-life Carl Denham. And like the mythical Kong himself, the film proved to be something 'the whole world will pay to see'. *King Kong* paid RKO's bills, raising the studio up from debt. It also became one of Hollywood's finest classics.

King Kong is not only one of the best fantasy pictures of all time but simply one of the greatest movies of any genre. The story is perfectly paced, the special effects superb. Only the acting and dialogue are dated by today's standards, but those supposed faults actually contribute to the picture's charm. Intellectuals have attempted to read certain symbolisms into *King Kong*. Kong represents a Depression-stricken people lashing out against society; Kong is a Christ figure crucified on a stage before an audience of spectators; Kong symbolises the black man and his conflict against his white oppressors; Kong on the Empire State Building depicts the most spectacular phallic symbol ever captured by film; and so on. Cooper has disavowed these 'insights' into his film; he was not the kind of person to consider injecting such messages into his productions. (The Empire State Building, for example, was simply the tallest structure in New York and paralleled Kong's own perch on Skull Mountain.) What Cooper and his associates accomplished was the creation of a masterpiece of cinematic fantasy – a picture made with care, skill and integrity. Whatever messages might lurk beneath the film's surface were entirely coincidental on Cooper's part or, at best, subliminal. Merian C. Cooper had endeavoured to give his audience a romantic and improbable adventure, something they had never before seen. He succeeded admirably.

King Kong has become a perennial success. Reportedly a theatre in Africa has been running the picture on a daily schedule for years. During the late 1950s a New York television station soared in the ratings by broadcasting the picture twice each day for a full week on its *Million Dollar Movie* series. (When *King Kong* was re-released in 1938, a number of scenes were deemed objectionable by the Hays Office and cut from American prints. The censored scenes included the apatosaurus chomping on sailors, Kong tearing the clothes off Fay Wray, Kong brutally attacking the natives on a scaffold, Kong flattening a native under his pressing foot, Kong chewing on various human beings and Kong discovering the wrong girl and dropping her to the pavement in New York. The scenes reveal a more brutal Kong. These outtakes have been shown in British prints of *King Kong* all along and were reinstated to the American theatrical prints in 1968 by Janus Films.)

The picture is unique though the giant monster style of motion picture has become a familiar cliché. Two of the better motion pictures to imitate *King Kong* were again the results of a group effort instigated by Cooper. But not even Delgado, O'Brien, Schoedsack and Robert Armstrong could surpass their original.

*Details pertaining to the prehistoric animals in *King Kong* have often come under criticism by palaeontology-minded film buffs. The apatosaurus is portrayed as an aggressive, possibly even carnivorous animal, while in real life it was a passive herbivore. Tyrannosaurus is portrayed with three claws on each hand while most palaeontologists agree that the animal possessed only two. The flying pteranodon, while shown in King Kong as capable of actual flight, was probably only a glider. In general all of the reptilian monsters of Skull Island were considerably larger than their fossil remains have proven. But their gigantism seemed appropriate for coexistence with the mighty Kong, especially when considering Cooper's constant demand to 'Make it bigger!'

INTERVIEW WITH RAY HARRYHAUSEN
By Lawrence French

In 1933 you saw the picture that changed your life.
Yes, that's when I first saw *King Kong*. I was only thirteen years old and I came out of the theatre absolutely amazed. It just goes to show you how much a film can impress a young person. It really did change my life – I haven't been the same since. It was at Grauman's Chinese theatre in Hollywood, with all the glamorous showmanship they used to put on back then for the opening of a picture. The forecourt was decorated in a jungle setting and they had a full size bust of Kong himself in the forecourt, with pink

Left: the Skull Island beach scene has a surreal quality that makes Kong seem like a beast from the recesses of the human psyche. Right: the behemoth that bestrode NYC.

flamingos roaming around pecking at the sand beneath him. Later on, after *King Kong* had made such a big impression on me, on the weekends Ray Bradbury, Forry Ackerman and I used to go down to the old Pathé lot in Culver City. You could still see the standing set of the of the Skull Island wall from the street, so we'd all look up at the wall and chant, 'Kong, Kong, Kong.'

Half the charm when I first saw *King Kong* was I didn't know how it was done. There were no books available at that time on stop-motion. In fact they tried to hide that stop-motion was a single frame process. I knew it wasn't a man in a suit, but it wasn't until later on that I discovered the glories of stop-motion. But nowadays everybody tells you everything about the picture before it's released and I think it spoils everything. It allows you to start picking the scenes apart.

You also mentioned that you once visited Indonesia to see the supposed location of Skull Island in King Kong.

Yes, I made a pilgrimage to Nias Island because in *King Kong*, Captain Englehorn says, 'I think they speak the language of the Nias Islanders.' So I looked up Nias Island, and by George, there actually is a Nias Island. It's right off the northwest coast of Sumatra. So [my wife] Diana and I took a tour boat there. We arrived early one morning on a launch, in a light fog, but of course there was no Skull Island, no wall on the beach with native drums beating, although I kept hearing Max Steiner's wonderful music in my mind. Nor were there any black natives, but there were a native Asian people. So when I came across someone who looked like a native I thought I'd try out some of Ruth Rose's dialogue on him. I said, 'Bala, bala kum nono Kong.' The man put his hands on his hips and said in perfect English, 'What are you talking about?' Ruth Rose liked to take languages and manipulate them. She told me once that she had based *Kong's* dialogue on an actual language, so there was a basic principle behind it and she was always noted for doing interesting dialogue.

King Kong *is a supreme example of what Pixar's John Lasseter defines as good animation. Namely, when you believe the creature is moving under his own thought processes and doesn't appear to be controlled by an outside force. Would you agree with that?*

Yes, of course. I've always felt that stop-motion adds a wonderful dream-like quality, which *King Kong* certainly had. So I've always tried to do that with my animation. There's something magical that goes on with stop-motion that gives it that quality. You know dinosaurs don't exist yet you're seeing them on the screen. If you saw that wonderful BBC documentary *Walking with Dinosaurs*, the dinosaurs were so real, it was the kind of thing you could never do with stop-motion. So whenever I animated a character, I tried to keep it in line with whatever the basic story idea was, but I didn't try to make it too real, or else it would lose that dream-like quality.

KING KONG
By Danny Peary

With the exception of *The Birth of a Nation* (1915) and *Citizen Kane* (1941), no picture has been the subject of more critical writing than the original *King Kong*, an irreplaceable part of twentieth-century American culture, the greatest, most popular, most intriguing horror-fantasy film ever made. As *King Kong* is a testament for those who believe film is a collaborative art, the majority of articles have dealt with the various achievements of the numerous individuals who worked on the project, with the tremendous contributions of special-effects genius Willis O'Brien and composer Max Steiner (who understood that *Kong* should be scored like a silent picture) being singled out most often. Because there is so much available material that documents the technical wizardry of *Kong*, I will confine myself to two other areas.

An Interpretation. Like most producers, Merian C. Cooper insisted that all his films, including *King Kong*, were strictly 'entertaining pictures', but *Kong* is so rich in implication that few critics haven't read added significance into it. It has been interpreted as: a parable about an innocent, proud country boy (probably a muscular, uneducated black) who is humbled and finally destroyed when he comes to the cold, cruel city; an indictment of 'bring 'em back alive' big-game hunters; a racist visualisation of the fears a white woman has about being abducted by a black – or, as Harry Geduld and Ronald Gottesman suggest, 'a white man's sick fantasy of the Negro's lust to ravish white women'; and a parable about the Great Depression, an interpretation I have never understood. Numerous critics contend that *Kong* was intentionally filmed as if it were a nightmare. (If the picture is indeed a dream, this would explain the frequent changes in Kong's size, according to scale.) R. C. Dale writes:

The film manages to bypass the critical, cenorious level of the viewer's consciousness and to secure his suspension of disbelief with what appears to be great ease. A number of French critics have attributed this phenomenon to the film's oneiric qualities, its pervasive dreamlike control of some subconscious, uncritical part of the mind. Indeed it does succeed in dreaming for us.

I agree that *King Kong* is dreamlike – in fact, our first view of Skull Island is an exact reproduction of Arnold Böcklin's dreamlike painting *Isle of the Dead* – but I don't think that it is *our* dream we watch on the screen. The film begins in the *real* world, in dark, cold Depression New York where unemployed, hungry people stand in soup lines; but from the moment the *Venture* leaves port for uncharted regions, I believe we are on a journey through *Carl Denham's subconscious*. Just as Pauline Kael described the landscape of Altair-4 in the *Kong*-influenced *Forbidden Planet* (1956) as being 'the caves, plains, and the towers of Dr. Morbius's mind', Skull (as in cerebral) Island's expressionistic landscape – fertile, overgrown, reptile-infested, watery, cave-filled – is Denham's fantasised sexual terrain.

And Kong, I believe, is a manifestation of Denham's subconscious. Much like Morbius's Id monster. Whereas Morbius conjures up his monster to kill off the men he fears will take away his daughter (likely his lover in his subconscious), Denham conjures up Kong as a surrogate to battle Driscoll for Ann's love and to perform sexually with her when he has never been willing (or able) to have a sexual encounter himself. Although young and virile, misogynist Denham has travelled to the far corners of the earth with an all-male crew to avoid intimate liaisons because he believes women will strip him of his masculinity ('Some hardboiled egg gets a look at a pretty face and he cracks up and goes sappy'). Kong is Denham's female-lusting side – his alter ego, which he keeps in the dark recesses of his mind, as remotely located as Skull Island, behind a figurative great wall. Kong is evidence of Denham's desperate need to possess Ann; his birth is a result of Denham's continuing to suppress his sexual/romantic drive even after he meets, and immediately falls in love with, Ann.

In New York, Denham tells Ann, 'Trust me and keep your chin up.' A few seconds of screen time pass, and Ann, now on board the *Venture*, is struck accidentally by Driscoll – on the *chin*. This is a sign that Denham can't be trusted to protect Ann's physical well-being even if he wants to. As his secret (even from himself) love for Ann increases, his Kong side overcomes his desire to protect her. He betrays his lack of concern for her safety (from Kong): for her screen test aboard the *Venture*, he dresses Ann in white – with her bee-stung lips and hair style she looks like one of D. W. Griffith's virginal Victorian heroines – as if preparing her for sacrifice, or perhaps a sexual initiation rite; then he takes Ann onto Skull Island before he knows if it is safe. Just as Denham saved Ann in New York from jail (for stealing an apple), unemployment, and starvation, Kong continues Denham's gallantry toward Ann on Skull Island, saving her from a tyrannosaur and a pterodactyl. But the difference is clear: the civilised Denham (the man) believes his interest in Ann is 'strictly business', while the primitive Denham (Kong) has placed no such restrictions on himself.

Since Kong is a side of Denham, *Kong* needn't follow the movie formula of having Denham and Driscoll vie for Ann's affections. Denham can allow Driscoll free reign with her because, in truth, the schizophrenic Denham is moving in on Ann from his Kong side. Also, through Kong, Denham tries to eliminate Driscoll and all other men who 'pursue' her. When Driscoll's kisses bring Ann to her height of sexual passion, and her breathing is heavy and her body is like jelly, he is conveniently (as far as Denham is con-

This classic Kong *poster is taken from the artwork of the original lobby cards that accompanied the film's March 1933 release.*

cerned) called to a meeting with Denham and the captain. Suddenly natives, who to Denham probably represent the link between civilised man (himself) and his simian ancestors (apes), climb aboard the *Venture* at the very spot where Ann stands, at the first moment she is alone, and kidnap her to be Kong's bride. Is it the natives' lucky night? Or were things so easy for them – being part of Denham's dream – because Denham's subconscious orchestrated the whole thing in their favour?

That Denham and Kong are rarely in the same shot further gives one the impression that Kong is being directed by some external force, namely Denham's subconscious. At one time Kong is on one side of the tree-trunk bridge that holds Driscoll (who climbs off to safety) and several other men pursuing Ann (who fall to their deaths) – while Denham is *out of sight* on the other side of the bridge and only emerges after Kong has left. Not coincidentally, a later scene in New York shows Kong reaching into a hotel room (to which Denham's subconscious must have directed him), snatching Ann, and knocking down Driscoll – while Denham is *out of sight* in the hall and only appears after Kong has left.

Denham and Kong do confront each other (the visualisation of Denham's internal struggle) when Kong breaks through the supposedly impenetrable door of the great wall (Denham's mental barricade) – just as the Id monster breaks through the supposedly impenetrable laboratory door in *Forbidden Planet*. Confronted with his bestial side, the civilised Denham – a model for Morbius, who at this point denies his Id monster, thereby making it cease to exist – puts it (Kong) to sleep with gas bombs. Back in New York, Denham still tries to control his sexual side by literally chaining up Kong. However, once Kong breaks out of his supposedly unbreakable chains, Denham's last barrier, we never see Kong and Denham together again until Kong lies dead.

Denham's words, 'It was Beauty killed the Beast,' make sense only if the beast he's referring to was part of himself. It is an understatement to say that Kong is too big for Ann, but we could overlook this except for the fact that Kong's size prevents him from considering her a beauty. That he can't even recognise Ann by her looks is evident when he pulls the wrong woman from the hotel and can only tell she's not Ann by hair colour and smell – not by beauty. That Kong reacts so violently when the photographers take pictures of Ann is not because he thinks they're trying to harm her – Kong probably doesn't recognise her – but because filmmaker Denham, a *voyeur* (as many critics have acknowledged), becomes filled with jealous rage because others are taking pictures of his actress/woman/property/beauty; and it is *his* subconscious that wills Kong to intervene by breaking his bonds and chasing the photographers away. Once loose, Kong is out of the civilised Denham's control and goes all out to succeed in his mission of having sex with Ann. On Skull Island, a snake (a Freudian sex symbol) attacks Kong – a symbolic act that shows Denham is trying to suppress his sexual instincts; however, in New York, Kong attacks the snake – the Third Avenue El – making it clear that nothing will get in his way this time. Having no penis – is impotence the reason Denham avoids women? – Kong has symbolic intercourse with Ann when he takes her up the world's greatest phallic symbol: the Empire State Building. Once this sexual act has been carried out (consummated), Denham is no longer sexually repressed (or a virgin). As his sexual self can surface at last, he no longer has to enjoy sex vicariously through a surrogate and Kong, now obsolete, can die. Therefore, it makes sense that in the Cooper-Ernest B. Schoedsack sequel, *Son of Kong* (1933), where Denham is the romantic lead and has a love affair with Helen Mack, the gorilla need not be and is not a sexual being.

Kong as Hero. That Kong is regarded as a hero rather than the prototype for all monster-villains is quite extraordinary, considering how many innocent people he kills and how much property he destroys, all done with the emotion of someone eating a melting

Bruce **CABOT** Fay **WRAY** Robert **ARMSTRONG**

KING KONG

Regia: **M. COOPER** e **E. SCHOEDSACK**

KING KONG

with
FAY WRAY.....
ROBT. ARMSTRONG
BRUCE CABOT..
FROM AN IDEA CONCEIVED BY
EDGAR WALLACE
AND MERIAN C. COOPER

A
COOPER-
SCHOEDSACK
PRODUCTION

RKO
Radio
PICTURES

DAVID O. SELZNICK
Executive Producer

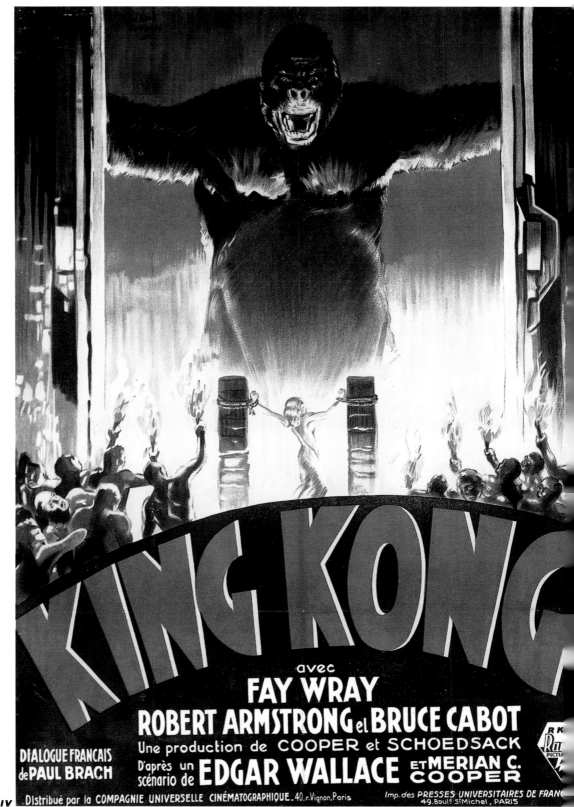

KING KONG

avec

FAY WRAY

ROBERT ARMSTRONG et **BRUCE CABOT**

Une production de COOPER et SCHOEDSACK

D'après un scénario de **EDGAR WALLACE** et **MERIAN C. COOPER**

DIALOGUE FRANCAIS de **PAUL BRACH**

R K O
Radio
PICTU...

IV Distribué par la COMPAGNIE UNIVERSELLE CINÉMATOGRAPHIQUE_40,r.Vignon,Paris

Imp. des PRESSES UNIVERSITAIRES DE FRAN...
49.Boul⁹ St.Michel, PARIS

KONG

KING

with
FAY WRAY
ROB'T ARMSTRONG
BRUCE CABOT
FROM AN IDEA CONCEIVED BY
EDGAR WALLACE

RKO
Radio
PICTURES

A
COOPER-SCHOEDSACK

v

Colour section. *These classic posters were created to publicise the original 1933* King Kong *(and 1933* Son of Kong*). Page I: if Fay Wray stands five-and-a-half feet in this pre-release ad, then Kong reaches no more than fifteen feet. Page II: Kong reaches familiar proportions in this Art Deco-style poster, but resembles a chimp more than a gorilla. Page III: the Great Ape, the dinosaurs, and the main characters rendered in 1930s pulp-mag or comic-book style. Page IV: Kong as 'a king and a god in the world he knew', in a vivid French poster by artist Roland Loudon. Page V: the defiant last stand atop the Empire State Building. Page VI: like an omnipotent force, Kong towers way above the city in this classic promotional painting. Page VII: top – Fay Wray, Bruce Cabot and Robert Armstrong in cartoonish close-up; right – the classic 1933 lobby card. Page VIII: while less gargantuan than his father, 'Kiko' still appears disproportionately small.*

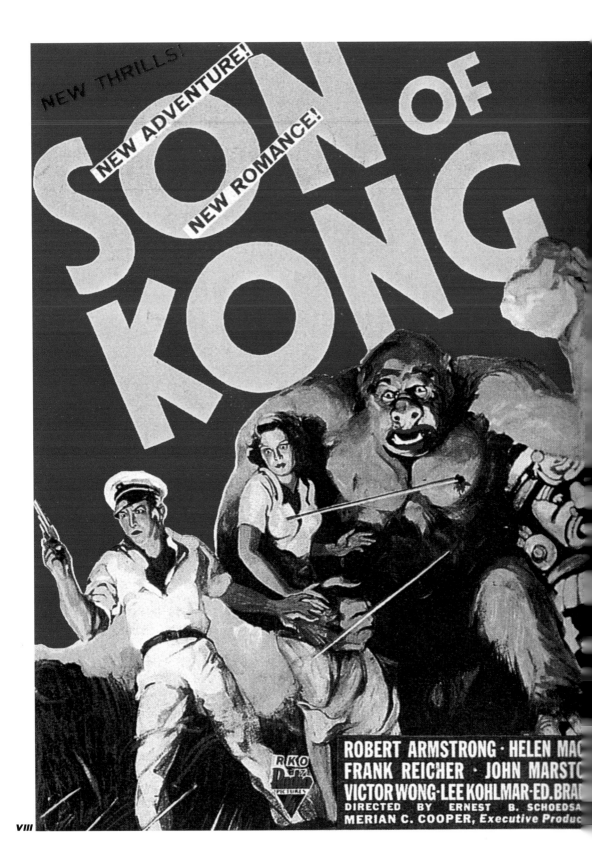

ice cream cone. His hero status is even more unusual since the recent reinsertion of scenes censored in 1938 from all prints of the film. These scenes of Kong partially stripping Ann (touching her and smelling his finger), viciously trampling and chewing on helpless natives, and dropping the woman he mistakes for Ann to her death from high above the city streets, make Kong's 'beastliness' much more pronounced.

Kong is a hero, I suspect, because he is a great fighter, capable of beating Tunney or Dempsey with his pinky, or the entire United States Air Force if it fought fairly; he gallantly risks his life for his woman; black people see him as a black character who fights White America; the poor see him as their champion who wreaks havoc on New York City, home of Wall Street and the least popular city during the Great Depression and not much more popular since; women see that he doesn't hide his feelings as most men do. And Kong is certainly sympathetic. We feel sorry for grotesque characters whose love for someone beautiful is not returned – Fay Wray earned her reputation as the screen's top screamer by shrieking *every* time Kong came near her. He is taken forcibly from his homeland, where he was god, to be, as Denham tells the theatre audience, 'merely a captive to gratify your curiosity.' He is destroyed by airplanes, something he can't understand, for reasons he can't comprehend. As his last act, he puts Ann in a safe place so she won't suffer his horrible fate – what is truly upsetting is that Ann doesn't verbally acknowledge the nobleness of this gesture. Kong dies so tragically and so theatrically (as a hammy silent movie star might) that we forgive and forget all that he has done. But for all this, as Robert Fiedel writes in *The Girl in the Hairy Paw* (Avon, 1976), 'Most critics have always been at a loss to give adequate explanation for the great feeling of tragedy evoked by Kong's death.' When the airplanes start firing on Kong we suddenly feel we are losing our best friend, when up till now we have thought Kong our enemy. I believe Fiedel pinpoints the reason for our dramatic reversal:

> The answer lies, in fact, in the musical score . . . . Nowhere is the score more manipulative than in the death scene. As Kong realises that his death is immediately impending, we hear a lamenting variation of the 'Ann Darrow' motif played passionately by the strings . . . . Then as Kong finally dies and loses his hold atop the Empire State Building, his motif is resolved by rest chords . . . signifying his acceptance of defeat . . . . Kong's actual fall is accompanied by a sustained blaring dissonant chord, and finally resolved by an orchestral outburst. It is interesting that his fall is resolved only by the score, and not by the visuals . . . . The score serves the vital function of resolving the tension of the actual fall and denoting the precise moment to trigger our emotional responses . . . . As Denham muses philosophically over the body of Kong . . . a celestial statement of the 'Ann Darrow' motif is played in the upper string register which makes a final tragic comment on the death of Kong. A final recapitulation of the resolved 'Kong' motif ensues, concluding the film on a negative, disturbing theme.

King Kong is an institution, a folk hero, certainly more real to us today than the defunct studio that created him. Kong has been resurrected so many times – initially by major studio releases in 1938, 1942, 1946, 1952, and 1956, and then by impossible-to-miss television and repertory theatre screenings – that he has become immortal. The King is dead!, etc., etc.

BEAUTIES AND BEASTS:
THE EROTICISM OF *KING KONG*

By Steve Vertlieb

When at last all of the great love stories throughout history have been transcribed for posterity, it is doubtful that any will have achieved greater cultural, sociological or romantic significance than Merian C. Cooper's cinematic re-telling of the 'Beauty and the Beast' fable, *King Kong*. Filmed in 1932, and released in March of 1933, this classic fantasy adventure remains a landmark of American cinema and a cultural icon. For more than 70 years this massive tale of unrequited affection has captivated the imagination of audiences throughout the world, and remains today as fresh and compelling as when it first burst through the forbidding jungles of primordial birth all those many years ago. *King Kong* was the embodiment of civilisation's worst nightmare – that the mannered, fragile pretence of civility we cling to so desperately could so easily be torn asunder from an assault by an agent of mindless brutality. The concept is as potent today as it was 70 years ago. Most of us lead double lives, wearing multiple faces, as we parade our wares before the outer world. This is the identity we put on display for acceptance by families, co-workers and friends, masking a darker, perhaps more sinister reality in the innermost sanctity of our private thoughts and yearnings.

Environment usually dictates that we don the proverbial cape of Dr. Jekyll, while masking the appearance of Edward Hyde. Others parade a more evil countenance before society, inwardly longing for or aspiring to the socially acceptable face of Henry Jekyll. We are the sum total of many diverse, complex parts. Some of these elements are outwardly attractive, and some are not, but they all contribute to who we ultimately become. It is preposterous to suggest that any individual is entirely pure and wholesome, or unsavoury and evil, and yet many often consciously and deliberately present one or the other simplistic appearance to their neighbours. It is considered somehow shameful for a warrior to admit sensitivity, or a seemingly cultured, civilised individual to acknowledge inherent inclinations toward depravity or debasement. This may explain the suspicion and mistrust separating cultures, countries and inner-city communities. We're holding a mirror to the world surrounding our own complacent environment and are confused, frightened and enraged by the disturbing, yet vaguely familiar imagery reflected back.

Kong expressed the raging beast within each of us. Repulsed by his apparently mindless brutality, we recoiled and proclaimed our own undoubted virtue. Kong was huge, darkly complexioned and deeply resentful. His own power and virility had set him apart from his fellow creatures and made him an outcast. He was both feared and envied for his great size and strength. Victorian morality, ever prevalent in America, reasoned that size similarly dictated the length of corresponding genitalia. Hence, Kong suffered the slings and phallic arrows of both penis envy and fear. If anatomically correct and beautiful creatures behaved properly and correctly, might not an anatomically incorrect being behave in the very manner in which he was perceived? If one is perceived as unattractive or ugly, his rage might well determine the ugliness of his actions. This would explain the great ape's displeasure with the physically (as well as morally) 'little' people who feared and attacked him.

It has been suggested by psychologists that women secretly long to be overpowered, and that white women yearn privately to be sexually dominated by an inordinately large black male. Might this be a reason for our unending fascination with King Kong's seem-

The curvaceous Fay Wray cowers theatrically from an unseen Kong. Miss Wray displays the unashamed voluptuousness of her era, alluring to both man and ape.

ingly hopeless romantic and sexual obsession with a small, apparently virginal white woman? The relationship is implausible, and yet darkly exciting. If black flesh upon white is a social taboo, it is probably the ultimate socio-sexual fantasy among men and women of both races. This may explain at least a part of our timeless fascination with the 'Beauty and Beast' aspect of a motion picture described alternately as a horror film, an adventure thriller, and a romantic fable. Surely, in greatness there is complexity. Everything thematically painted in *King Kong* is larger than conventional life, and if larger is somehow better, then we can see some of the reasons behind its enduring popularity and mythological status.

From the moment in the early reels when Ann Darrow reveals her plight to motion picture entrepreneur Carl Denham, it is apparent that she is, culturally speaking, a fallen woman. Societal expectation and monetary pressure have combined to cause her fall from grace. She attempts justifying her loss of employment, and near theft of a piece of fruit from a street vendor, by remarking that she could get by in good clothes, 'but when a girl gets too shabby . . . ' The unfinished sentence suggests darker implications than mere theft. What, indeed, might a traditional good girl feel compelled to accept should hunger make it necessary? Robbed of pride and dignity, is there the unspoken suggestion of self-abasement or prostitution lurking menacingly in the darkness? Sexual power is, undoubtedly, a disturbing and recurring theme in the picture. The Old Arabian Proverb written by Merian C. Cooper for the introduction of his filmic fable is clearly indicative of the notion that sexual preeminence can topple mountains, and the giants who dwell within. 'And lo, the Beast looked upon the face of Beauty, and it stayed its hand from killing. And from that day, it was as one dead.' David killed Goliath, while a frail, hungry girl of the street tempted a rampaging beast to its premature demise. 'It wasn't the airplanes,' after all. 'It was Beauty killed the Beast.'

Robert Armstrong's Carl Denham is a ruthless hero. He'll do anything he can to make his picture and achieve the realisation of his desires. 'I'm going out and make the greatest picture in the world, something that nobody's ever seen or heard of. They'll have to think up a lot of new adjectives when I come back,' he rants. Angered by critics and exhibitors demanding a love interest in his next picture, Denham proclaims to his crew that he'll find a girl to take along to the island, even if he has to marry one. When he encounters Ann for the first time, and saves her from the wrath of the disgruntled vendor and unseen policeman, she surrenders to his will, nearly fainting in his arms. After buying the famished girl a meal, he bluntly comments that he isn't just bothering about her out of kindness. He might just as well be a white slaver, as a film producer. Ann, as portrayed by Fay Wray, is, in fact, enslaved by her poverty. Agreeing to accompany virtually anyone anywhere who will offer her a job, she willingly suspends her disbelief and journeys halfway around the globe on a dilapidated tramp steamer, in the company of a crew of embittered and hardened seamen.

It's difficult to imagine that Ann Darrow's appearance aboard the dismal ship is not premeditated, either by Merian Cooper, or by the character herself. Filmed one year prior to Hollywood's infamous, mandatory production code, the actress's nipples can clearly be observed beneath a sheer white blouse. Surely this remarkable revelation hasn't gone unnoticed by the ship's all male crew. As the first mate and principal romantic interest, Jack Driscoll, enters the scene, Ann arches her back to greet him. Soon Denham

Ann takes momentary refuge in Jack's arms, while the fleshy Skull Island natives barely cover their modesty in a manner that would have been too risque for Fay Wray.

joins the pair on deck, and asks Ann to go below and put on her Beauty and Beast costume in order to shoot some tests while the light is still right. As Ann leaves the two men, walking toward both the camera and the audience, her breasts heave and jiggle uncontrollably, leaving one to suspect that the actress is not wearing a bra, and that this too is deliberate. When Ann reappears in a full-length white gown her shoulders are bare, revealing a discreet suggestion of cleavage. Here too, the actress is apparently naked beneath her virginal gown and, as the narration is dictated by Denham for the test reel, Ann obligingly pants and heaves her bosom once more, leaving the crew and audience drooling.

Driscoll, sensing danger for the girl, protests to Denham, who mockingly castrates his young companion. Denham accuses Driscoll of 'going soft'. 'The Beast went soft too,' he chides, 'and the little fellas licked him.' In both allusions, men are rendered 'soft' and presumably impotent by a woman's influence. We'll leave the imagery of licking and being licked to other interpretations.

While white female nudity was considered too inflammatory for the time, the same taboos did not seem to apply to women of colour. When the ship's crew ventures forth to Skull Island for the first time, they encounter a frenzied, ritualistic native sacrifice in progress. A decidedly nubile young black woman, half naked and whimpering in confusion and fear, is being prepared for her impending marriage to Kong. Presumably, this entails a momentary courtship, a quick honeymoon, and the quivering virgin being fed to their god for dinner. Not unlike a scene out of *The National Geographic*, black female nudity is somehow perceived as educational, rather than sexual or erotic. Little has changed, in fact, in the 70-odd years since *King Kong* was produced. When Alex Haley's mini-series, *Roots*, was prepared for ABC Television, American audiences were treated each night for a week to the spectacle of naked African women in their living rooms. The women were, more often than not, young, healthy and attractive. Presumably, television's dedicated band of network censors might have suffered massive coronaries over nude white women in prime time every evening, but thought nothing of this endless stream of well-endowed black women parading across their television screens, in the highly suspect, and sanctimonious, name of education. Millions of teenaged boys, however, remained eternally grateful.

Such is the perceived value of white flesh in America that, when the natives of Skull Island first see Fay Wray, they quickly offer to trade six of their own tribal women for Ann. Shaken from the religious fervour of a ceremonial dance, they can only gape in wonder and proclaim, 'Look at the golden woman.' Denham, nonchalantly racist, casually responds, 'Yeah, blondes are scarce around here.' Both tribes, black and white, appear to regard tribal women as so much meat, utilised only for barter, sexual gratification, or virgin sacrifice. The men of each philosophical or sociological background are either racist, sexist or both. At least they share that much in common.

Meanwhile, after returning to the ship, Jack professes his love for Ann. In the style of early American sound films, Jack is inarticulate, stumbling over both his words and their intent. He is naïve, boyish, and devoid of sexual passion or guile. Ann, however, is literally ripe for picking, breathless with desire, heaving and panting in erotic expectation. Since sexual fulfilment is inherently evil in this wholesome environment, it is left to the black natives of the island to consummate the relationship, and bring a violent climax to the sexual tension. The rhythm of primitive drums, pounding and pulsating through the night, is alive with testosterone explosions and raging hormones. As Ann is left alone on the deck of the ship, she grows more excited with every beat of the island drums. Her breathing has quickened. Her arms long to hold Jack, but he has been summoned to the bridge. After all, duty before sex. Meanwhile, slim, narrow, and pointedly erect canoes quietly approach the ship. Ann is standing alone on deck, her back arched against the railing of the old freighter, when the native tribesmen steal aboard, attacking from behind and abducting the virginal white goddess. Still in the throes of sexual rapture, she struggles against the darker reality of her imagination. She is to be punished for her desires. Her marriage will be consummated not with the boyish Jack Driscoll but, rather, with the huge, hulking, black beast whose home they dared to enter.

Ann is drugged on the island and prepared for the ultimate sacrifice. Intoxicated and overpoweringly virile, the natives of Skull Island dance into the night in sensual abandonment. Triumphant in their conquest of Ann, and exhilarated by the promise of the monumental rape that awaits their fragile captive, the ceremony is frenzied and orgasmic. Throbbing, pulsating, and ultimately terrifying, Max Steiner's overwhelming score enhances every emotion on the forbidding island with raging intensity. At its climax, Ann is dragged through the imposing gates that protect the village from the vast jungle beyond, and tied, spreadeagled, to the massive sacrificial pillars. The gate, spread wide in invitation, leaves the girl exposed and vulnerable, like a great vaginal tunnel waiting to be plundered. As the doors of the mighty gate close behind her, an elongated pole slowly, deliberately enters its awaiting chamber, an open receptacle in which the great pole will find penetration and climax. Lost in masculine bravado, the natives pound a ceremonial gong, as if they were pounding their chests in primal excitation and victory, preparing to welcome their god in fear, curiosity and awesome expectation.

Like mischievous boys, caught masturbating by their parents, the natives peer furtively into the jungle foliage, vicariously enjoying the terror vibrating from the frail maiden below. As the ground begins to tremble, great footsteps can be heard. While brushes part and trees topple, a huge, ferocious beast roars in defiance of the insignificant people who worship him and call him god. Kong is an awesome spectacle to behold, a monstrous ape the size of a house. Angered, yet appeased by the petulant tribe paying him homage with virgin sacrifice, Kong snarls, hurling his great fist toward the towering battlement. He could burst through their puny fortress, decimating these impotent adversaries at his slightest whim, for he understands all too clearly that he is the cowardly instrument of their imagined virility. He could capture and hold a woman in ways that remain elusive to these pygmy slaves. This is his island, his woman, his captives. Kong is the dominant force, and no one dares challenge him. He is the semen of their ejaculation, and will possess any female of his choosing. He 'was a king and a god in the world he knew', and these tiny pretenders to his carefully guarded throne were merely pawns in a game of his own design and manipulation.

Turning his attention to the miniature, struggling doll at his feet, Kong's eyes widen in curiosity. She is like nothing he has ever seen before, a lovely creature, milky white, with golden hair. She obviously dreads his enormity, screaming in terror at the thought of this terrible violation. Will he be gentle, or will he mindlessly ravage her body and tear her apart? For his part, the great ape has been humbled and tamed. His formidable heart has melted. There is an unfathomable aching deep within his chest, and a palpable yearning in his groin that he has never known before. Gently, he undoes the bonds of Ann's imprisonment, and lifts her from the ground. What is this strange, sensual creature he holds dearly in his paws? His fury spent, his anger dissipated, the once ferocious beast must now acknowledge feelings of tenderness and chivalry. He must find a way to protect this vulnerable toy thrust unexpectedly into his care. Turning once more to the chanting natives, leering and drooling in sexual excitation, Kong roars his contempt, returning proudly to the jungle with his precious new prize.

In a fight over female flesh, Kong wrests a pterodactyl away from his sacred prize, atop his Skull Mountain lair.

Emotions have been stirred within the hulking creature's soul that he's never experienced before, and he is startled by them. How will he respond to his growing passion? She is too small, obviously, to penetrate and yet his warrior's masculinity has been touched. Surely, there must be a way to arouse her feelings as well? To have come so far, only to be anatomically rejected, would be unthinkable. While he is pondering his impossible dream, exploring the mysteries of sensual pleasure, Kong stops and, momentarily, places his whimpering captive within a fully erect tree stump, vaguely suggestive of an open penile cavity. Calm, relaxed, his defence mechanisms at rest, the imposing ape is viciously attacked by a rampaging allosaurus. Humiliated before the woman for whom he has a growing affection, Kong defends his bruised honour and wounded pride with equal measures of brutality and bravado. The dinosaur had fancied Ann as his luncheon appetiser until Kong gallantly stepped between them. Aware that all eyes are upon him, he capitalises on an opportunity to both impress and protect his intended bride. As much a performance as a battle, Kong challenges his rival with obvious relish, roaring, pounding his chest, and dancing around the perimeters of his stage with an assuredness Muhammad Ali might covet. His vanity in crisis, Kong's would-be rival strikes back. Kong, however, is grimly determined to prove his mettle and win the heart of the golden woman. In a terrible battle to the death, Kong is triumphant, breaking open the leathery jaw of his avowed enemy, prying open his mouth and playing with the dislocated parts, suggesting an oral fixation.

At home once more, the battle of the sexes continues as the weary gorilla walks through the cavernous opening to his vast estate, a gaping cavity he enters confidently. Once inside, however, the waters of discontent bubble over, as a slithering serpent crawls out of a primordial lake, stalking Ann like a writhing, putrid, elongated phallus. When Kong forces his way between the serpent and its prey, the giant eel wraps itself tightly around Kong's neck, attempting to crush his windpipe, giving new meaning to the term Deep Throat. Kong delivers a crushing blow to the serpent, rendering it lifeless and impotent.

Alone at last, Kong takes Ann to the innermost domain of his personal sanctuary, and sits with her atop the ledge of a great precipice where, his curiosity satiated, he gingerly inspects her tattered undergarments, and commences her seduction. Often referred to as the 'rape scene', to the everlasting consternation of the film's late creator, Merian C. Cooper, the once excised sequence seems to illustrate Kong's innocence, and utter isolation from civilisation. Whether he had ever explored his own awakening sexuality in the presence of previous female companions, or merely ravaged and eaten his captives, remains speculative. Ann Darrow represented a portion of humanity hitherto unknown to him. He had never before encountered a white woman and, as Denham had callously pointed out earlier, blondes were indeed scarce on the native island. Call it white America's particular conceit, if you will, but the noble animal was undeniably aroused by, and enamoured of, Ann's sensual beauty. Their colouring was different, as was their species, but here was most certainly a wondrous example of animal magnetism. If oppo-

The scene where Kong's paw invades the bedroom of an anonymous woman, represented in the production art. This expressionistic drawing makes it the stuff of nightmares.

sites attract, was there ever a male and female with greater opposition to one another? Was Kong's inquisitiveness mere curiosity borne of ignorance, or was there a deeper, more profound yearning in his heart for this woman? If we naturally ignore the familiar, striving instead for the unusual or the different, or if opposites truly do attract one another, then Kong's fascination with Ann is entirely normal and plausible.

Left free to explore his fantasies, Kong peels layer after layer of Ann's clothing from her body, gently prolonging the moments, inhaling her intoxicating scent and ignoring her feeble protests. The animal is an inquisitive child, a probing innocent uncovering each new revelation, each new discovery, with unbridled joy and fascination. He tickles her breasts as she wriggles expectantly beneath his dark fingers. His nostrils twitch gleefully, as though tickled themselves by the alluring aroma of her provocative scent. Caught with his pants down by Jack Driscoll, the great simian may as well have been discovered masturbating by his stern parents. The disapproval and resultant anger at having been caught would seem just as potent. Leaving the isolated perch to investigate an unwelcome intrusion on their privacy, Kong leaves Ann alone. Her solitude is momentary at best as a great pterodactyl swoops down from the skies, its beak erect, protruding, lifting her up from the plateau to feed her supple flesh to its young. Hearing her screams, Kong races back to the ledge where he rips the airborne reptile out of the sky, wrestles his prize from its perverted grasp, and hurls the creature to the jagged rocks and raging river below.

During the battle, Jack ascends the mountain top. Seeing the promised land and their steamer in the distance, Jack steals Ann away and commences their precarious descent from Kong down the wall of the mountain. They hold onto one another, intertwining their legs around a thick vine hanging from the cliff. Ann's dress has been shredded, exposing her bra and panties. Jack, looking for a discreet part of Ann's anatomy to hold onto, protectively cups his hand over her breast. The intimate proximity of the coarse vine to Ann's panties and vagina surely adds to both her anxiety and excitement as she clings desperately to Jack, and makes her daring escape. Discovering the 'abduction', Kong finds the offending vine and begins pulling it back up toward the ledge. Using both paws, he plays with and massages the elongated rope, pulling gently upon it until he loses control. Ann and Jack dive into the river below, bringing both the scene and Kong's anticipation of the outcome to a watery climax.

Ann and Jack, spent and exhausted, crawl out of the river together and race through the primordial jungle to the relative safety of the distant native village. There they collapse in frenzied perspiration while Denham, not to be undone by his young friend, lifts Ann off of the ground, nearly cupping his own hand over her breast. Fear and masturbatory excitement inflame the night sky high atop the turrets of the gate, where men can be heard screaming, 'It's Kong . . . Kong's coming.' Reaching the massive structure from the jungle, Kong hurls his body into the wooden barricade, pushing himself against it repeatedly, until the rigid pole holding the gates shut nearly explodes from unrelieved tension and pressure, ripping it asunder. All is calm in the eye of the hurricane, in the infinite seconds leading to the thunderous clap of the exploding rod, ejaculating splinters into the air, and raining jagged remnants onto the bloody beach below. The massive gates open wide, leaving the village naked and vulnerable to the rampaging attack by the great, marauding beast. Kong's fury is a terrifying spectacle, as he savagely plunders the village and its populace in search of his stolen bride. Kong tears natives brutally from their huts, ripping their heads from their torsos, until gas bombs finally bring the enraged animal to his knees where he collapses, unconscious, on the beach. Denham, triumphant in victory, orders his crew to send for anchor chains and tools. They'll build a raft and float him to the ship. 'In a few months it'll be up in lights on Broadway,' he cries. '. . . KONG, THE EIGHTH WONDER OF THE WORLD.'

Abducted in the darkness of night and taken in chains to New York, Kong is enslaved and put on display, a carnival freak in a world of greedy human animals. Seated in the theatre, a woman asks her date the nature of the performance. 'I hear it's a kind of gorilla,' he replies. A boorish theatre patron steps on her feet, attempting to reach his seat. Glaring at him contemptuously, she wisecracks, 'Gee, ain't we got enough of them in New York?' The roots of superiority blur as one wonders which is more animalistic, the loutish captor or the noble beast – taken unwillingly from his native land and sold into slavery, a stranger in an even stranger land.

Backstage, newsreel cameramen are given an opportunity to take the first photographs of Kong and his captors. As Denham supplies them with the more lurid aspects of their harrowing adventures on the island, the photographers leer knowingly at Ann, their imaginations fabricating the sensational, humiliating spectacle of a lovely young woman degraded and, perhaps, violated by animal lust. Denham encourages the newsmen to take pictures of Ann and Jack together, for 'they're going to be married tomorrow.' Jack, it seems, has finally mustered the courage to ask Ann for her hand. It remained for Kong to take the rest of her.

With the curtains open on the stage, and Kong glaring menacingly at his audience, the largely white, upper and middle class patrons squirm uneasily in their seats. Denham, in his arrogance, proclaims from the stage that Kong was 'a king and a god in the world he knew . . . now merely a captive to gratify your curiosity.' Pulled violently from his jungle throne in the unspoiled purity of the islands, 'the little fellas licked him.'

Ever protective of his fragile, golden flower, Kong reacts threateningly as flash bulbs light the stage. 'Look out,' Denham warns, 'he thinks you're attacking the girl.' Oblivious to his cries, the photographers continue shooting the couple until Kong shatters his chrome steel bondage, breaking free of his chains, leaping off of his metallic crucifix into the crowded theatre. Terrified patrons race screaming through congested streets, while Kong begins searching for the woman he loves. Societal taboos are decimated as the brooding, dark creature wreaks havoc on the well-mannered avenues of the largely Caucasian community. Free of constraints, the rampaging of the noble savage serves as a bleak, uncomfortable remnant of a past too easily forgotten.

Ascending artificial mountains at the epicentre of urban paranoia, the simian suitor peers through the window of a sleeping innocent, blissfully unaware of the danger just beyond her grasp. Searching for Ann, Kong reaches his great paw through the window, pulling the bed toward him. Awakening to the horrifying vision of a giant gorilla, its fangs bared in her darkened bedchamber, the woman screams in terror. Alone and vulnerable in her flimsy nightgown, she is lifted out of the window dangling, feet first, high above the flaming neon city, held tightly within Kong's massive paw. Sensing that the grief-stricken woman is not his beloved Ann but, rather, the object of his revulsion for humanity, the beast allows the strange female to slip callously from his fingers, falling horribly to her death amidst the tangled streets infinite storeys below. She matters, after all, no more than the thousands of faceless, chanting 'natives' on this urban island and is blithely expendable. Such is the danger lurking eternally, beneath the shadows of civility, when night must inevitably fall.

Suspended beneath the clouds, yet over the panic-filled pavements of the city, charged with energy, a metallic bullet hurtles along its tracks, impregnating the darkness with calculated ferocity. Slim, elongated, packed with throbbing, teeming life, the elevated train shoots toward its destination, confidently unaware of the danger below. Kong is attracted by the primal vibration of the serpentine creature roaring in the distance, breaking apart the electrified tracks, derailing the broken cars, hurling their bewildered passengers plummeting into the vast darkness. The aborted missile has itself been mercilessly violated, rendering it flaccid and ineffectual.

Finding momentary respite from the inherent madness of civilisation, Kong climbs the tallest penile structure in the city, the awesome Empire State Building, straddling its tower, placing Ann within the silver pouch inside its foreskin. The pointed tip of the virile sack glistens in the sunrise, sparkling and moist. Kong has reached the climax of his long, perilous journey. He has conquered the very top of the world, and there is nowhere else to go. Is that ominous rumble in the sky the sound of thunder, he wonders, or the terrible cry of some perverse pterodactyl flying in the clouds? In seconds the source of the thunder is tragically revealed, for soon the sky is filled with great metallic birds, predatory machines sniffing the air for the scent of animal prey. Military biplanes circle the prone, naked beast, ravenous sharks anticipating the taste of martyred blood. Kong roars in heroic defiance of the growing threat from the clouds, but his bravado merely inflames the airborne vultures, intoxicated by their own boiling passion. His eardrums shattered by the sudden, monotonous repetition of thunderous claps, the sky explodes in blinding flashes of light, and he grasps his chest in sudden, excruciating pain. Warm streams of liquid begin seeping from his body, as Kong realises that the brownish semen lingering curiously on his fingers is his own blood. Lightning explodes the air once more, his shoulder burning in anguish. Attacked from all sides now, fiery projectiles deeply penetrate his flesh. His genitalia discreetly camouflaged behind the tower of the scarred skyscraper, erect and pointing to the stars, Kong waits naked in the sun for his last castration. He has been humiliated, spat upon by the ammunition spewing forth from the flying reptiles. He will pay dearly for his sins against humanity, for he has been judged 'different'. He is an outcast from a smug, self-righteous society that would rather eradicate his memory than admit his existence, for to acknowledge his being might awaken a primordial memory of a shared bloodline, a spiritual heritage created by a single deity, in which we might have been brothers.

Sensing the end, Kong reaches down, softly, lovingly stroking the golden hair of the creature who, perhaps, in another reality, might have grown to love him. Standing proud and tall once more, Kong lashes out at the ravenous buzzards circling his blood-soaked body, pulling one of the airplanes in his fist, sending it crashing to its explosive destruction, in a final act of masculine defiance. It is too little and too late, however, for society has deemed him an anachronism, sealing his fate. He is doomed.

Weakened by incessant attacks, Kong is barely able to grasp the dome of the gleaming tower at the world's end. Grown tired at last, resigned to his inevitable fate, his paw loosens its grip, and his fall from grace is complete. Rendered impotent, he pays dearly for his individuality, crashing heartbreakingly to the concrete street so many hundreds of feet below. Denham, representing the guilt of structured, unforgiving society, attempts to shift the blame for Kong's betrayal and ultimate martyrdom . . . or perhaps he is nearer the truth than we realise. If sexual repression and psychological castration are basic tenets of mannered society, while isolationism, loneliness and the torment of unrequited romantic love share the penalty for naivete and innocence then, indeed, 'It wasn't the airplanes . . . It was Beauty killed the Beast.'

In fairness to the creative men and women responsible for the gestation and birth of this most timeless of classic films, it should be noted that little, if any, of the preceding sexual or sociological speculation was consciously intended by the various film makers.

Merian C. Cooper was a pioneer explorer, aviator, journalist, writer, producer, director and Brigadier General in the Air Force of the United States. He was a simple, direct and honourable man. Great art, however, lends itself to philosophical interpretation. That Merian Cooper's adventure odyssey can still inspire enthusiastic, metaphorical discussion, more than 70 years after its inception, is a testament and tribute to the vision of this gifted, influential artist.

UNTOLD HORRORS OF SKULL ISLAND
By Paul Mandell

What remained of Carl Denham's search party fled through the primordial jungle. One of his men had just been plucked out of a tree by a charging bronto and was bitten to death. 'Come back with those bombs, you fools!' Denham screamed as the sailors raced aimlessly through the mud.

In the distance, Kong could be seen cradling Ann Darrow in his paw, making his way to a dry mound near an asphalt pit. 'Down, down!' Driscoll whispered to the men as they crouched behind some shrubbery. Then, his jaw dropped at the sight of three bull tricer-

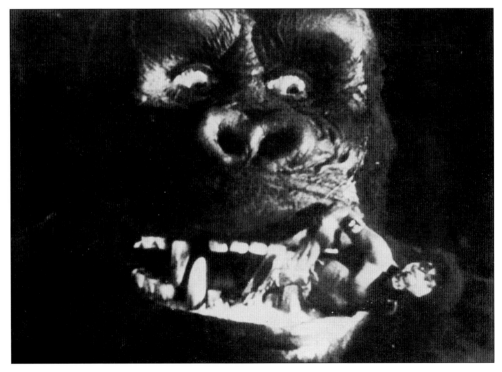

This hapless Skull Island native tried to spear Kong from a platform close to the Great Ape's eye level. Hoisted by his own weapon, he ends as shish kebab.

atopses heading toward the asphalt. Putting Ann down on a dry slab, the ape picked up boulders and hurled them at the horned behemoths, killing two. A third retreated into the jungle.

Cautiously, the men backed away and darted in the other direction. Some tripped and fell. The renegade animal caught their scent and stampeded. One sailor in striped trousers, separated from the party, screamed for his mates and hid behind a tree. Furiously, the beast rammed into the trunk, pinned him down and gored him to death.

The men ran toward a ravine bridged by a huge log end, stopped dead in their tracks. From a distance, they saw the giant ape carrying Ann across the log. A styracosaur lumbered behind them. Driscoll pointed to the ravine and waved the men on, exiting to the right. In no time, they gathered at the edge of the abyss.

Kong came to a clearing and placed his golden prize in the fork of a tree. The shouts of the men distracted him. Enraged, he made his way back to the ravine.

Driscoll and the sailors raced across the log. Denham, the last man, was about to cross when he looked up and saw the simian hulk looming on the other side, beating his chest. 'Look out!' he screamed, trying to reverse the sailors' course. Then, Denham turned and saw the styracosaur approaching from behind with alarming speed. In the nick of time, he ducked back into the shrubbery.

Driscoll had already reached the left bank. Within seconds of Kong's grasp he caught a vine at the ravine's edge, swung down to a ledge, and flung himself into a shallow cave ten feet below.

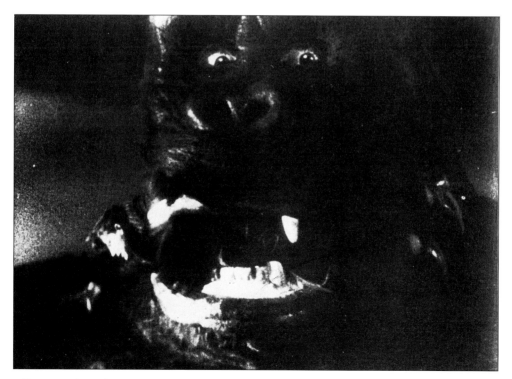

All scenes where the carnivorous Kong chows down on human victims were censored from US prints between 1938 and the 1960s.

KING KONG COMETH!

The men were panic-stricken. Flanked by two monstrosities, they clung to the log, screaming for their lives. The styracosaur bellowed on, trying to dislodge the tree with its long nasal horn. Seeing the animal fuelled Kong's wrath. Reaching down, he grabbed the log and rocked it back and forth. One by one, the sailors fell to the bottom of the gorge. Driscoll watched in horror as his friends plummeted into the slime. The styracosaur retreated while Denham gaped through the thick, verdant cover.

Only one man remained, clinging to a stump and kicking wildly. The ape-god roared in defiance, thumping his fist hard on the slope. With one mighty heave, he hoisted the log into the air and watched it careen into the abyss. The sailor's scream wailed on endlessly as he bounced off the log and landed in the mud.

Scenario sound familiar? No doubt you've seen *King Kong* a hundred times. But doesn't it read a little strange? Not exactly the way you remembered it?

Believe it or not, the above narrative is not an enhanced novelisation of the movie – rather, according to *Kong*'s shooting script, it's a scene-by-scene continuity of how the film actually appeared *prior* to its release! Realising this is a surrealistic experience in itself, for only in our dreams do we extrapolate new vistas from the most fantastic action sequence ever devised.

Of course, no triceratops or styracosaur appeared in the final film. It was producer Merian Cooper's idea to salvage the most dramatic aspects of Willis O'Brien's *Creation* footage, filmed in late 1930 and early 1931, and intercut it with the stunning Dunning process shots of Kong rocking the log, which had been part of *Kong*'s demonstration reel. Only certain sections of *Creation* had been shot, including a sequence in which a hunter

Venture crew members suspended over a ravine between a pursuing triceratops and Kong. *The Great Ape will shake them off the log, sending them to their deaths below.*

The scene where the sailors who fall into the ravine are eaten by giant spiders and lizards – as seen in this production still – has attained the status of a lost classic.

(Ralf Harolde) mercilessly shoots a baby triceratops, gets chased by its enraged mother, and is gored to death when the animal pins him under a toppled tree. To maintain continuity, Cooper had one of Denham's men dressed like Harolde. This scene from *Creation* was spliced into *Kong*'s rough cut and was retained up until the final editing stage.

Also built for *Creation* by Marcel Delgado was an arsinoitherium, a colossal ancestor of the rhinoceros. *Creation* called for this beast to charge two jungle explorers and kill them, leaving their carcasses to be devoured by a swarm of pterodactyls. Part of this attack was also sutured into *Kong*'s rough cut, and O'Brien planned additional scenes of the arsinoitherium cornering Denham's men at the ravine. For some reason or other, Cooper was unhappy with the look of this animal and suggested that O'Brien and Delgado change it to a styracosaur. Presumably this merely required redressing one of the larger triceratops models with more ornate facial armour. Eventually, all the scenes of the styracosaur described in the narrative went before the animation camera, only to become orphans of the cutting room.

The queasy notion of having some of the sailors *survive* their fall into the ravine and encounter unspeakable horrors was no mere pipe dream in Cooper and O'Brien's minds; it all happened on film in gruesome detail. Some audience members of 1933 claimed to have seen the forbidden spider pit sequence. Undoubtedly, such tales were products of an overworked imagination – not only did Merian Cooper reconsider their dramatic value before release, the scenes never got past the Motion Picture Board of Censors! It was a bold, audacious idea, an attempt to squeeze as much sensation out of the audience as possible, but one that ultimately proved too show-stopping and repugnant for anyone's taste.

Described here are the nine lost cuts of the pit sequence, cited verbatim from the script. Due to the ghastly nature of the action, scenarist Ruth Rose penned only the essence of each shot, leaving the details to Cooper's second unit direction and Willis O'Brien's stop-motion ingenuity:

EXT. RAVINE BOTTOM – LONG SHOT – DAY:

The men at the bottom of the ravine are attacked by giant insects which come out of caves and fissures to eat them.

EXT. RAVINE BOTTOM – CLOSE UP – DAY:

The surprised face of a sailor lying in the mud as he sees this.

EXT. RAVINE BOTTOM – CLOSE UP – DAY:

Face of another sailor staring up in horror from the mud. [The suggestion, according to the Delos Lovelace 1932 novelisation, was that the sailor had landed *feet first* in the mud, buried to the waist and immobilised.]

EXT. RAVINE BOTTOM – CLOSE UP – DAY:

Face of a third sailor in the mud, horrified as he sees –

EXT. RAVINE BOTTOM – MEDIUM SHOT – DAY:

An insect with octopus arms takes a man (miniature projection).

EXT. RAVINE BOTTOM – SEMI-CLOSEUP – DAY:

Its arms wind around the struggling man.

EXT. RAVINE BOTTOM – SEMI-CLOSEUP – DAY:

Two men on their backs staring up at a spider monster who attacks them (miniature projection).

EXT. RAVINE BOTTOM – CLOSE UP – DAY:

The face of a fourth sailor, fallen in mud, staring in horror as he sees –

EXT. RAVINE BOTTOM – FULL SHOT – DAY:

A giant lizard takes a man.

After devouring him, this final anomaly climbed a vine hanging from the top of the ravine and made it way toward Driscoll hiding in the cave. Part of the shot survives as Driscoll cuts the vine, sending the lizard to its death.

Bert Willis, who functioned as OBie's animation cameraman, vividly recalled the sequence. 'The bottom of the ravine was a miniature set about four feet wide, built in plaster, with a few tiny projection screens behind the log. I don't know *how* many days we spent on that set animating those terrible animals! Spiders, snakes, horrible things! The Pennsylvania Board of Censors demanded that the scenes be taken out. The Board was aimed at women and children, and these things were just too horrible to show.'

The octopus-insect was the most loathsome creature to deal with. Delgado built it in miniature based on O'Brien's design. According to Bert Willis, 'That thing made everybody a little nervous. OBie wanted *real snakes* for the closeups. So, a lady was brought in with a cage full of them. I must say she knew how to handle them. She had been to South America and had picked them up there. I remember we filmed stuntmen screaming as the snakes wrapped around their bodies. Fortunately, no one was hurt. The censors ordered those scenes removed, too.'

The sequence retained only the long shots of the men falling into the chasm. The camera rolled at eight times normal speed for a slow motion effect. Originally, close-ups of the men landing in the slime were intercut with the actors to suggest the possibility of survival. Because the six-inch jointed dummies refused to react properly during the fall, lead weights were placed inside, causing them to bounce realistically at the point of impact.

Interestingly, anguished screams were actually those of sound effects man Murray Spivack, whose shrieks could be heard in *The Most Dangerous Game*, filmed back to back with *Kong*.

The crab monster from the undergrowth that attacks the sailors. The scene remains lost, but restored prints clearly show the men falling to their deaths.

Only weeks before *King Kong* premiered at Radio City Music Hall on March 2, 1933, Cooper and his superiors were buckling under the strain of the picture's length. Fourteen reels had been shot, far too long to suit RKO's New York office, which frowned on a running time of more than 100 minutes. More importantly, there seemed to be too many points where the pace lagged and the peripheral monsters drew too much attention away from Fay Wray's plight. After heated sessions with *Kong*'s editor Ted Cheesman, Cooper ordered chunks of footage removed and brought it down to eleven reels.

Great sacrifices were made in the jungle scenes. Gone forever were the arsinoitherium, the triceratops, and the styracosaur, although the latter was revived for *Son of Kong* somewhat gratuitously, and a publicity pasteup showing the men on the log flanked by Kong and the horned monster confused devotees for years.

Fortunately, the jungle chaos moves so swiftly, one hasn't time to wonder *why* the men stay on the log, instead of retreating to the right bank. Only during the aftershock does Denham's absence seem conspicuous, since his scenes evading the styracosaur were removed.

Still, the greatest casualty of all to afficionados and film historians were the creatures of the pit, lost for the ages. Perhaps one day in some technician's attic, or in a mislabelled film can buried deep in the RKO vault, a print of the episode will be unearthed and screened, fulfilling the original vision of its makers. Or, as Denham would have pitched it, 'merely a show to gratify your curiosity.'

SONS OF KONG

HIS MAJESTY, *KING KONG* — V
THE KING'S SUCCESSORS
By Donald F. Glut

The same month that *King Kong* was premiering in New York and Hollywood, Schoedsack and Cooper were already at work on a mysterious film project called *Jamboree*. The budget for the picture was $250,000, which meant that whatever the nature of the film it could not be another *King Kong*.

But, in a way, it was. *Jamboree* was actually a sequel to *King Kong*, a quickly made comedy followup described by one advertisement (depicting a smiling ape wearing a sandwich board with the picture's final title) as 'A Serio-Comic Phantasy'. The title *Jamboree* had been used to keep curiosity-seekers off the set. When the film was released in 1933 its title '*The Son of Kong*' was descriptive enough.

The Son recreated the grandeur of the original, albeit on a smaller scale. The sequel ran only 70 minutes (as opposed to the 100 minutes of its predecessor). Cooper and Schoedsack were producing and directing again, with Robert Armstrong returning as a more sympathetic Carl Denham. Marcel Delgado created some new prehistoric creatures for the second Kong production which Willis O'Brien animated. Recycled were an apatosaurus and styracosaurus left over from *King Kong*, scenes of the latter model being one of the casualties of Cooper's final editing job on the original picture. The music in *The Son of Kong* was again Max Steiner's (and was titled 'Runaway Blues', 'King's Theme', 'Ship at Sea', 'In Dakang', 'Hootchie-Kootchie', 'Fire Music', 'The Warning', 'An Offer of Help', 'Chinese Chatter', 'Love's Awakening', 'The Forgotten Island', 'Monotony', 'The Quicksands', 'The Old Temple', 'The Stegosaurus', 'The Black Bear', 'First Aid', 'The Coconuts', 'Evening Quietude', 'The Discovery', 'Johnny Get Your Gun', 'The Comedian', 'The Lizard Fight', 'Mazeltof', 'The Earthquake' and 'Calm Sea').

Carl Denham now lives in a sleazy boarding house room adorned by a theatrical poster depicting *King Kong*, the monster who created so much damage in New York that the former film producer is now haunted by creditors and reporters.

With a grand jury indictment and several lawsuits also threatening him, Denham leaves the country with Captain Englehorn (Reicher again), operating the *Venture* in the China Sea as a cargo vessel. While in the port of Malaya, Denham attends a performance of a cheap tent circus operated by an old alcoholic named Peterson (Clarence Wilson) and his songstress daughter Hilda (Helen Mack). The show's main attractions are the girl's songs and, to Denham's amusement, a monkey act. After nightfall the down-and-out Captain Nils Helstrom (John Marston) argues with Peterson, strikes him with a bottle and inadvertently sets fire to the tent. Peterson perishes in the flames.

Helstrom is now afraid that he will be arrested for murder. Coincidentally, he is the

Son of Kong (1933) transformed Carl Denham (Robert Armstrong) into a romantic hero.
The eponymous 'Kiko' is a white ape barely resembling the Sasquatch creature on the poster. **91**

Son of Kong is more of a seafaring adventure than a horror movie. Like King Kong, it holds back the monsters for much of its (much shorter) running time.

same Norwegian captain that had originally sold Denham the map to Skull Island. Helstrom tells Denham that the people who had built the Great Wall had also left behind a vast treasure, thereby inspiring Denham and Englehorn to return to the island with Helstrom accompanying them. As the new voyage of the Venture gets underway, Denham discovers that Hilda has stowed away. Helstrom, meanwhile, excites the crew to mutiny, which they do on the morning of the vessel's arrival at Skull Island. Certainly not a loyal bunch, the crew then casts Helstrom overboard, leaving him, Denham, Hilda, Englehorn and Charlie the Chinese cook (Victor Wong, another survivor from the previous film) stranded on Kong's former home.

Naturally the natives are not too receptive, recalling the damage to their village the last time Denham and company visited their island. The chief (Noble Johnson, recreating his part from the first Kong film) drives them away, forcing them to gain access to the island via a narrow inlet. Once on the island, Denham and Hilda set off on their own, coming upon a flight of stone steps. But they also encounter something quite unexpected – a huge albino gorilla (about fifteen feet tall), the apparent Son of Kong, trapped in a pool of quicksand.

Marcel Delgado constructed his 'son' models over the armatures that once formed the metal skeletons of the original King Kong. There were three such models of the little Kong, all capable of registering considerable expressions. (No full-size mock-up of the ape's head and shoulders was built for *The Son of Kong*; O'Brien animated the facial expressions on the miniature for the close-up cameras.) Since *The Son of Kong* was essentially a comedy, the white-furred Kong was often animated in fulfilment of the old adage 'Monkey see, monkey do.' Little Kong rolled and blinked his eyes inquisitively, scratched his head in puzzlement and reacted with human 'takes'. More than a monster, he was a giant and lovable teddy bear, entirely sympathetic and perfectly suited to the tongue-in-cheek flavour of the picture.

Denham, feeling a sense of responsibility to Little Kong because of what happened to his father, pushes over a tree so that the ape can extricate himself from the quagmire. Meanwhile, Englehorn and the others barely escape death on the horns of a spike-frilled styracosaurus. When Denham and Hilda are menaced by a huge prehistoric cave bear, Little Kong engages the beast in a furious battle. After he kills the animal, the small version of King Kong nurses a wounded finger, bandaged with a strip of material from Hilda's slip.

The next morning Denham, Hilda and Little Kong come upon an ancient temple. Inside, draped across the stone face of a demon-like idol, are the jewels which Denham assumes to be the treasure of Skull Island. Unnoticed by the threesome, a strange long-necked reptile (a creation of Delgado not found in any palaeontology book) enters the cave which houses the temple. The battle between Little Kong and the saurian is exciting and at the same time humorous. Apparently killing the monster, Little Kong dangles its neck and peers into its open mouth. But as the ape turns away to join his human friends, the reptile lifts its head to bite him in the rump. Kong finishes the creature with a well-placed blow to the head.

When Englehorn and the others arrive on the scene, Helstrom is astounded by the discovery of the treasure, admitting that he had invented the legend in order to escape Malaya. Upon first seeing Little Kong, Helstrom tries to escape in the lifeboat, only to be devoured by a hideous sea serpent (another invention by Delgado).

The Son of Kong utilized the *deus ex machina* climax so familiar to the 'lost world' motion picture or story. Skull Island has existed since Mesozoic times, but now that modern Man has journeyed there the island is suddenly attacked by an angered Nature. The traditional volcano was replaced with an earthquake and flood as Skull Island begins to sink beneath the sea. Denham again rescues Little Kong, whose foot is caught in an earth fissure. But Kong's salvation is brief as he returns the favour, holding the former film producer high above his head as the waters continue to rise and the final vestiges of the island vanish below the waves. Denham is pulled into the rowboat occupied by Captain Englehorn, Hilda and Charlie, after which Little Kong's hand disappears beneath the depths. Soon four persons, all rich now from the treasure of Skull Island, are picked up by a ship. At last Carl Denham reveals himself to be more than a motion picture entrepreneur. He and Hilda are destined for marriage before the fade-out.

The Son of Kong was a fine sequel though it suffered in comparison to the grandeur of the original *King Kong*. (A scene showing animated birds from *The Son of Kong* later appeared in a background shot of the celebrated *Citizen Kane* [RKO, 1941].) Willis O'Brien would have preferred a more serious approach to *The Son of Kong* and, in the years that followed, spoke little about the film. Part of O'Brien's reticence in this matter was probably due to his own personal tragedy that occurred during the production of the movie.

O'Brien had been married to a mentally ill woman, Hazel Ruth Collette, whose problems were compounded further by tuberculosis and cancer. Hazel was under narcotic sedation when, in a state of severe depression on October 7, 1933, she fatally shot both of their sons and then turned the weapon upon herself. The boys died that day while she survived but a year longer. (In 1934, O'Brien married Darlyne Prenette and lived a happy life with her until his death in 1962.)

For a while Cooper considered making yet a third Kong epic, flashing back to before Denham transported the original ape to New York. King Kong was to escape in the Malay Archipelago for an untold adventure. It remained unfilmed.

ORPHAN IN THE STORM: *THE SON OF KONG*

By Gerald Peary

While Franklin Roosevelt first occupied the White House in spring 1933, Americans went in droves to see *King Kong* in its original release. The film was such an immediate financial (and also artistic) success that it became apparent that the dead would not rest. It was time for Regeneration, Hollywood style: a sequel. Prodded into activity by an anxious RKO, the *King Kong* artistic crew (Merian C. Cooper, Ernest Schoedsack, Willis O'Brien, Max Steiner and scriptwriter, Ruth Rose) went scurrying back to work.

KING KONG COMETH!

Before any other studio could capitalise by jumping on the bandwagon of 'big ape' movies, RKO did so itself, making best of the realisation that Kong's agonising demise before the camera possessed such finality that to risk a *Return of Kong* would be a bit ridiculous. The filmmakers instead resorted to a simpler device of inventing an orphaned foundling child for the late monster, appropriately deemed for the title *Son of Kong*. Six months after *King Kong*'s release, the sequel was already playing the neighbourhoods.

Looked at today, *Son of Kong* still begins imposingly enough with ominous, dramatic jungle music and a close-up of Kong himself at his most vindictive and frightening best, spewing forth muscles, hair, teeth. But the camera dollies back for a most disappointing revelation. Kong is only a picture on a poster, an inanimate artefact, hung on a wall. In place of the cosmically energised, tempestuous jungle stomping grounds of *King Kong*, the locale introduced is the drab, confined living quarters of a cheap New York rooming house.

Who lives here? *Son of Kong* is full of surprises, for it is nobody other than Carl Denham himself, though hardly recognizable. He has fallen on terrible times in the month since Kong took blocks of New York with him to his final destiny, leaving his business manager full responsibility for his damages. 'Tell the public that Carl Denham, the smart guy who was going to make a million dollars off of King Kong, is flat broke,' he informs a reporter. 'Everyone in New York is suing me.'

Denham is not only impoverished but, even less characteristic of him, penitent and remorseful about the havoc caused by Kong. 'Don't you think I'm sorry for the harm?' he asks, and not without feeling. 'I wish I'd left him on the island. I'm paying for what he did.' Denham is now a spiritless, guilt-ridden man, hiding away in this obscure rooming house from a host of creditors, finally fleeing to safety incognito on the back of a junk wagon.

This first cluster of events in *Son of Kong* is strangely apart from the heroic plain of its predecessor. In fact these opening sequences seem almost closer in association to the slapstick comedy of a Buster Keaton one-reeler than to the heightened world of a film of the fantastic. Why this incredible shift in tone between the two *Kong* pictures? The answer cannot be offered in total confidence, but somehow the few months difference in their respective production schedules, from early to late 1933, holds clues to a viable historical explanation.

Franklin Roosevelt assumed the presidency three days after the release of *King Kong*. But by the time *Son of Kong* arrived in the movie houses, Christmas 1933, FDR had been in the executive office for half a year. The glamour and mystery and, for many, the trepidation surrounding Roosevelt's sweep into the White House slowly had dissipated in witnessing of the familiar, day-to-day grind of Roosevelt running the country. Likewise, his New Deal programmes became demythologised as they took pragmatic form.

In answer to the most paranoid anti-Roosevelt fears from the right, these policies, obviously were not wrecking the capitalist foundations of the country. But it became equally clear to even his most fervent admirers that Roosevelt, as Hoover before him, possessed no instant panacea for the acute ailments of the Depression. In fact, life for millions in the USA was destined to become worse before getting better, as more and more Americans became unemployed during the first years of Roosevelt's administration than ever before. While the New Deal slowly passed through Congress for approval, then moved with bureaucratic sluggishness out into the country to take effect, there was nothing for many Americans to do but stick out the miseries until rescued someday.

King Kong had opened boldly with a frontal attack on the Depression in the form of New York City souplines, then expanded its horizons outward into an open-ended, adventurous world in which anything, from the delightful to the disastrous, could occur in an instant. Thus was the eve of Roosevelt's presidency. But *Son of Kong* tells a different story

Unlike his belligerent old man, the son of Kong is benign and friendly – as Robert Armstrong and Helen Mack will soon discover.

six months afterward, this of financial circumstances so oppressive that they can't be beaten by even the most resourceful of individuals.

The seemingly indomitable entrepreneurial spirit of dynamic Carl Denham has receded into the past. Instead, Denham in *Son of Kong* is weary and helpless, victimised by his impossible financial obligations. He has become reduced in status to a penniless Depression Everyman, whose last gasps of energy and imagination are devoted not to combating the Depression but to fleeing from it. *Son of Kong* finally reveals its true reason to be: it is an escapist film, expressing through Denham's subsequent actions a wistful yearning (probably on a national level in late 1933) for a fantasy alternative somewhere to the hard times of America.

Denham locates his old sea buddy of *King Kong* days and together they drop out of the Depression, taking off on the ocean for places unknown, never returning to the shores of the USA for the rest of the film. And while the names of exotic, romantic places flash across the screen – Lombak, Makassar, Singapore, Colombo – superimposed on a shot of splashing ocean waves behind the ship's rudder, the music of Max Steiner's score swells with excitement for the first time in *Son of Kong* since its opening moment.

In retrospect, *King Kong* was a pacesetter: bold of conception, unique of content, pushing its way effortlessly toward new frontiers unexplored either in reality or previously on the screen. But *Son of Kong* is conservative and cautious, a movie of quiet excitements, leisurely pace, and also predictably derivative of the filmic past. Not only are many of its scenes variations on similar sequences in its parent film, but huge chunks of its plot are lifted directly from a lost, absolutely unknown silent of the Tiffany

Corporation called *The Enchanted Island*.

For the record: *The Enchanted Island* concerned a man and his daughter stranded for fifteen years on a tropical island with only their trained animals as companions. The peace is broken by the sudden invasion of three men: the hero, Bob Hamilton; the villain, 'Red' Blake; and Ulysses Abraham Washington, a Negro cook. Hamilton falls in love with the young girl and teaches her about the outside world. 'Red' Blake kills off the father in a quarrel, but he is in turn done in by Ulysses in a fight during a volcanic eruption. The lovers escape from the molten lava and are rescued by a cruiser.

Son of Kong retains in its script by Ruth Rose all of the plot elements listed above for *The Enchanted Island*, with some minor adjustments. A young girl, Hilda, and her alcoholic father, a refugee from the circus, have lived for years as expatriates at the port of Dakang, supporting themselves through a sideshow trained monkey act. Into this locale comes the hero, Denham, the villain, Helstrom, and a Chinese cook, Charlie. (Also the captain.) Helstrom quarrels with Hilda's father and murders him. Denham becomes enamoured of Hilda. Later in the movie, Helstrom is killed and buried beneath a volcanic explosion. Denham and Hilda escape from both the lava and an island sinking into the sea. They are picked up by a cruiser and rescued.

The Dakang of *Son of Kong* is hardly, however, an idyllic, 'enchanted island' setting; rather it is pictured as a dank, impoverished port town, a hangout for derelicts and shiftless drifters. Denham's own rejuvenated romanticism is swiftly undercut here. He and the captain follow a sign pointing out the way to an exciting musical interlude with the mysterious 'Belle Helene', a trip which ends for them on a flat bench in a tent crowded with the lowest native element. They sit in stony silence watching a monkey orchestra perform its dreadful act. The tiny animals, dressed like miniature bellhops, pound on their instruments in a rhythmic, atonal counterpoint, an unnerving baroque introduction to the show's main attraction.

The 'Belle Helene' in person proves equally unsettling. Instead of the sultry, husky-voiced continental probably anticipated, 'Helene' turns out to be the inexperienced and awkwardly misplaced American, Hilda, who strums a Hawaiian guitar in a clumsy attempt to appear exotic and sings badly in a high-pitched voice, 'Oh, I've got the runaway blues today . . .' Denham and friend have been taken.

The existence of the rich atmospheric details in this strangely compelling scene result quite obviously from the filmmakers' personal acquaintances with such locales during global travels in the 1920s. In fact, Merian Cooper (whose uncanny resemblance to actor Robert Armstrong, the movie Denham, is too close for coincidence) speaks at length of exactly

The son of Kong fights an unspecified prehistoric reptile on behalf of his human friends, for the treasure of Skull Island. This is one of very few dinosaur scenes in the film

such happenings in his autobiographical journal, *The Sea Gypsy*, a 1924 account of an around-the-world voyage with the famed explorer, Captain Edward Salisbury. It was a trip much like the one Denham makes in *Son of Kong*.

Cooper had landed in Jibuti, an Abbyssinian port, and wandered with a friend into the native quarters, where they were confronted with an invitation to 'See Arab dance, de Somali dance.' Taylor, Cooper's companion, remarked excitedly, 'Well, here's a chance to see the famous and beautiful and sensuous dances of the East.' They followed their hosts through crooked streets and finally into a tiny tent where, in place of a lavish stage show, three Arab women pathetically attempted to sway their bodies in the floor space between the beds. The disenchanted Cooper wrote in his diary, 'These dancers and the fly-ridden cafe are Jibuti's only amusements. Absolutely nothing else.'

Back in *Son of Kong*, Carl Denham, the avowed misogynist and producer of all-male adventure movies, the man who told sexy Ann Darrow in *King Kong* that their relationship would be 'strictly business' and meant it, this same Denham is in love. *Son of Kong* allows with complete tolerance for Denham to fall for the shy, naïve young woman, as he disregards in true romantic fashion the embarrassing inadequacy of her show business personality. And when Hilda's father is murdered, Denham takes her willingly aboard for a return voyage to Skull Island. This bashfully grinning middle-aged courtier finds time to flirt with Hilda under the moonlight once the ship is again at sea.

At last, with the exposition done away and romance brewing, *Son of Kong* brings its plot around to the concerns for which people presumably paid their money, the strange and fantastic doings on Skull Island. The heroes sail up on the beach to be greeted in warning by Willis O'Brien's eerie black apparitions floating through the air like furies. It is *King Kong* over again, including that flamboyant and chilling Max Steiner jungle music.

The excitement quickly passes, however, as the neighbourhood seems cleaned up a bit since the last sojourn, with most of the rougher prehistoric beasts, from tyrannosaur to pterodactyl, apparently in migration. (Only the monstrous underwater dinosaur from *King Kong* remains to gobble up the villain at an opportune moment, thus revenging the death of Hilda's father without need of Denham to bloody his hero hands.) All in all, the rejuvenated Skull Island isn't a bad place even to bring up a kid, unless the youth happens to be the son of Kong.

Denham and Hilda come across a most distressing sight, the titular star of the movie up to his neck in quicksand and yelping like a puppy for assistance. It is in this long delayed, rather anticlimactic moment that the son of Kong finally reveals himself, and he proves immediately less both in size and stature than his fearsome late father.

This twelve-foot Kong will not trample on native villages nor rampage through the streets of New York. Perhaps more disappointing in contrast to the provocative subconscious Freudian levels of *King Kong*, the son is clearly prepubescent and shows no more interest in sexual possession of the heroine, Hilda, than in searching out his strangely nonexistent Mom, the 'missing woman' of the Kong pictures. Yet in his favour, the son of Kong certainly is consistent in his character with the more gentle, mellow, and sexually subdued mood of this second movie.

Denham and Hilda come to the rescue. They pull the trapped youngster out from the mire, for, as Denham later explains, 'I felt I owed his family something.' Kong, Jr. follows after them in gratitude as an overgrown child trailing his parents; but in this case it is the adults who require protection against the more insistently carnivorous of the neighbourhood animals.

In parody imitation of the astounding Darwinian battle to the death between King Kong and the fierce tyrannosaur, the little Kong takes on a nasty-tempered bear in school-

CHAPTER SIX: There on the peak of Skull Island were Denham and Son of Kong, helplessly surrounded by the waters of an immense tidal wave which had followed the earthquake. On the waves of the choppy seas Denham could see Hilda, Englehorn and the Chinese cook, standing by in the small boat in which they had eluded the cataclysm. But Denham was unable to join them now, even if he had wanted to.

Still the waters rose about him and Son of Kong, the latter held fast by the foot, which was pinched in a cleft of the rock by the quake. The great dumb beast "with

the heart of a man" again proved its benevolent nature by holding Denham above the rising waves.

But still the waters rose—rose until they submerged the brave beast. And still he held his human companion aloft. The small boat made a desperate attempt to approach—succeeded! With King Kong's expiring gurgle the beast tossed Denham into the boat. And then the ocean closed upon Son of Kong forever!

Denham and his party of refugees were picked up by a steamer, which became the scene of his and Hilda's honeymoon. *(THE END)*

99

The final frames of a comic-strip synopsis of Son of Kong, *produced by RKO publicity. The gentle giant ape dies to save his friends, as Skull Island sinks beneath the sea.*

yard brawl fashion. They box, wrestle, and stumble about the terrain more noisily than with physical damage, as Denham and Hilda root on their new friend to victory in the mock heroic tousle. An admiring Denham comments, 'Gee, can he scrap. Just like his old man.'

Skull Island seems safe for the time being. It is the end of the day's wandering through the forest maze, and *Son of Kong*'s heroes have found themselves conveniently separated from the other party of sojourners. As the new lovers bed down near each other for the night, with Kong, Jr. secretly keeping watch over them (like the lion in Rousseau's painting of *The Sleeping Gypsy*), the movie begins to assume a tranquil beauty reminiscent of Shakespearean romance.

This feeling is reinforced by the sudden splitting of the movie into a double plot, complete with ironically paralleled events. The enchanted jungle greenery brings the romantic couple closer and closer together, a relationship further sanctified through the harmonious alliance of man and beast – a 'B' movie Holy Trinity of Denham, Hilda, and Kong, Jr. The reward for these is a restful night of sleep and sanctuary from the turmoil surrounding them, followed the next day by discovery of the treasures and hidden riches of the island.

Markedly different is the night time fate of their three companions – the captain, the Chinese cook, and the villain, Helstrom, who have holed up against their wills in a bare stone cavern. The reason is the unwanted outside presence of a raging prehistoric behemoth, pounding against the rocks trying to get at them. These three get no sleep at all, not even the chance to sit down. Perhaps they are plagued by the unlucky presence among them of a secret murderer, Helstrom, killer of Hilda's father.

Son of Kong appears at this point finally to have found itself, evolving out of its previously loose, rambling, and even haphazard form into a work of some purposeful structure. Unfortunately, everything gained is lost again in a split second, in the blowing of the wind. Literally from nowhere a mighty storm breaks on the horizon; and without the slightest motivation, Skull Island, its volcanoes erupting everywhere, crumbles into the sea, taking with it the last vestiges of prehistoric culture and also the body of the evil Helstrom.

The virtuous protagonists – Hilda, the captain, the Chinese cook – all row away in the nick of time. (What happens to the black native populace on the other side of the island? Their plight is ignored.) And Carl Denham is plucked from Davey Jones' Locker by way of the most valiant (and also contrived and sentimental) heroic sacrifice since A *Tale of*

Two Cities. Little Kong, noble savage until the end, holds Denham above the waves in his fist until the rescue. Then, with Max Steiner's mournful elegy of strings soaring and moaning passionately in the background (the same music that lay King Kong to rest), this well-meaning young giant gorilla finds death at a too early age at the bottom of the sea.

The harsh, dislocated ending to *Son of Kong* cannot be explained by any stretch or twist of the story. Quite clearly there were outside, nonaesthetic factors at work influencing the last of the filming. Perhaps the budget ran out. Or, more likely, RKO insisted on cutting short the shooting schedule in order to rush *King Kong*'s sequel onto the market.

Whatever the case, *Son of Kong* suffers to the point of near ruin in this abrupt halt to the narrative after only 62 minutes. The slow and deliberate build of the story for nearly an hour deserves much better than five minutes of packaged apocalypse followed, in Kong, Jr.'s ostensibly heroic drowning, with brief seconds of the most vulgarised cinematic apotheosis.

Hardly more satisfactory is the concluding tag of Denham and Hilda cooing together aboard a rescue vessel, bantering in cute innuendo about an impending marriage between them. Has the hero of the movie become wiser and more perceptive from living through this harrowing adventure? 'Poor Little Kong. Do you think he knew he was saving my life?' asks Denham with the most blank-faced seriousness.

Luckily this absurd inquiry is not answered, as the animated conversation turns to more important issues for Hilda and Denham at the fadeout: love, and portioning out the treasure money. Kong, Jr. becomes a forgotten memory for them, perhaps the inevitably adverse conclusion for this orphaned, then deceased gorilla giant. He was already denied artistic immortality by the callous mercenaries of RKO, who released a half-baked, virtually sabotaged movie so that it arrived in the theatres in time for the quick profits of the 1933-34 Christmas season.

The implications of this foul, commercial deed stretch immutably into the cinematic future. 40 years later hardly anyone remembers that King Kong had a son at all.

HIS MAJESTY, *KING KONG* — VI
By Donald F. Glut

In 1935, O'Brien joined Cooper and Schoedsack again, this time to create the spectacular destruction sequence (all executed in miniature) of *The Last Days of Pompeii,* another RKO epic. Four years later Cooper, O'Brien and Delgado began an ambitious project titled *War Eagles.* The premise was that natives living in a prehistoric world have tamed gigantic eagles and ride them on saddles made from the skulls of the horned dinosaur triceratops. Astride these great feathered monsters, the natives battle such adversaries as tyrannosaurus. Eventually they invade New York where they engage in aerial combat with a number of dirigibles. O'Brien animated Delgado's eagle and tyrannosaurus models for some colour test scenes. But the project waned, primarily because of Cooper's stint in the armed services. During the interim dirigibles had already become passé and *War Eagles* dropped into oblivion, existing today only in the form of a script, a few stills and some frames of colour nitrate motion picture film.

War Eagles was but one of many such aborted projects; *Gwangi*, which had been in the planning stages as early as 1942, was another RKO project about a Delgado-built allosaurus, to be animated by O'Brien as it fought against capture by a group of lariat-casting cowboys. O'Brien's successor Ray Harryhausen finally brought the project to the screen more than 25 years later. The new version of the story was called, again, simply *Gwangi* during its early stages and went into production in 1968 under two titles, *The Lost Valley* and *The Valley Where Time Stood Still.* But it was *The Valley of Gwangi* that finally reached the theatres in brilliant colour in 1969. *Gwangi* is an allosaurus, one of several prehistoric animals inhabiting a lost valley in North America during the early twentieth century. In tribute to O'Brien, Harryhausen had his allosaurus pause to scratch its 'ear' as had the tyrannosaurus in *King Kong.* The allosaurus is finally captured and exhibited at a circus, from which it breaks loose to terrorise a Mexican town. *Gwangi* finally meets destruction inside a burning cathedral. *The Valley of Gwangi* was directed by James O'Connolly and released in colour by Warner Brothers-7 Arts. (Though *Gwangi* never enjoyed the popularity of *King Kong*, there was some merchandising in association with the picture, including a record album, a Gold Key comic book, colouring book and a plastic allosaurus assembly kit obviously modelled after the Harryhausen creature.)

Though Delgado's original allosaurus model apparently never went before O'Brien's stop-motion camera, elements of the *Gwangi* project were finally salvaged as Cooper (teamed with producer John Ford) and Schoedsack enlisted the talents of the two men for a film that went into production in 1946 at RKO. It was motivated by a desire by the producers and director to give the public another *King Kong*, which they almost did.

The picture was originally entitled *Mr. Joseph Young of Africa*, though it was released in 1949 as the more commercial *Mighty Joe Young.* (The movie is also known as *The Great Joe Young* and, in Germany, as the misleading *Panik um King Kong* ['Panic Around King Kong'.]) Structurally, the story bore strong similarities to *King Kong.* Even the irrepressible Robert Armstrong was hired to re-enact his Carl Denham performance, though now he was almost a comic figure, a show business entrepreneur named Max O'Hara. The real star of the film, however, was Mighty Joe Young himself, another huge gorilla, though he was more the size of the son of Kong than the King himself.

O'Brien actually did only some fifteen percent of the animation in *Mighty Joe Young.* The remaining 85 percent went to a capable newcomer named Ray Harryhausen, a young man who had worshipped O'Brien since his first of countless viewings of the original *King Kong.* After mustering the courage to show O'Brien some of his 16mm footage of animated dinosaurs and fairy tale characters, Harryhausen was made the master's assistant for *Mighty Joe Young.* (Harryhausen later acquiesced to the position vacated by O'Brien after the latter's death and created the special visual effects for some of the finest fantasy pictures ever made.)

The model for Joe Young was the celebrated gorilla Bushman,* the star attraction at Chicago's Lincoln Park Zoo. Bushman was photographed so that O'Brien and Harryhausen could later study his movements, frame by frame, and attribute to Mighty Joe the gait and mannerisms of a real gorilla. It was Harryhausen who designed the metal armature for the new giant ape, basing it directly upon an authentic gorilla skeleton.

The animation in *Mighty Joe Young* proved to be much smoother than that in *King Kong.* Willis O'Brien even won an Academy Award for the special visual effects. Still, *Mighty Joe Young* never garnered the critical acclaim or popularity of its 1933 inspiration. Though a more realistic gorilla than Kong, Joe Young was more lovable than monstrous and his screen adventure lacked the spectacle of its two predecessors.

Joe Young, unlike Kong, was simply an oversized African gorilla, thereby lacking the exotic appeal and mystery of the King of Skull Island. (One criticism of both *King Kong* and *Mighty Joe Young* is that the sizes of the apes are sometimes inconsistent from one shot to the next. Joe, for example, ranges from slightly bigger than a real bull gorilla to

Mighty Joe Young (1949) is a 'King Kong for children', best remembered for setpieces such as seen in this exposure test of 29 June, 1948: 'Joe Holds Jill on Piano.'

approximating the enormity of Kong himself.) An African native trades the infant gorilla to Jill Young, a child who had given her father's flashlight in return. Joe, as Jill names him, grows up as a relatively gentle pet on her father's African estate.

When Max O'Hara gets the idea of having American cowboys roping wild animals in Africa for his new nightclub, the Golden Safari, the group makes the unexpected acquaintance of Joe. In a sequence originally planned for O'Brien's *Gwangi*, the cowboys attempt to rope the huge gorilla. (In reality they were lassoing a jeep, the ape figure being later inserted into the scene.) But when the gorilla lashes back, only the intervention of Jill, now a young lady played by Terry Moore, saves their lives.

O'Hara, like Denham, has big plans for Joe and soon the mysterious name of 'Mr. Joseph Young of Africa' is in lights above the Golden Safari in the United States. The club has an African setting, with live lions prowling in their glass cages behind the bar. Mighty Joe Young makes his public debut on the stage of the Golden Safari. The gorilla holds above his head a platform upon which Jill sits playing 'Beautiful Dreamer', Joe's favourite song, on a grand piano. After the audience has stopped gasping at the awesome sight, O'Hara and Jill put Joe through such routines as engaging a group of strongmen in a tug of war.

Joe's only real opportunity to be monstrous in the film occurs when several drunks slip backstage and get him intoxicated. The drunken simian goes on a rampage that wrecks the Golden Safari in an incredible display of special effects and stuntwork. During the conflict O'Hara's lions are freed from their enclosure, only to meet the full violent fury of Mighty Joe Young. Regarding him now as a dangerous beast, the police order him destroyed, after which O'Hara, Jill and cowboy Tex (Ben Johnson) smuggle him away in a truck. On their way to the airport, the group passes a burning orphanage. Joe Young charges to the rescue, saving the trapped children from death and redeeming himself before a blazing tree to which he clings splits in half, sending him falling to the street with two youngsters hanging onto his hairy back. Joe, unlike Kong and his son, survives to return to Africa with Jill and Tex, living out his days peacefully and bringing to a fade-out the last of the great films about a giant ape. One of the Mighty Joe Young models was eventually displayed at the special effects exhibit at Hollywood's Lytton Center in 1966. The model was identified as King Kong. *Special Effects*, an 8mm film of this exhibit, was made available by this author. Mighty Joe Young was also worked into the lyrics of 'Ape Call', a song recorded by Nervous Norvis during the 1950s.

* Born approximately 1928, Bushman was a Cameroon gorilla. During his early years, the baby Bushman was walked about the zoo on a leash. By adulthood the ape was six feet, two inches tall when standing erect and weighed 550 pounds. Bushman, was, perhaps, the finest gorilla specimen ever to live in captivity. He was known for a rather pleasant disposition though he became rather cantankerous in his later years. The magnificent ape survived until New Year's Eve, 1951, and all Chicago mourned his passing. Today, thanks to the art of the taxidermist, Bushman can still be viewed in Chicago's Field Museum of Natural History.

FATHER OF KONG FAREWELL —
WILLIS O'BRIEN IN MEMORIAM,
2 MARCH 1886 — 8 NOVEMBER 1962

By Forrest J Ackerman

When I told Ray Bradbury that Willis O'Brien had died, he was temporarily too taken back and too saddened to say anything for print. But a few days later he wrote me:

Willis O'Brien was known to me only by his work, which speaks sufficiently for the man. No one born in this century can fail to have encountered him at least once through his monsters. I cannot see how it would be possible for anyone to forget The Lost World, *once encountered. This film, with a few others, coloured and changed my life. And my colouration and change were completed by my introduction to* Kong *through the genius of O'Brien. I saw* Kong *at least twelve times from the age of twelve until my thirties. I still believe it to be the supreme action myth of our day, a wonderful blend of the implausible made plausible by people, especially O'Brien, who obviously cared about what they were doing. Their love for high romance, grand adventure, enabled them to make an immortal film. This is the true monument O'Brien built for himself. No one can take away from it or add to it. It is there now and will always be there in the history of the cinema.*

They called him the Sphinx of Hollywood. One publication of the early thirties stated: 'He makes even the Sphinx seem talkative. Not even his employers know his secrets. Willis O'Brien, wizard of prehistoric lore, makes things live – he's a miracle man who can relive the past! He pulls prehistoric monsters 75 feet long out of a hat! He makes today yesterday – yesterday today.

'He is the man of the hour on the RKO lot for without him that studio's great bid for screen immortality would be impossible. The bid is *King Kong*, completed after more than two years of production effort conducted behind locked and guarded stage doors. The process for making *King Kong* required the ultimate in precision craftmanship. Nomore than a total of twenty feet of film could be photographed in the best ten-hour day, so laborious was the task.

'For *King Kong* O'Brien conjured, magically, among other things, animals that thrived from seven to 35 million years ago, including a tyrannousaurus, a stegosaurus, a brontosaurus and a pterodactyl. The largest of these, the tyrannosaurus rex, weighed 30 tons, was twenty feet high and measured 30 feet in length. The flying reptile known as the pterodactyl had a wingspread of 25 feet.

'But the foregoing can be considered mere samples of O'Brien's ingenuity, for he created an ape 50 feet tall, 36 feet around the chest and weighing between fifteen and twenty tons!

'The fight to the death between a brontosaurus and tyrannosaurus (the combined weight of the creatures estimated to be 100 tons) was difficult enough to tax the inventive powers and ingenuities of O'Brien and his staff of technicians but this was simple compared to the scene showing Kong, with struggling Fay Wray in his grasp, wringing the neck of a pterodactyl!

'The mysterious powers of O'Brien, which are not even known by Merian C. Cooper and Ernest B. Schoedsack, producers and directors of *King Kong*, made all that possible.' Mark McGee of Arcadia, California, is president of the Ray Harryhausen Fan Club.

Harryhausen, as is well known, was a 'student' of O'Brien. McGee was among the first to know of the passing of O'Brien, and at a meeting of monster fans in his home young Mark said: *I am more than sorry to hear about the death of Willis O'Brien. I had great hopes of meeting the pioneer of the animation world. There will never be another like him as there will never be another* King Kong. *Long live them both.*

Hopes for another genuine high-class *King Kong* spread with wildfire enthusiasm a couple of years ago when announcements came out of Hollywood over a period of a couple months to the effect that Willis O'Brien was preparing to revive his mightiest creation and pit another imaginary monster against him. But hopes for a new monster classic died aborning; after a few months of publicity the project was heard of no more; and now with the death of O'Brien, *King Kong vs. Prometheus* has gone to the grave, to the Vault of Films Unmade.

Present at the McGee monster-fans meeting was Jim Danforth, the talented young animator whose work has been featured in *Jack the Giant Killer* and *The Wonderful World of the Brothers Grimm*, and Danforth proved so knowledgeable about O'Brien that the following list of his screen accomplishments was prepared on the spur of the moment from young Jim's memory:
1914 – *The Dinosaur and the Missing Link*.
1918 – *The Ghost of Slumber Mountain*.
1925 – *The Lost World*.
1933 – *King Kong* and *Son of Kong*.
1935 – *The Last Days of Pompeii*.
1949 – *Mighty Joe Young*.
1955 – *The Animal World*.
1957 – *The Black Scorpion*.
1958 – *The Giant Behemoth*.

In addition *The Beast of Hollow Mountain* was acknowledged to be from an idea of O'Brien's dating back to *Ring Around Saturn*, a film title which was announced for production several years earlier. *Ring Around Saturn* was to have had, as its climax, a fight in a Mexican arena between a bull and a dinosaur.

Weaver Wright, reminiscing about O'Brien in the home of the president of the Harryhausen Club, recalled that originally, while it was in production, *King Kong* had three alternative titles: *Creation*, *The Eighth Wonder of the World* and *The Eighth Wonder*. 'And *Son of Kong*, while it was being "shot",' he recalled, 'was called *Jamboree*.' This caused me to remember hearing (approximately 30 years ago) a good deal about an O'Brien picture-to-be which it seemed to me was to have been called *White Eagle* or *War Eagles*. Jim Danforth said *War Eagles*. *White* or *War* or whatnot, it was not, alas, ever made. Thru the mist of a memory (half-remembered things perhaps once told me by Ray Harryhausen) I have a mental vision of a flock of giant eagles, big as rocs, with fighting men astride their backs, attacking New York, with aerial battles between the birds from Brobdingnag and American planes high above the skyscrapers, machine-gunned birds and wing-smashed planes crashing into the man-made canyons below, destroying buildings and automobiles, panicking and killing thousands of people . . . What went wrong a quarter of a century or so ago to rob us of another O'Brien masterpiece? Unfortunately now, we shall probably never know.

Via Danforth we learned of another lost bit of O'Brieniana: Jim had never seen the name written so he couldn't say how it was spelled but he had heard of an O'Brien project called *Gwangi* or *Gwonjee* featuring a triceratops and a tyrannosaurus rex found alive in the bottom of the Grand Canyon. One drawing of Gwangi/Gwonjee is believed to exist and we at *Famous Monsters* are attempting to track it down (if we have to go to the bottom of the Grand Canyon, pen in one hand, atom bomb in the other) to show it you.

I am suddenly reminded, right while I'm writing, that about ten years ago a motion picture producer contacted me concerning a property I represented as an agent: *The Image and the Likeness* was a fantastic story about a Japanese mutant named Kiazu Takahashi who on his first birthday was nearly 30 feet long and weighed 30,100 pounds. 'By his second birthday,' wrote the author, 'he could walk, and now surpassed all land animals save the monsters of the Jurassic age, with a height of 51 feet and a weight of 158,000 pounds. In June of 1950 . . . he exceeded the capacity of our million pound scale.' At the time that the action of the story takes place (1965), the Living Buddha, age nineteen, towers 590 feet high (twelve times the height of Kong!) and weighs 198,000,000 pounds! This film project, like a score of other spectacles, never reached fruition, but the potential producer did astound me with one piece of information: 'If I can swing the picture,' he said, 'we've got *the* man for our special effects, the man who made the original *Lost World* – Willis O'Brien.'

Mighty Joe Young won O'Brien an Academy Award (1950) for his construction and animation of the supergorilla, 'a lineal descendant of King Kong, who towered so menacingly on the screen but actually stood only sixteen inches high and consisted of a metal frame padded with sponge and covered with rubber skin.' As Ezra Goodman cleverly put it, 'Through

Mighty Joe Young *was full of spectacle, but lacked the dark drama of* King Kong. *Alongside this poster is a dedication to the great Willis O'Brien by SF author Ray Bradbury.*

hocus-pocus, Joe loomed ten feet high on the screen.'

Reader Alan Gianoli has done us the favour of forwarding several pertinent quotes from the Goodman book, *The 50 Year Decline and Fall of Hollywood*. Goodman characterises the late O'Brien as 'a white-haired, bespectacled, soft-spoken gentleman, who has been in the movie monster business since 1918. His first monster movie, *The Dinosaur and the Missing Link*, was a prehistoric comedy which ran five minutes on the screen and took two months to make. The dinosaur and the cavemen in it were constructed of modelling clay over wooden joints and chunks of granite were used for a Mesozoic background. The stop-motion photography animation was jerky, but the picture was a success.'

For his more recent movies, Goodman revealed, O'Brien constructed his creatures about the size of a baby's doll, on an average half-inch to one-and-a-half-inch scale to the foot.

For *Mighty Joe Young* O'Brien was assisted by a crew of a quarter hundred (Harryhausen prominently among them), according to Goodman, and it took these technicians three years to complete the picture. 'Joe and the other monster models were moved from a quarter-inch to one inch to more than an inch at a time to achieve the illusion of animation. After each move, the film was exposed and the camera stopped. The model was then moved another portion of an inch and again photographed. When these individual action segments were run together on the screen, they gave the impression of movement.

'There have been refinements in O'Brien's technique down the years but this is substantially the same method he used in his first monster movies. It is a technique requiring time, patience and great skill. 25 feet of film per day is a good output even though that footage speeds by on the screen in about 30 seconds.

'O'Brien, not an over-talkative fellow, will tell you, when pressed, that monster pictures never go out of style. In his opinion they appeal to the adventurous streak in all of us and constitute an imaginative escape from a world of reality populated by too many human monsters. Among his recent creations has been *The Black Scorpion*, a 100-foot long animated specimen, and *The Giant Behemoth*, about a prehistoric marine monster activated by atomic propulsion that sets out to destroy London. Latterly, O'Brien even did some work on a remake of *The Lost World* – but this one had live lizards and iguanas doubling for the prehistoric monsters. O'Brien was not too happy about it.' Probably 'not too happy' is the understatement of two generations for a specialist who devoted 40 years of his life to perfecting his art of animation.

His best friends called him 'O'B' (Oh-Bee), this man from Oakland, California, who did considerable serious scientific work for the American Museum of Natural History in New York in addition to his film work. I was not privileged to know Mr. O'Brien personally but I have the vaguest recollection that as a teenager I may have been taken to visit him in his Hollywood home by a sci-fi author friend of the time, one Joseph William Skidmore who, ironically, met his end in an auto crash. So I can't check with Joe but I have the feeling he took me many many years ago to meet a friend where I saw magnificent great pieces of original artwork illustrating scenes from *King Kong* and that I was in the home of either Merian C. Cooper or Willis O'Brien.

Willis Harold O'Brien died in Hollywood of a heart ailment on 8 November, 1962. He was 76. Because his acolyte, Ray Harryhausen, 'the man who saw *King Kong* 90 times', was abroad at the time, we could not get a statement from him in time for publication but we can well imagine Harryhausen's keen sense of loss at the passing of the man who was the idol of his youth and the inspirator of his vocation.

We will not say goodbye to Willis O'Brien in our pages but only *au revoir* because we know that all the rest of our lives we will continue to enjoy revivals in theatres and on television of his *Lost World* and *King Kong*, and that babies born this year of 1963 will in 1975 – and *their* children in the years 2000 – discover anew and thrill to and love the Wonderful Prehistoric World of Willis O'Brien.

INTERVIEW WITH RAY HARRYHAUSEN – II
By Lawrence French

Animator Phil Tippett told me he would try to think like a dinosaur, in order to get a feeling for how they actually might have moved. It's what might be called 'method animation'. Did you ever do that?
Oh, sure. When I was animating *Mighty Joe Young*, I ate carrots and celery on my tea break in order to feel what it was like to be a gorilla. You had to put yourself into the animation of the creature; otherwise it's just mechanical movement. Knowledge about acting certainly helps you, because it's important that your animated creature can act and react to the live action characters involved in the scenes. So early on I took some acting classes at Los Angeles City College and I also used to go to the ballet to study the dancers' movements and see how one movement flowed gracefully into another. As for the timing of the creature's moves, that's usually something that comes from experience. In the early stages of *Mighty Joe Young* I used a stopwatch to time the scenes out and I had a canvas on the floor to act out all the motions myself. However, I soon found that to be rather cumbersome, so I abandoned it, because by that time I already had the experience of animating the puppetoons. It really became a matter of intuition, as to how many moves I'd make, or how far I should move a puppet in any given scene. Over the years I used all that experience for animating many different types of creatures.

You mention in An Animated Life *that you even named your favourite Joe Young model after producer David O. Selznick's wife.*
Yes, we had four model gorillas that Marcel Delgado had made for the animation, but he didn't make them exactly alike. Each one of them was slightly different. He used a basic process of sponge rubber and cotton to build them up, with rubber for all the muscles. He used unborn goat fur to cover them, because it didn't shift as much as the rabbit fur he used for *King Kong*. Anyway, the model I liked best looked the most like a real gorilla to me – I had studied gorillas at the zoo – so I named it Jennifer, because while we were making *Mighty Joe Young*, Selznick was shooting *Lust in the Dust* – I mean *Duel in the Sun* – at the same studio and we always had to wait to see our rushes. So while I was watching the rushes of *Duel in the Sun* from up in the projection booth, I saw Jennifer Jones crawling over the rocks (after she's been shot by Gregory Peck), and her little quivering hand was coming up from behind a rock and I thought, 'This almost looks like it has been animated.' So I named my favorite gorilla Jennifer. I don't think Jennifer Jones would appreciate that, so I hope she never finds out.

Did you meet John Ford during the production of Mighty Joe Young?
Oh yes. John Ford didn't actually have anything to do with the making of the picture, but

The Animal World *(1955) features a ten-minute dinosaur sequence devised by O'Brien and animated by Ray Harryhausen – whose posthumous dedication to his mentor is seen here.*

he was a partner of Merian C. Cooper's [in Argosy Productions], so he occasionally came over and saw the rushes. I met him while he was shooting a picture over at Columbia and he went out of his way to come over and congratulate me on my work on the lion cage sequence.

I did a cameo with Terry Moore in the remake of *Mighty Joe Young* [1998], because we were the only people from the original one still alive. We shot for eleven days, and on the last day we had to crawl on the floor trying to get away from Mighty Joe Young. I had to do six takes of that scene, crawling on my hands and knees and when you are past 75, that isn't as simple as it sounds. But the cameraman couldn't keep up with us, so they cut the scene out of the picture. There's only about 30 seconds left of the two of us talking at the reception. Of course, the re-make was a different interpretation. I think they took all the fantasy out of it and the pivotal character – which in the original was Max O'Hara. The original was about the exploitation of a gorilla, and the remake was about animal conservation, which is a serious subject, but it was a much different approach.

The Valley of Gwangi *was originally a project developed by Willis O'Brien, wasn't it?*
Yes, it was a picture he was working on around 1941 at RKO. John Speaks was writing it, and they even had the historian Harold Lamb working on the script. I remember going over and seeing all these cardboard dioramas OBie had made, and OBie explained to me that Gwangi was the Native American Indian word for 'lizard'. But, like *War Eagles*, the project collapsed.

Is there a particular reason why both you and Willis O'Brien always seemed to favour an allosaurus, rather than a tyrannosaurus rex?
That's something I got from Willis O'Brien. One time he told me that he'd rather animate an allosaurus than a tyrannosaurus, because he thought the tyrannosaurus was a sort of

clumsy creature. He felt the allosaurus was a much more agile dinosaur. Later on, I sometimes crossed the two together, as in *The Valley of Gwangi*. OBie had originally written Gwangi as an allosaurus, but because the allosaurus isn't as big as the tyrannosaurus, I made him into a combination of the two.

How did your first meeting with Willis O'Brien come about?

I first learned about Willis O'Brien from an exhibit at the Los Angeles Natural History Museum. They had several of his miniatures on display in the basement. Then while I was still in high school, one day during study period I looked over at a girl who had this big book with all these wonderful illustrations from *King Kong*, and I almost flipped. I went over to her and introduced myself and told her about my desire to do animation and she said her father had worked with Willis O'Brien on *The Last Days of Pompeii*. She told me that O'Brien was now working at MGM on *War Eagles*, and I should call him up there. So the next day I called him at MGM and he kindly invited me down to the studio. When I got there I was in complete awe at all the pre-production drawings that were covering every inch of the walls. They showed all these giant eagles, who at the climax of the picture were seen perched atop the Statue of Liberty. So after that I kept in touch with O'Brien and he became my mentor, from whom I learned many things.

Was Willis O'Brien the first person to use stop-motion animation?

It's hard to track down, exactly. There may have been people before him doing it in Europe. But OBie started it way back in 1914, or even before that in some of his early experiments. He started right here in San Francisco, on top of the Bank of America building, using two clay figures. He worked for the Edison Company and tried many different things. He ran away from home when he was very young and became a cowboy, then a cartoonist and he loved boxing and wrestling. When we were preparing *Mighty Joe Young*, we used to go to quite a few boxing matches, because there was a time when we thought we'd have two gorillas let loose in San Francisco, beating the heck out of each other on top of a cable car that had broken loose and was going down a hill. OBie made several big drawings of that sequence, because he loved San Francisco, but unfortunately it was discarded in favour of the burning of the orphanage.

In An Animated Life *you talk about the many projects Willis O'Brien had planned that unfortunately never materialised.*

Yes, a lot of pictures he planned folded under him because of budgets and things like that. *War Eagles* collapsed at MGM when Merian Cooper was called into the Army to join the Flying Tigers. Then OBie had *Gwangi* set up at RKO, until it was cancelled and replaced with *Little Orphan Annie*. He had a lot of personal tragedy in his life, as well.

After working with Willis O'Brien on Mighty Joe Young, *did you hope to continue collaborating with him on future pictures?*

Yes, because initially Merian Cooper was going to produce H. G. Wells' *The Food of the Gods*, but that was dropped, and I think Cooper also had in mind *Mighty Joe Young Meets Tarzan*, because we had made *Mighty Joe Young* at the old Selznick studio, and at the time Sol Lesser was making the Tarzan pictures there. Then OBie had a story idea he had sold to Jesse H. Lasky, *The Valley of the Mist*. But we were unfortunate, because we got caught in a change of management at RKO and all the overhead of the studio got dumped onto our picture. It made *Mighty Joe Young* appear to be far more costly than it actually was. So nobody wanted to touch animation. OBie's technique also involved using these large glass paintings about ten feet wide and he painted all the scenery on the glass so you could get this wonderful jungle, like you saw in *King Kong*. But that was a very costly process because of all the time it took to paint the scenery. You had to have a staff of two or three very good artists to make a painting of a tree actually look like a tree. It was just too costly.

In your Film Fantasy Scrapbook, *you mention that O'Brien's story idea for* Valley of the Mist *somehow won an Academy Award later on.*

Yes, there was a big problem with that, involving lawsuits and everything else. I don't know all the details, because I heard the story secondhand, but OBie had originally prepared a story about a boy, a bull and a dinosaur. The story ended up in a bullring with the boy's pet bull fighting an allosaurus. OBie had made a thick book of production illustrations that was very impressive and Jesse L. Lasky was going to produce it for Paramount. Jesse Lasky, Jr., who had written *The Ten Commandments* for Cecil B. DeMille, was writing the final screenplay based on OBie's outline, but once again it was one of those projects that never matured. Somehow it went through various hands, and I think it came back to O'Brien and he sold it to Eddie Nassour and then it went somewhere else. There were all sorts of problems with the rights to it, until eventually they took the dinosaur out of it and made it as a separate picture in 1956, called *The Brave One*.

The Valley of Gwangi *(1969) was an O'Brien project he never lived to see, realised by his disciple Harryhausen. Gwangi himself was an allosaurus rather than a t-rex.*

And the story credit for The Brave One *was given to 'Robert Rich', who was actually Dalton Trumbo hiding under a pseudonym, because at the time he was blacklisted for supposedly being a communist.*

Yes, so nobody knew who the author was. There was a lot of talk, then a lawsuit with the Nassour brothers, who made *The Beast of Hollow Mountain* [also in 1956], which was a sort of modification of OBie's story.

None of O'Brien's films dealt with mythological subjects, did they?

No, most of his animation dealt with either a gorilla or dinosaurs. He made that wonderful silent version of *The Lost World* by Arthur Conan Doyle, with Wallace Beery and Bessie Love that had many dinosaurs, I think 25 dinosaurs. He had always been associated with the prehistoric world, which is wonderful. It's earlier mythology than Greek mythology.

OBie was working on this picture, *Creation* at RKO, when Merian Cooper took over as head of the studio. RKO was failing, because they had made a lot of duds, and the studio needed boosting. So Cooper came in and brought this idea of a gorilla with him, which he wanted to shoot in the Komodo Islands. But when he saw O'Brien's work for *Creation*, he thought he could use many ideas from *Creation* for *King Kong*, which O'Brien had developed before Mr. Cooper took over at RKO. So many ideas from *Creation* were incorporated into the script of *King Kong*. OBie would go into a story conference and bring his ideas on how to stage a certain scene, then the writer would incorporate that into the script and they become his ideas. So the writer got the credit for them.

HIS MAJESTY, *KING KONG* — VII
THE SECOND BANANA KONGS
By Donald F. Glut

Just one year after the release of *King Kong* and *The Son of Kong*, parodies of the concept were in production. *Hollywood Party* (1934) featured a man in an ape costume who is introduced at a party as 'Ping Pong, the son of King Kong.'

Charles Gemora, who made a career of portraying some of the most realistic gorillas on film, gained some publicity before his death as the actor who had played the original King Kong. He did not, of course, at least in the 1933 motion picture. Yet Gemora's confusion might well have been the result of the passage of years since his participation in two spoofs of *King Kong*

The Lost Island was an ambitious project, a planned musical comedy from the Christie Studio, directed by LeRoy Prinz in 1934 and filmed in the old three-strip Technicolor process. Technically the picture was a reverse on *King Kong*: the giant gorilla was played by a human actor (Gemora) in a gorilla suit while the fanciful dinosaur that inhabits a great cavern was also a costumed performer. All the human characters, however, were now marionettes in the image of famous screen personalities. Wah Ming Chang, Blanding Sloan, Mickey O'Rourke and Charles Cristadoro designed the puppets. A Mae West marionette filled in for Fay Wray and was bound to a pedestal from which Kong abducted her. When *The Lost Island* proved overly expensive, the project was terminated before completion.

Gemora was also suited up to play a giant legendary ape in the comedy *Africa*

Screams (also known as *Abbott and Costello in Africa*) directed by Charles Barton for United Artists in 1949. While Mighty Joe Young was appearing at the Golden Safari, Frank Buck and Clyde Beatty were heading an expedition into the jungle in search of a monstrous missing link. Lou Costello inadvertently discovers the creature when he finds himself standing between its shaggy legs.

During the 1930s and 1940s, Gemora's major rival in the portrayals of gorillas was Ray 'Crash' Corrigan, a star of Western movies who moonlighted as a screen anthropoid. Corrigan's ape suit was a shaggy, monstrous creation, more a product of the imagination than were Gemora's more authentic costumes. Corrigan's association with *King Kong* is only peripheral, beginning with his performance in the PRC programmer *Nabonga*. The film starred Buster Crabbe with Julie London as a white jungle woman whose protector is a bull gorilla. The Belgians must have considered the ape suitably Kong-like for they retitled the picture *Fils de King Kong* ('Son of King Kong'). (The picture is also known as *Gorilla*, *The Girl and the Gorilla*, *Nabob*, *Jungle Witch* and *The Jungle Woman*. *Nabonga* was filmed in 1943 and released the following year.

A similar change in title was made by the Italians for the 1945 PRC movie *White Pongo*. Corrigan played a dual role in this film, his standard gorilla plus a highly intelligent white ape believed to be the missing link. Though neither anthropoid was of gigantic size the film was known as *La sfida de King Kong* ('The Challenge of King Kong') in Italy. (Other titles include *Congo Pongo*, *Blond Gorilla* and England's *Adventure Unlimited*.) Both films were produced by Sigmund Neufeld and directed by Sam Newfield.

Corrigan assumed a more authentic Kong-type role in *Unknown Island* (Film Classics, 1948), another variation on the 'lost world' theme, directed in colour by Jack Bernhard. Among the denizens of a prehistoric island is a giant ground sloth, presumably similar to the extinct megatherium. Yet ground sloths were passive creatures with thick tails. Corrigan's aggressive, tailless sloth seemed to be merely a strange looking ape. The snorting and gorilla-style lope added to the simian effect.

In a scene obviously influenced by the battle with the tyrannosaurus in *King Kong*, the shaggy sloth fights a flesh-eating dinosaur (another costumed actor) and finally shoves the reptile off a cliffside to its death. The victorious monster then lumbers off-screen to nurse its wounds. Many viewers of *Unknown Island* would have preferred instead another screening of O'Brien's ape vs. dinosaur fight.

When Merian C. Cooper became head of production for the Cinerama organisation in the early 1950s, he considered remaking *King Kong* in the three-screen process and under the title *The Eighth Wonder* – but his plan never reached fruition.

Two strange Kong creatures did reach the screen in 1959. *Gekkoh Kamen* ('The Moonbeam Man'), a Japanese picture made by Toei and directed by Satoru Ainuda, was one in the series of films featuring a superhero known as the Man in the Moonlight Mask.

Also known as *The Monster Gorilla*, this fourth entry to the adventure series featured Mammoth Kong, a giant ape armed with a horn protruding from its forehead. To combat Mammoth Kong a scientist creates an equally monstrous Robot Kong, equipped with deadly laser beam vision.

The British *Konga*, directed by John Lemont and released in colour by American International Pictures in 1961, was more traditional, though it hardly validated its advertising. ('Not since *King Kong* has the screen exploded with such mighty fury and spectacle!') *Konga* was produced by Herman Cohen, the man responsible for *I Was a Teenage Werewolf* and *I Was a Teenage Frankenstein*, so it is not surprising that his giant ape movie went into production the year before its release under the inane title *I Was a Teenage Gorilla*. (An even more misleading title for *Konga* was ascribed to the picture for release in Germany, where it became known as *Konga – Frankenstein's Gorilla*. A Chicago drive-in theatre advertised the picture as *Theory of the Evil Satan*, with 'Congorilla Konga'.) *Konga*, however, did not even begin his career as a gorilla, teenage or otherwise.

The plot of *Konga* was standard mad doctor fare. Dr. Charles Decker (Michael Gough), a botany professor, returns to London from the African jungle with slips from carnivorous plants that seem to be a link between the animal and plant kingdoms.He also brings back a friendly chimpanzee which he calls Konga. Back in his laboratory, Decker tests a growth serum extracted from the weird plants on the ape after which Konga grows and evolves into a full-sized gorilla.

While Charles Gemora and Ray Corrigan essayed most of the gorilla roles in films made during the 1930s and 1940s, George Barrows provided some stiff competition during the next two decades. Barrows' costume was less the mythical monster created by Corrigan, but still not as authentic a gorilla as that played by Gemora. Yet it was his costume and not Barrows himself that went to England where *Konga* was to be filmed. (In 1963, Barrows and Michael Gough teamed-up for *Black Zoo*, another horror film produced by Herman Cohen; Barrows played another gorilla that suspiciously resembled Konga.) Konga (another actor wearing Barrows' ape suit) carries out the orders of his insane master, namely murdering his enemies. When Foster (Austin Trevor), the dean of Decker's college, reproves him for discussing his growth theories with the press, he becomes a victim of the hypnotised Konga. After Decker learns that an Indian botanist, Professor Tagore (George Pastell), might steal his glory by working on a similar experiment, Konga claims his second victim. The third person to be crushed to death by the ape is Bob Kenton (Jess Conrad), the boyfriend of Sandra (Keire Gordon), a blonde and shapely student on whom Decker has licentious designs.

Posters boasted that the picture was filmed in 'SpectaMation', though this cinematic 'miracle' was nowhere to be seen during the final minutes of *Konga*. Decker has brought Sandra to his home for dinner and then lures her into his greenhouse where he declares his love for her. But his proclamation is overheard by Decker's assistant and fiancée Margaret (Margo Johns). Vengefully she injects Konga with an overdose of the growth serum. Suddenly Konga's head reaches the ceiling of the laboratory. Konga's disposition has also changed for he destroys the laboratory, creating a traditional horror-film inferno, then tosses Margaret into the flames.

The only impressive shot in the film depicts Konga bursting through the roof of the laboratory, his size still increasing. The rest of the picture is hardly memorable, as he spots Decker through the greenhouse windows forcing his kiss on Sandra and then snatches him up in his enormous paw. Sandra falls victim to a flesh-eating plant while Konga lumbers off through London's streets still clutching Decker. The army makes its not unexpected appearance, blasting Konga with rockets, rifles and machine guns, as the ape is trapped near Big Ben. Unlike King Kong, this gorilla does not climb the towering structure. Fatally wounded, Konga dashes his former master to the street, then shrinks to the size and form of a dead chimpanzee. The brief sequence with the Kong-sized Konga was surely not worth the wait.

At least some executives in the publishing industry considered *Konga* a commercially viable product. In 1960, Monarch Books published a novel *Konga*, written by Dean Owen. The book was based on the storyline of the film with some mild (by today's standards) sex scenes added. Monarch Books was a division of Charlton Publications.

Another branch of the company, the Charlton Comics Group, issued a *Konga* comic book based on the movie in 1960. Steve Ditko provided the artwork. Some changes were made in the film's storyline: Margaret is now Decker's wife, Konga begins his career as a small monkey instead of a chimpanzee, there is no attempted love affair between Decker and Sandra (hence, no deaths of either Sandra or Bob) and Konga injects himself with the serum that makes him as tall as King Kong.

Konga proved to be a popular one-shot comic book and Charlton soon realised the possibilities in issuing it as a series. *Konga* no. two was dated August 1961 and featured the story 'Return of Konga'. Bob and Sandra marry, carry on Decker's experiments and adopt another monkey called Konga, which soon follows in the paw prints of his predecessor. The friendly monster is then taken to an island inhabited by prehistoric animals and, after killing a tyrannosaurus, presumably dies during a volcanic eruption.

But Konga did not perish. He returned for a total of 23 issues of *Konga* comic books in which he aided people in distress and battled a long list of monsters, aliens, Communist spies and evil dictators. A lapse in the series' continuity occurred in 'The Lonely One', *Konga* no. twelve (May 1963), wherein it was explained that the current Konga was synonymous with the creature spawned by Dr. Decker. The original Konga, we are now told, never really died! The last story in the *Konga* comic book series (dated November 1965) was 'The Creature of Uang-Ni' and pitted the lovable giant ape against a Godzilla-type, fire-breathing, prehistoric reptile. What would have been the 24th issue of *Konga* became *Fantastic Giants* (September 1966), which reprinted the first movie-based story.

Charlton also issued special edition comic books featuring their monster star. *The Return of Konga* (1962) presented 'A Mate for Konga'. A Russian scientist clones a female gorilla giant called Torga from a cell scraping of Konga's hide. Torga becomes a rampaging monster, shot to death in a city by a Russian gunboat. With the second issue of this series (summer 1963), the magazine's title became *Konga's Revenge* and featured a tale in which the giant ape shrinks down to miniature size. *Konga's Revenge* survived two more issues, the last of which saw publication in December 1968.

An Indian motion picture entitled *King Kong* was made in colour for Santosh in 1962. It was directed by Babubhai Mistri and starred Kum Kum and wrestler Darasingh. Whether the picture was a fantasy or featured an ape of any sort is not known. *Tarzan and King Kong* was another Indian production, made in 1963 by Saegaam Chittra Ltd., and starring Darasingh, a wrestler, in the role of Edgar Rice Burroughs' Apeman. Because of difficulties with copyright the picture has rarely been screened.

Willis O'Brien had been intrigued with the possibilities in animating a Frankenstein movie as early as 1928; in 1961 he expanded the concept to include his beloved Kong. *King Kong vs. Frankenstein* was to have been a tongue-in-cheek conflict between the great ape and a new version of Frankenstein's creation, shot in full colour. O'Brien wrote a treatment and a sampling of the script and later changed his title to *King Kong vs. the Ginko* (the word 'Ginko' being a play on both the words 'King' and 'Kong'). O'Brien also prepared some watercolour paintings of Kong and the Ginko.

The story itself was an unusual one. Carl Denham explains that Kong never really died but was smuggled, after his plunge from the Empire State Building, back to Skull Island. Denham's idea is to retrieve the mighty gorilla and stage a boxing match between him and some other monster in San Francisco. That 'other' monster is created by Dr. Frankenstein's grandson from the organs of rhinoceroses, elephants and other ponderous African animals. In a San Francisco auditorium a girl walks a tightrope held high in the hands of the Ginko. When the rope breaks, Kong, believing the Ginko to be harming the girl, breaks free of his cage and attacks the towering Frankenstein creature. The battle of the beasts continues through the San Francisco streets until both King Kong and the Ginko fall from the Golden Gate Bridge and into the sea.

When O'Brien took his project to producer John Beck, the latter eliminated the animator altogether and assigned the property to George Worthing Yates, who wrote a new version of the story in 1961 known both as *Prometheus vs. King Kong* and *King Kong vs. Prometheus*. The old Ginko was now called Prometheus while Denham's part in the film was dropped entirely. 'Prometheus V' is the creation of Kurt Frankenstein who had dreamed of manufacturing an army of giant workers. But after the monster demonstrates his abilities in San Francisco's Candlestick Park, he reveals himself to be a crafty being who kills the man controlling him. King Kong, also in the park, and Prometheus then battle their way to O'Brien's original climax.

When Beck could not get financing for the project in the United States, he took *Prometheus vs. King Kong* to Toho International in Japan. Toho was interested in the basic theme, the staging of a battle between King Kong and some other gigantic monster. But national chauvinism dictated the removal of the Frankenstein characters in favour of Japan's own King of the Monsters. Thus the flame-breathing prehistoric reptile Godzilla was brought out of retirement for his first and only bout with America's monster King. *Kingu Kongu tai Gojira* went into production in 1962 (the same year O'Brien died), directed in colour by Inoshiro Honda and (American scenes) Thomas Montgomery. The following year it was issued in the United States by Universal under its translated title *King Kong vs. Godzilla*.

Devotees of the original *King Kong* shuddered at the thought of it. First, though a giant gorilla, Kong's 50-foot height could in no way even approximate the size of the 400-foot long Japanese sea monster. There was also the problem of Kong's survival after his drop from the Empire State Building. Most ominous of all, however, was the knowledge that Toho traditionally used actors in monster costumes rather than the more satisfactory animation process.

Kingu Kongu tai Gojira proved to be neither a direct sequel to *King Kong* (though it was to the previous Godzilla epic) nor a serious picture at all. Whether or not the King Kong who appeared in the Japanese film was the King Kong of RKO fame was never revealed. If they were one and the same, Kong had mysteriously grown, for now his head reached as high as Godzilla's. (The publicity was that King Kong was 148 feet tall and weighed a massive 55 million pounds.) Somewhere along the way he also developed the ability to thrive on electricity. One thing is certain; the shabby Kong suit worn in the new picture ranked alongside some of the worst gorilla outfits ever seen on film, even those in silent movies. The Japanese King Kong was so ridiculous in appearance that the film's advertisers wisely chose to paste-up shots of the original 1933 Kong over scenes of Tokyo for their display stills and lobby cards.

Thankfully, *Kingu Kongu tai Gojira* was played tongue-in-cheek. The owner of a pharmaceutical firm wants a live monster to publicise his products. The answer to his dream comes when reports of a giant monster god existing on remote Faro Island reach him. One stormy night the natives (all Orientals wearing blackface make-up rather unconvincingly) are menaced by a giant octopus. The scenes of the huge cephalopod are very atmospheric and realistic as the tentacled monster slithers about their village. When Kong appears, beating his breast, he battles the octopus to the death.

The victorious King Kong is given some wine made of Faro Island berries which makes him groggy enough to be floated on a raft back to Japan.

Godzilla is discovered in an iceberg (where he had been hibernating since his last Toho adventure) by the crew of a nuclear submarine. After destroying the ship, the prehistoric reptile proceeds to Japan, following a kind of homing instinct. Kong revives as

Konga (1961) is one of the best of the ultra-cheap Kong rip-offs – faint praise indeed. But at least the man in the gorilla suit makes an impression against a miniature Big Ben.

he is being floated near to the coast of Japan. Sniffing the scent of Godzilla, a natural enemy, Kong wades to shore in pursuit of the scaly creature.

Inevitably the two monsters meet, lashing into one another in slapstick style like a pair of monstrous sumo wrestlers. In an imitation of a famous public-ity still from the original King Kong's fight with the tyrannosaurus, the ape rams a tree trunk down Godzilla's throat. But Godzilla retaliates with his radioactive breath, scorching Kong and rendering him unconscious. Then Godzilla goes off on his own spree of devastation.

A bolt of lightning revives King Kong. In Tokyo the ape monster attempts to reclaim past glories by re-enacting some of his New York scenes. He destroys an elevated train. Then he snatches a lovely young woman off the street and, while a sentimental melody plays over the soundtrack, promptly falls in love. Since there is no Empire State Building in Japan, he carries her instead to the top of Tokyo Tower where more of the Faro berries render him unconscious.

When the authorities deduce that the two monsters can be used to dispose of each other, the drugged Kong is floated by balloons to the top of Mount Fuji, where he and Godzilla engage each other in their most spectacular (and ridiculous) fight. After much kicking, biting and monstrous 'laughing', King Kong and Godzilla fall into the sea. The hairy figure of a giant ape rises to the surface and swims away, probably back toward Faro Island. The rumour has persisted since the film's release that two endings were filmed, with Oriental countries seeing Godzilla rather than the 'foreign' King Kong emerge the victor. However, according to Saki Hijiri, a fantasy film buff living in Kyoto, the endings of both the Japanese and American versions of the film are the same. It is understood among Japanese movie fans, said Hijiri, that Godzilla merely went back into hibernation underwater until his next screen appearance.

Kingu Kongu tai Gojira is an unpretentious fantasy comedy. Making no claims to rival the 'real' *King Kong*, the picture stands on its own merits. Surely it is an entertaining hour and a half or more and the special effects (the ape suit notwithstanding) of Eiji Tsuburaya are impressive.

The title *Frankenstein vs. King Kong* surfaced in 1965. This time the film was to be another Toho spectacle. But the picture was not made and Kong did not appear in another Japanese epic until 1967. *Kingu Kongu no Gyakushu* ('King Kong's Counterattack') went into production at Toho that year, again directed by Honda with Tsuburaya handling the visual effects. Shot in colour, the picture was issued in America by Universal the next year. The American title became *King Kong Escapes*. (Other titles for the picture include *Kingukongu no Gyaskushu*, *Revenge of King Kong* and Germany's *King-Kong Frankensteins Sohn* [son]. Scenes from the film later appeared in the 1968 Godzilla sequel,

From the sublime to the ridiculous: The Mighty Gorga *(1970). (Courtesy of Something Weird Video and Distributors Production Organization.)*

Kaijû Sôshningeki.)

The American press-book for the film blatantly pronounced: 'The 35th birthday of the most famous monster in films is marked by the Universal release of the Toho Production in Technicolor, *King Kong Escapes*, now at the . . . . . Theatre. It was in the early thirties that *King Kong* burst upon the scene to become one of the most success-ful movies of the era. The all new *King Kong Escapes* is far superior in its technique showing the tremendous advances made in the cinematic art, and is in beautiful Technicolor.'

One thing was certain: the picture was in 'beautiful Technicolor'. But the production did not even approach *Kingu Kongu tai Gojira* in either quality or entertainment value. A new Kong suit was built for this second Toho outing into the giant ape genre. If this new Kong seemed more of a cartoon-like character, with its sleepy eyes and its absurd face, perhaps Honda and Tsuburaya were attempting to achieve that effect upon the screen – which certainly has some validity. The plot itself is like something found in a comic book, or more accurately, an animated cartoon, the true origin of this particular King Kong movie. For *Kingu Konguno Gyakushu* is actually based on the animated car-toon *King Kong* television series which had debuted on American television a couple of years earlier. The new Toho live action film was a full-blown expansion of one of the tel-evision programme's individual episodes. Both were aimed directly at the juvenile mar-ket. Unfortunately the point was missed by the American distributor who packaged *King Kong Escapes* as just another monster movie.

The evil Dr. Who (the arch-fiend from the *King Kong* cartoon show) is out to conquer the world by means of a huge robot in simian form called, after its hairy inspiration, Mechani-Kong. But Dr. Who's mechanical monster fails to mine Element X, the radioac-tive material the mad doctor needs to carry out his plan. Meanwhile, Captain Nelson (Rhodes Reason playing the same heroic figure from the television cartoons), and his United Nations nuclear submarine crew, come upon Mondo Island. There an old hermit warns them to keep away, shouting the legendary name 'Kong!' The explorers, including a pretty young technician named Susan (played by Linda Miller), are menaced by a sea ser-pent and then by a huge green dinosaur (called Gorosaurus when he returned in the multi-monster picture *KaijQ Sôshingeki* in 1968). Not surprisingly, King Kong also inhab-its this island and promptly makes his appearance. Kong fights the flesh-eating reptile and finally kills it, then, as is traditional, seizes and falls in love with Susan.

Dr. Who learns of the great discovery after Nelson's press conference. The megalo-maniac's henchmen subdue Kong with tranquilising bombs then utilise a helicopter fleet

This French poster for King Kong Escapes *dignifies the schlocky movie by allusions to the original Kong, Fay Wray, and the Empire State Building.*

to transport the animal to their Arctic secret complex. Hypnotised by Dr. Who, Kong then proceeds to dig out Element X. But as the mighty gorilla continues to claw at the radioactive material, an explosion occurs which severs Dr. Who's hypnotic bond. Kong, free of the madman's mental bondage, jumps into the icy water and swims to Japan. There, in perhaps the world's most monster-beset city, he encounters his robot counterpart. Decidedly Mechani-Kong has the advantage; he feels no pain and is equipped with beams of mesmeric light. Still, the real Kong puts up an impressive battle which eventually brings both monsters to the top of a sky-scraping television tower (another attempt to at least suggest the famous Empire State Building scene). This time, however, the real Kong survives as his mechanical double falls to crash on the street below in a pile of useless junk. In an amusing epilogue, Kong runs down the waterfront alongside the speeding car with our heroes and then destroys the evil Dr. Who in his submarine.

Kingu Kongu no Gyakushu was neither as entertaining nor as successful as *Kingu Kongu tai Gojira* and Toho abandoned the giant ape for any later productions. Besides, RKO, the owners of the simian property, demanded payments for use of the character. Toho found greater profits in continuing the screen adventures of their own Godzilla and other monstrous behemoths.

But King Kong films were still being made by other companies. *Hor Balevana* ('A Hole in the Moon'), an Israeli film of 1965, included a fantasy sequence featuring King Kong. Uri Zohar directed it for the Navon company.

Mad Monster Party (1967) climaxed with a *King Kong*-spoof sequence in which a giant brown gorilla rises from the sea to attack Baron von Frankenstein's castle. As per custom, he falls in love with the Baron's pretty daughter. During the final moments of the picture the ape has all of the monsters held in his gigantic arms and, like Kong atop the Empire State Building, is perched high on a mountain peak. The Baron and his fleet of old-fashioned airplanes attack the creature while von Frankenstein destroys everyone with his newly developed explosive. The animation of the models was crude in comparison to that in *King Kong, The Son of Kong* and *Mighty Joe Young*. Still, it was refreshing to see a new film with a stop-motion giant gorilla. (The ape returned with a giant mate in the television feature cartoon *Mad, Mad, Mad Monsters* in 1972. This go-round he fights the Frankenstein Monster for possession of the latter's newly-assembled bride.)

The Italian colour film *Necropolis* (Cosmoseion & Q Productions, 1970), written and directed by Franco Brocani, was made up of plotless episodes about life starring various movie and historical villains. The Minotaur appears as King Kong unwinds a string that marks the way through a labyrinth to the picture's opening set. *The Mighty Gorga* (American General Pictures, 1970) was a less pretentious offering directed in colour on a modest budget by David Hewitt. A group of treasure hunters discovers a prehistoric plateau, like that in *The Lost World*, somewhere in Africa. Ruler of this dinosaur land is a 50-ton gorilla called Gorga (played by an actor in a shoddy ape suit) which one member of the expedition, a circus owner, decides to capture. (In 1976, with a number of studios vying to remake *King Kong*, plans were initiated to re-shoot the special effects scenes of *The Mighty Gorga* using model animation and to reissue the film.)

Flesh Gordon (Griffiti Productions, 1972), a sex spoof in colour of the old Flash Gordon movie serials, paid tribute to *King Kong* as the huge alien 'god' Porno (an animated model) seizes heroine Dale Ardor (Suzanne Fields) and carries her to the summit of a tower. Mike Light directed. John Landis wrote, directed and starred in the colour *Schlock* in 1972, released the next year by Jack H. Harris Enterprises. *Schlock* spoofed virtually all ape movies and referred to Kong (and Godzilla) as if he were an historical figure. A prehistoric Schlockthropus, part man and part ape, is thawed out, goes on a murderous rampage and falls in love with a teenage girl named Mindy (Eliza Garrett). In one scene 'Schlock' admires a poster from *King Kong vs. Godzilla* on a movie theatre wall. Finally he climbs a building before receiving the fatal gunfire of the National Guard. Rick Baker, who four years later would literally become King Kong, created the apeman costume. *Closed Mondays* (1974), a colour short subject by Will Vinton and Bob Gardiner, also paid tribute to *King Kong*. Among its cast of animated clay characters was a miniature gorilla sculpted in the image of Kong. In Germany *Gojira tai Megaro* was called *King-Kong, dä Monen aus dem weltall* while *Gojira tai Mechagojira* became *King Kong Gegen Godzilla*.

'KING KONG APPEARS IN EDO' (A LITERAL TRANSLATION): THE TOHO KONG YEARS
By Ken Hollings

The title couldn't have been simpler, the prospect more straightforward. *King Kong vs. Godzilla* pretty much said it all, leaving no room for either shading or ambiguity. 'Onward and upward with the arts,' *Variety* dryly remarked on the film's US theatrical release in 1963.

You cannot, however, manufacture conflict without also manufacturing a history to go with it. The outcome might otherwise be meaningless. It was, after all, King Kong and not Godzilla who became the first giant monster to gaze down upon the fleeing, terror-stricken people of Japan. That was back in 1938, barely five years after his original appearance in the classic RKO feature. *Edo Ni Arawareta Kingu Kongu*, which translates into literal English as 'King Kong Appears in Edo', is a lost film, existing as little more than a title and a cast list these days. What evidence survives suggests that Japan's earliest known giant monster movie took the form of historical drama set during the Edo Period.

For his second cinematic appearance, the mighty Kong was represented by an actor wearing an ape costume moving against a miniature landscape of buildings, forests and fields: a preliminary attempt at creating the illusion of scale most closely associated with *kaiju eiga*, or Japanese giant monster movies. Special effects pioneer Fuminori Ohashi, responsible for creating the Japanese version of King Kong, would later assist in the fabrication of the giant monster suit seen in Toho's 1954 movie *Gojira*, released in the West as *Godzilla: King of the Monsters!*

King Kong has always cast a second shadow over Godzilla and his origins. The theatrical reissue of the original *King Kong* in 1952 triggered a wave of giant monster movies in the US, having a direct influence upon the commercial thinking behind Godzilla's existence. No surprise therefore to discover that Gojira, the name by which the creature is known in his country of origin, is derived from the Western word 'gorilla' coupled with '*kujira*', the Japanese word for 'whale'.

Exit the Ginko: Enter Godzilla

A relatively stable time in Japan's history, characterised by military rule, clear division of the social hierarchy and self-imposed isolation from all foreign influences, the Edo Period embodied all those things to which monsters in general, and King Kong in particular, would find themselves intrinsically opposed. With Godzilla and King Kong directly confronting each other, however, things would not be so sharply defined. The two giant monsters had far too much in common for that.

In 1960, probably as a consequence of *King Kong*'s successful theatrical reissue, Willis O'Brien had developed the outline for a sequel, originally to be called *King Kong vs. Frankenstein*. It would open with showman Carl Denham revealing that Kong did not die in New York but had been secretly returned to Skull Island. Denham was now planning to stage a public contest in San Francisco between the great ape and a monster sewn together by Dr Frankenstein's grandson using skin and organs taken from rhinos, elephants and other African animals. The inevitable mishaps would then occur, leading to the film's climax in which the two creatures would fall to their deaths from the top of the Golden Gate Bridge.

O'Brien would later change the projected film's title to *King Kong vs. the Ginko*: 'Ginko' containing a scrambled allusion to King Kong in the same way that Gojira's name did.

O'Brien ended up pitching the idea to independent producer John Beck, who had formerly been at Universal International: Beck's production credits at that time included monster movies *The Creature from the Black Lagoon* and *The Deadly Mantis*, and *Harvey*, which made a movie star out of a giant invisible rabbit. Beck took the project over from O'Brien, effectively removing him from any future involvement, and hired George Worthing Yates to flesh out his original treatment.

Yates, who had screenwriter credits for *Them!*, *Earth vs. the Flying Saucers* and *It Came from Beneath the Sea*, turned in a script called *King Kong vs. Prometheus*, eliminating Carl Denham but retaining the Frankenstein monster: hence the thinly veiled reference to Mary Shelley's novel (*Frankenstein: or, The Modern Prometheus*) in its title.

Unable to find backing in Hollywood, Beck took the project to Toho in Japan. Toho liked the idea of King Kong's return but passed on nearly everything else. Out went the Ginko, and in came Godzilla. What the arrangement came down to was that Toho would be leasing the rights to King Kong from RKO for a guaranteed $200,000, with Beck and the studio picking up the US distribution.

Such a large outlay meant that location shooting for *Kingu Kongu tai Gojira*, as it was to be known in Japan, was already severely curtailed before a single frame had been shot. 'King Kong was a really expensive actor!' one cast member would later remark, 'King Kong took all the money!'

All the same, the deal could not have come at a better time for Toho. The studio was preparing to celebrate its 30th anniversary with a number of prestige productions, such as Akira Kurosawa's *Sanjuro* and Hiroshi Inagaki's *Chushingura*. The film with the broadest appeal, however, would be *Kingu Kongu tai Gojira*, selling over eleven million tickets on its release in August 1962.

Even after King Kong had taken his cut, there had still been enough left of the budg-

Battle of the titans: Toho's King Kong vs. Godzilla *(1962) was an international hit with the young, despite the disapproval of Merian C. Cooper and Willis O'Brien's widow.*

et to wow audiences. For what was only Godzilla's third movie in almost eight years, Toho had assembled a top ensemble cast, as well as reuniting the original team behind the creation of Godzilla – most notably director Ishiro Honda, composer Akira Ifukube and special effects maestro Eiji Tsuburaya, with stuntman Haruo Nakajima putting on the rubber suit once again as Godzilla. This was also the first Godzilla film to be shot in wide-screen Tohoscope and Eastmancolor, and the first to be released with a stereophonic soundtrack.

And yet when *King Kong vs. Godzilla* opened in the United States the following year, Willis O'Brien's widow refused to attend the premiere. Acting for his uncle, who had died on November 8, 1962, a nephew feild a lawsuit over the use of O'Brien's ideas in the film, while fans of the mighty Kong were outraged at what they saw up on the screen. Although the lawsuit was later dropped due to the large legal fees involved, *King Kong vs. Godzilla* lost just about every other argument made against it. Derided as one of the worst movies ever made, rarely screened, it was to become another film doomed to exist more fully as an evocative title than a legitimate cinematic experience.

'A Brain About This Size'

One fact lost on Western audiences at the time was that *Kingu Kongu tai Gojira* was the first Godzilla film to acknowledge that its audience was starting to change, and to be deliberately played for laughs as a result. 'There was a huge fall in the average age of Godzilla fans,' director Honda would later recall, 'so Toho decided it would be a good idea to make him more heroic and less scary. I didn't like the idea, but I couldn't really oppose it.'

Given Honda's frustrations, it's somewhat ironic that most of Toho's steady income during this period was derived from '*salaryman* comedies': light-hearted movie satires that poked fun at the plight of the increasing number of office workers busily contributing to Japan's post-war economic recovery. Not so ironic, perhaps, was the decision to extend the formula, effectively transforming King Kong's confrontation with Godzilla into one gigantic knockabout salaryman comedy.

When a rival show sends out a camera crew to investigate a glowing iceberg from which Godzilla is subsequently seen to emerge, top executive Tako of the Pacific Pharmaceutical Company, sponsors of the *Mysteries of the World* TV series, finances an expedition to Farou Island in the Pacific to bring King Kong back to Japan.

'It will be in all the newspapers,' Tako enthuses. 'King Kong pitching Pacific Pharmaceuticals with a big smile on his face.'

'King Kong's going to smile?' an underling objects.

'If we ask him nicely,' comes Tako's blithe response.

Played by top Japanese comedian Ichiro Arishima, making a rare appearance in a monster movie, Tako's grotesque optimism is in grave danger of taking over the entire film. When Kong shows signs of breaking free from the giant raft being used to tow him back

Kong battles with t-rex Gorosaurus, in King Kong Escapes *(1967). Note the cheesy bug-eyed ape suit, a deterioration since Kong's previous Toho outing.*

to Japan, Tako refuses to let one of his staff blow it up. 'You can't!' he objects furiously. 'King Kong is under my sponsorship.'

By then Godzilla is already heading back to Japan and his first encounter with Kong. The film's satirical approach to the mass culture of commercial TV extended into the staging of the fights themselves, with the two monsters grandstanding and hurling themselves around like a couple of professional wrestlers. 'I used the elements of pro wrestling, as well as the movements of Godzilla,' Nakajima said of his bouts with Shoichi 'Solomon' Hirose as his adversary in the King Kong suit. 'I modified the way he moved.'

The balance between broad comedy and dark fantasies of destruction is a delicate one, but it exists nonetheless. The one thing King Kong, Godzilla and the salaryman have in common is that, from the fluctuating bar charts of the American Depression during the early 1930s to the tower blocks of post-war Tokyo, they presided over periods of perceptible economic reconstruction. To lose this aspect to the Kong-Gojira encounter is to lose a whole dimension to the film.

The American version didn't even bother to acknowledge it. Whole new sequences were shot on a Hollywood soundstage and inserted into a reworking of the original narrative, so heavily cut that the US print still ended up running eight minutes shorter than the Japanese one. Needless to say, none of the dialogue quoted above appears in *King Kong vs. Godzilla*. Instead a United Nations news reporter and a scientific expert offer infantile commentary on the proceedings from the relative safety of the 'UN newsroom', a bare box of a set containing little more than a desk, a phone and a map of the world. 'Godzilla has a brain about this size,' the scientist helpfully explains, holding up a child's marble. 'He is sheer brute force.' Science was, of course, a great deal simpler back then.

The Battle of the Centuries
But so too was the art of illusion. A lot depended on what you were looking at. In the opening sequence of *Kingo Kongu tai Gojira*, an obvious model of the Earth rotates in space while a voiceover ominously speaks of the mysteries of the universe. It's quickly revealed, however, that we are actually watching part of the network TV show sponsored by the Pacific Pharmaceutical Company, and that the spinning globe is just what it appears to be: a cheap studio prop. In *King Kong vs. Godzilla*, no such contextual explanation is given: a quotation from Shakespeare's *Hamlet* accompanies the same view of the Earth but without the subsequent telling cutaway, giving the impression that this unrealistic representation is our actual planet seen from outer space. This shift in per-

spective hints at the true nature of the conflict played out in *King Kong vs. Godzilla*: one between two different animation techniques.

A number of false assumptions about the special effects in Japanese monster movies have persisted over the years. There's a longstanding myth, for example, that special effects maestro Tsuburaya resorted to a man in a rubber suit to play Godzilla solely because he couldn't figure out the stop-motion technique used by Willis O'Brien in the making of *King Kong*. Not true: rejecting stop motion as too expensive and time-consuming, Tsuburaya developed instead a complex amalgam of techniques to create his special effects that ranged from highly detailed miniatures and matte shots to wirework and puppetry. Stop motion does actually feature in *Gojira* but only to convey violently rapid motion, such as the flicking of the monster's tail. It even appears briefly in *King Kong vs. Godzilla*, when Kong gets kicked in the stomach during the monsters' second bout on Mount Fuji.

All the same, there's no denying that King Kong is most evidently a man in a gorilla suit, and not a particularly convincing one at that. If anything, Kong's sagging physique resembles that of an aging, out-of-shape athlete, already long past his prime, which by 1962 would undoubtedly have been the case. Kong had changed in more remarkable ways too: he could get drunk on wine made from berries found growing on Farou Island, while bolts of lightning helped revive and increase his strength. More significantly, the mighty Kong's height had increased eightfold to a strapping 400 feet, the better to face his new, far taller opponent.

Whichever way the fans chose to look at it, Kong was in Godzilla's world now. And yet he was still the same ape in essence. In *Kingu Kongu tai Gojira*, Kong has become a series of conventions that exist independently of scale. Those familiar with the original *King Kong* will quickly recognise what has been retained in translation. King is still worshipped as a god by the natives of Farou Island. He attacks Godzilla by shoving a tree down his throat, just as he had done to a similar opponent almost 30 years previously. He also derails an elevated train, peers in at a beautiful young girl through a window and then falls in love with her, scooping her up in his huge paw.

'I didn't know what was going on,' actress Mie Hama said of her experience playing the girl in question. 'I was put in the palm of King Kong's hand in front of a blue screen running away. I had no idea what it was all going to look like.'

To know what is going on, or at least to have the impression of doing so, you have to be outside the illusion: a spectator, in other words. Viewed from this dimension, Kong's climbing of the Diet Building in Tokyo, a replica of Mie Hama in his hand, evidently re-enacts his ascent of New York's Empire State Building.

For the makers and consumers of *kaiju eiga*, reality becomes a series of commonly accepted gestures – that is to say, a ritual. The star of a film that was ostensibly about the making of a film, a subject of spectacle that dramatically runs riot in the streets of New York, King Kong had been ready to enter Godzilla's world as far back as 1933.

King Kong's Counterattack

A rumour persists, quite possibly started in the pages of *Famous Monsters of Filmland* magazine, that two different endings were shot for *King Kong vs. Godzilla*: one intended for the Japanese market in which Godzilla wins, and one for the US in which King Kong is victorious. The outcome of their fight, with both monsters plunging into the sea but with only Kong surfacing to commence his long swim back to Farou Island, is actually about the only thing the two versions have in common.

Almost all of Akira Ifukube's rousing score was dumped from the American sound-

track, replaced largely with stock music lifted from *The Creature from the Black Lagoon* and even *Frankenstein Meets the Wolfman*. Scenes of a satellite orbiting in space, mass panics, an earthquake and a flood, originally part of *The Mysterians*, a 1957 Toho production released in the US by RKO, were also added. The American prints were also poor, making the mattes more glaringly visible; and both the dubbing and continuity were quite atrocious. Character names change during the course of the movie, a microphone attached to a tape recorder is referred to as a 'light meter', and individual lines are given wildly inappropriate delivery. As this was the usual fate met by Japanese monster movies released in the US during this period, however, it seems unfair to complain when Kong receives similar treatment.

The processes that had brought the two giant monsters together in the first place told a tale remarkably similar to the one unfolding up on the screen. Their conflict was ultimately played out in the promotion of the film. 'I may be a stranger to the younger people,' King Kong announced in Toho's bilingual press release, 'but have quite a number of fighting adventures to my credit.' Godzilla made equally bellicose statements in return. *Variety* compared the bout with the Liston-Patterson fight and the Nixon-Kennedy TV debates of 1960, adding that it 'could only be described by Don Dunphy'.

'It's cataclysmic!!! It's catastrophic!!!' the US theatrical trailer declared in tones that wouldn't be out of place in Madison Square Garden. 'So gigantic in scope, it dwarfs every wonder the screen has ever shown before. Don't miss the battle of the centuries! *King Kong vs. Godzilla*!'

Was its outcome really that decisive, however?

Eiji Tsuburaya won a Japanese Film Technique Award for his special effects in *Kingo Kongu tai Gojira*, which proved to be the most successful Godzilla movie ever made. The film also broadened Godzilla's appeal considerably, transforming him from a mindless terror to the star of over 30 more releases, most of them featuring his name in the title. Now that the formula had been so successfully established, Godzilla would quickly return opposite Mothra in Toho's *Mosura tai Gojira*, released in the West as *Godzilla vs. the Thing*.

King Kong was not quite as fortunate. He wouldn't appear in another Japanese monster movie until four years later in *King Kong Escapes*, an unashamed kiddies' fantasy put out by Toho in 1967. An examination of the film's original Japanese title suggests that Kong did not emerge entirely unscathed from his bout with Godzilla. *Kingu Kongu no Gyakushu*, which translates literally as 'King Kong's Counterattack', is a direct copy of the title to the first ever Godzilla sequel, *Gojira no Gykusu*, released in the US as

KING KONG COMETH!

Gigantis, the Fire Monster but subsequently known as *Godzilla Raids Again.* King Kong's counterattack had turned out to be Godzilla's victory.

Exit King Kong: Enter King Ghidorah

'The Japanese, who show the greatest delicacy in arranging flowers and manufacturing transistor radios, are all thumbs when it comes to making monster movies like *King Kong Escapes*,' sniffed Vincent Canby in the *New York Times*. Thanks to a series of Hollywood co-productions, starting with *Kong vs. Godzilla*, it might also be argued that they were getting some extra help from the West.

King Kong was effectively the first American movie star to exploit his status in Japan. The collapse of the studio system back home, compared with a Japanese film industry that remained highly productive well into the 1960s, meant that a lot of Western faces were now showing up in Toho productions. Whereas fading talents and thrusting mediocrities had formerly been edited into American versions of such Japanese monster films as *Godzilla, King of the Monsters!* and *Gamera the Invincible*, companies like Toho could now afford to include their own shop-worn American stars. Where the mighty Kong led, others soon followed: most notably Nick Adams, Russ Tamblyn, Joseph Cotten, Cesar Romero and, in the case of *King Kong Escapes*, television actor Rhodes Reason.

'Everybody's bigger than life, you know,' Reason subsequently revealed about his time on the film, 'and it gets to the point where it's ridiculous. I had to work to underplay to bring the film some credibility.' As the movie was derived from the *King Kong* children's animated cartoon series that ran for over 78 episodes in the US, he could have saved himself a lot of trouble. In collaboration with the show's producers, Rankin-Bass, Toho pitted the great ape against Mechani-Kong, a robot replica of himself. Mie Hama was back from *King Kong vs. Godzilla*, playing the villainous Madame X this time, and Haruo Nakajima had taken over inside the King Kong suit.

Elsewhere the established conventions prevailed: on Mondo Island Kong battles with a giant tyrannosaurus rex, referred to as Gorosaurus the following year in Toho's *Destroy All Monsters*, and falls in love with a pretty young nurse played by Linda Miller, while Mechani-Kong takes a fateful tumble from the top of Tokyo Tower.

The movie ends with Kong swimming back to Mondo Island. 'I think he's had enough of civilisation,' Rhodes Reason's character remarks as he watches him go. It was to be King Kong's last appearance in a Toho production.

He would, however, continue to exert a perceptible influence over the career of archrival Godzilla. While Ishiro Honda and Akira Ifukube were busy working on *King Kong Escapes*, director Jun Fukuda and composer Masaru Sato took over their respective roles on *Ebirah, Horror of the Deep*, the first Godzilla movie to be set on a South Pacific island, and intended originally as a King Kong vehicle according to some Japanese sources. Next came *Son of Godzilla*, a film that echoed RKO's 'serio-comic phantasy' *Son of Kong* in more than just its title.

By then, Godzilla was being portrayed as a heroic figure, and his presentation pitched at an increasingly younger audience. What helped to make this possible was the introduction during the 1960s of King Ghidorah, a three-headed intergalactic terror who allowed Godzilla to develop more recognisably human characteristics by displaying none of its own. Such a thing would have been unthinkable in a bout featuring Godzilla and King Kong; an audience's sympathies, once established, are extremely hard to shift. But Kong's second shadow had now become a Japanese icon.

Catch a lizard by its tail: King Kong vs. Godzilla *was the last movie wherein the radioactive dragon was the villain, coming off worse against the more sympathetic Kong.*

AN OPEN LETTER TO UNIVERSAL AND DINO DE LAURENTIIS

By Paul Mandell

Author's note: This piece was originally written in 1973 as a tribute to King Kong. *It was reworked into 'An Open Letter' in* Cinefantastique *when the two remakes were announced. The story is reprinted here as it first appeared, with some redundancies deleted for clarity.*

43 years after its premiere engagement at New York's Radio City Music Hall, *King Kong* remains as timeless as classical music and as enthralling as it was during its initial release. The reasons for this phenomenon are varied: some of them are not as obvious as others. The film is a technical *tour de force*: one of the most unusual escapist fantasies ever filmed; a surreal adventure driven by a relentless momentum; and in terms of a subgenre, the most ambitious stop-motion animation film ever made.

Today's demanding audiences won't think twice about paying a hefty price of admission to see *King Kong* again and seem to enjoy it as much as the audiences of yesteryear – people who paid their 50 cents by the thousands in the midst of economic chaos. And yet *King Kong* isn't viewed as a museum piece but rather as an eternal experience. The obvious drawbacks of the film are dated acting techniques which evoke titters in some of the segments while the real protagonist – Kong himself – awaits his entrance or is busy doing other things. Nevertheless, viewers seem to relish these overplayed bits. It was woven into the fabric of the film and welcomed with that air of familiarity. In fact, the snickers that often arise during key pieces of dialogue in Merian Cooper's process of creating 40-odd minutes of buildup may well have occurred during its presentation in 1933. But who cares? All the charm and anticipation is still there. Ruth Rose (Mrs. Schoedsack) apparently knew what she was doing behind the typewriter. It worked. And Kong himself became somewhat of a grotesque culture hero to a new generation of moviegoers and television addicts. It is remarkable how the masses can always manage to extract profundity out of the absurd. Yet *King Kong*, preposterous as it may be, has the unique capacity to justify its own absurdity. It really deals with epic themes: consequently, it deals with the hardware of important literature and of important films. Other effects films have survived because they seem to have been well-mounted. Still, even with today's technology in Hollywood, no other film has ever approached *King Kong* in terms of action and pure showmanship.

Recently, the inevitable was announced. Dino De Laurentiis would remake *King Kong*. So too, apparently, may Universal Pictures, who hope to follow the De Laurentiis version with their film after an eighteen-month grace period. With the De Laurentiis ver-

The promise of this poster for the De Laurentiis remake of King Kong *(1976) was not fulfilled by the film. But its use of the Twin Towers is grimly portentous, with hindsight.* **127**

sion due on movie screens in less than six months, for Christmas '76, anyone with an ounce of respect for the original film feels their anxiety mounting. Every few years someone has thought of remaking *King Kong* because of its classic status and built-in publicity. Basically, *King Kong* was a lavish exploitation film which happened to work out splendidly. It seems to occur to certain people as a remake for all the wrong reasons. Looking back at what the Japanese had done to Willis O'Brien's indelible creation is disheartening enough: Toho Films produced *King Kong vs. Godzilla* (1962) and *King Kong Escapes* (1967) using a man in an ape costume. That degenerative development certainly warrants no further exploration but illustrates just what happens when a classic film creation is purchased from the original source and blasphemed by the purveyors of schlock. This also brings up the very important question of technique. It's disturbing to consider that an enterprising producer like De Laurentiis could even begin to undertake a project as vast as a new *King Kong* without fully realising the delicate artistry that made *King Kong* such a success. But could anyone with such an understanding even contemplate a remake using costumed actors and mechanical models as De Laurentiis plans?

Every professional animator, weaned on the techniques pioneered by O'Brien, has at some time dreamed of re-doing *King Kong* in its classic style. Some have clearly demonstrated the possibilities of bringing such a dream to fruition. But could a new production stand up today and be accepted by contemporary audiences? Would it undermine the integrity of the original? Is it not grave-robbing of the highest order?

The idea of a remake has been toyed with seriously on at least one other occasion. It had been reported that both Cooper and O'Brien were seriously investigating the possibilities of a new production in Cinerama in the early fifties when setbacks occurred, forcing the project to be abandoned. (Actually, what Cooper planned to do, instead of an outright remake, was to film an additional sequence, floating Kong on a raft to New York using doubles in long shots, as odd as that sounds!) Then in 1965, Hammer Films approached Ray Harryhausen to animate a remake in colour. Due to legal problems, Harryhausen did a remake of *One Million B.C.* instead. But perhaps it was for the best. There are many sound reasons why a remake of *King Kong* would not be a very feasible venture to undertake. The 'thirties charm' and the innate absurdity of it all that was so lavishly mounted would be enormously difficult, if not downright impossible, to transpose to today's standards. De Laurentiis plans to update his version to modern times; Universal plans the impossible, keeping to the period setting and details. One vital point is the niche in time in which *King Kong* was produced, something that proved to be an element of its immediate success. Americans who were seized by the Depression years embraced this preposterous piece of escapism. As author Carlos Clarens put it: 'Through an extravagant and quite mad process of identification, the audiences of 1933 were plainly gratified by scenes of urban destruction . . .'

No better said, really. The audacious, whopping mayhem of some mythical super-simian of gigantic proportions, brought back to urbana, shackled by his captors and frustrated by an outrageous eroticism that he can't quite understand, brought some bastard form of gratification to audiences, particularly to New Yorkers who almost seemed to welcome the mass destruction of the metropolis that did nothing for them other than radiate the *ennui* of economic despair. So the point made is that the authenticity of that niche in time and the uncanny foresight of Cooper and Schoedsack in putting it together during such a critical period could never really be duplicated, and the updating approach being taken by De Laurentiis seems bent on corrupting the values that made the original so successful. *King Kong*, like a fine old wine, has mellowed with age; it is doubtful if today's audiences would want to accept a new production merely for the sake of wide-screen colour and new dialogue, although I fear they could be *promoted* into accepting it through the flamboyant, almost immoral tactics of an enterprising movie mogul.

But if a remake is to be done at all, the delicate stop-motion artistry that endowed old Kong with remarkably human characteristics would certainly seem to be the only logical technique available. Animator David Allen displayed the possibilities when he refilmed the Empire State Building finale for a TV commercial. It would be virtually impossible to find a satisfactory substitute for stop-motion animation. Moreover, anyone remotely familiar with the overall design and 'feel' of *King Kong* must realise that any sincere attempt at recreating the grand atmosphere of the original would require an enormous amount of matte paintings as opposed to projected backgrounds (the tedious process of producing these paintings on glass for each miniature setup largely accounted for the amazingly organic jungle of O'Brien's masterpiece). It is a technique that Ray Harryhausen abandoned in the fifties due to low budgets and time constraints imposed on him. Harryhausen realised his limitations and proceeded accordingly, using live back-grounds in place of the netherworld that could only be rendered by the skilful artist's brush. Hence, Dynamation. But so much was lost in the process. Harryhausen himself would be the first to agree with this. Viewers of *King Kong* are always surprised to learn that much of what they have marvelled at in the film is nothing but paint. And yet matte painting today is virtually a lost art, castrated by a film world geared to economy, and per-petuated by only a handful of Hollywood artisans who fully realise its applications to clas-sical or fantastic themes. Albert Whitlock, today's most acclaimed matte artist and soon to retire from the business, expressed his regrets to me on several occasions concerning the prejudice and ignorance of filmmakers and producers towards matte painting. It is clearly a case where fantasy suffers from a hard reality, and art and commerce generally don't mix.

What about Kong himself? There is always the school of aesthetic judgement that sees dimensional animation as jerky as it is costly. To get away from this technique, the producers of *The Land that Time Forgot* (1975) used mechanised costumes operated by men in trenches. The laughable results of this and other technical travesties should dis-courage any sensible producer from trying to cut corners on expense again. The limited mobility of the costumes make them totally infeasible on the mammoth scale required by a film such as *King Kong*.

Any producer seeing dollar signs in a remake of *King Kong* should fixate himself on a viewing screen, seriously examine the technical genius of Willis Harold O'Brien, and realise how disastrous it would be to attempt to recreate the work that went into it. Creating the effects on an almost *carte blanche* basis, free of union interference, the variety of shots and angles, all necessitating different setups, probably could never hap-pen again. With a relentless drive for realism and perfection, O'Brien would marry com-posite shots of matte paintings and live action by superimposing silhouetted birds over the scene. Such a scene would in turn be used as a process background for foreground actors. Who could forget the breathtaking initial vista of Skull Island as the SS *Venture* approached the beach? Likewise, O'Brien's own avian creations were animated in long shots which may have been totally unnecessary but added that special primeval touch. His technique of painting foreground, middleground, and background on large panes of glass in conjunction with miniature projection and model work resulted in dawn-of-the-world landscapes, unsurpassed even until this day. If Harryhausen's technique of elimi-nating the miniature setups and matte paintings by inserting animated creatures into projected backgrounds were to recreate some of the key sequences of the original, the so-called 'magnificent grandeur' that watermarked Willis O'Brien's work would be severely compromised. Animator Jim Danforth, contracted as part of Universal's remake team, has made serious attempts on various occasions to reinstate some of OBie's techniques in feature films, but oddly enough, none of O'Brien's scholars have been able to approach the wonderful mystique that dominated his *King Kong* compositions.

A closer examination of some of these compositions reveals astonishing bits of technical ingenuity that are so minute, one wonders why O'Brien went through the pains of putting them there in the first place. Consider the scene atop the cliff where Kong proceeds to examine his fair-haired treasure. An astute eye can pick up the sun's rays slowly dissipating behind a cloud, inexplicable when you consider that the background is a static painting! Illuminating the miniatures with rim light and diffusion gave an atmospheric haze to jungle scenes and the animals themselves. And it all worked perfectly in black and white. The fight between Kong and the allosaurus is *still* the most spectacular interaction of animated miniatures, heightened by Murray Spivack's dynamic sound effects. I, for one, cannot imagine this sequence being redone more dramatically than the way it was achieved in 1933. It is relentless, awe-inspiring imagination at its best. When Kong knocks the tree Fay Wray is perched on to the ground, that vertigo is felt by every spectator in the theatre, even if it is an obvious process shot. Of course, the essence of O'Brien's work was characterisation. The great ape displayed rage, curiosity, sorrow, and valour. Even the often-criticised fur dance (the bristling effect of Kong's fur caused by manipulation of the model between exposures) added that special *elán* to Kong's character. Kong was a living entity, as far as audiences were concerned, even in spots where the animation was less than perfect. He kicked, breathed, and fought to the finish. Willis O'Brien was able to make an inanimate sculpture emote on the screen. Somewhat even more remarkable is that the audience believed it and reciprocated.

King Kong has become a group experience; every line is anticipated by the viewer. Audiences are always amused by Sam Hardy's quip, 'Everybody knows you're *square*, Denham'; by Robert Armstrong's hammy role, a personification of Cooper himself; by the chauvinist attitude of Bruce Cabot ('Women . . . made that way, I guess . . .'); by the ethnic stereotypes ranging from the old Jewish fruit peddler to Victor Wong's Chinaman; by Armstrong's almost psychotic response to Fay Wray's query regarding the voyage ('It's money and adventure and fame, the thrill of a lifetime!'); and by Fay's fainting spell as Denham hails a cab and makes the fastest pickup in town! But as the natives of Skull Island summon up our super-simian hero and we catch our initial glimpse of Kong, our disbelief is suspended as we wonder at the size, shape, and mobility of the thing. From that point on, we are caught up in a relentless series of nightmarish episodes. As biplanes spit their lead into Kong's chest and he looks down, tired and weary, puzzled at the sight and feel of his own blood (perhaps for the first time), we all shed a tear for the old guy. Or at least for some, it wells up.

As the reader may have guessed, *King Kong* and I are old friends. Having been born and raised in New York City, I harbour a very special prejudice for a certain colossal ape. He was introduced to me via television at the tender age of ten, scared the hell out of me, and remained with me ever since. In that regard, I'm sure that I am not alone. When RKO released *King Kong* in the fifties to *Million Dollar Movie*, thousands of young New Yorkers were fed a constant diet of the film for weeks on end. I don't know of one child at the time who didn't feel apprehensive or even petrified to take an elevated train for fear of confronting a huge ape ripping up the track ahead. Even a stroll down 34th Street evoked a certain queasiness. Kong was that real to us; we were that impressionable. It was a time when the full impact of *King Kong* had been felt by kids like myself who were

'He was a king and a god in the world he knew.' This scene from the 1976 remake makes literal Denham's words from the original film, to an absurd degree

too caught up in the narrative to question its credibility, with *no* knowledge of model animation or photographic effects, precisely the reaction that Cooper and Schoedsack and O'Brien had hoped for back in 1933. Somewhere in my youth, I came to realise that Kong was indeed a trick, engineered by a group of artists and craftsmen. Fear transformed into utter fascination. That sense of wonder has never left me.

What was responsible for that special sense of wonder? Within that dreamlike primeval world, the answer must certainly be traced back to Kong himself. Gigantic on screen, King Kong was a stop-motion anthropoid with a unique kind of movement. We were aware that we were not being cheated by the obvious antics of some Hollywood acrobat in an ape suit, nor were we bored by the stiff movements of an oversized mechanical toy interacting incongruously with humans in the same scene. We were looking at something extraordinary, a different-drummered type of life force. It is not the intention of this commentary to merely make a pitch for stop-motion techniques to the moguls it is addressed to; rather, it is to make them realise how well stop-motion models worked in the original film, and how it still manages to produce a strange psychological effect on the viewer. The phenomenon of *King Kong* should be examined on this psychological level in order to fully understand its effectiveness. Yet the narrow-minded, money-hungry film producers who refuse to do so, who could care less about the chemistry that made the original *King Kong* work, who are out merely to exploit it for a fast buck, are doing the film world and the public a grave injustice.

Of the two proposed remakes, the Universal period-piece approach seemed the lesser of two evils. Negotiations had been made to use Max Steiner's musical score from the original. Jim Danforth had completed a series of detailed drawings depicting key scenes that would have been lensed in something close to the Willis O'Brien tradition. Due to some legality over the storyline, new prehistoric creatures were to replace the originals: an arsinoitherium for the tyrannosaur, a huge centipede in place of the lizard, another form of prehistoric bird as a substitute for the pterodactyl, and so on. Emphasis was to have been placed on the extinct civilisation responsible for the Great Wall. One key scene on the drawing board was that of the heroine (tentatively Susan Blakely) positioned high atop a column among ancient ruins as Kong does battle with a prehistoric adversary. Though stop motion techniques would have been employed, it almost seemed as a way for the producers to add a footnote of respect, just a little way to buy some integrity. But at least Universal is striving for some fidelity, although some of their decisions seem strange indeed. Casting developments had led the studio to seek Peter Falk, *sans Columbo* raincoat, to play Carl Denham. (Imagine his meeting Ann Darrow at the fruitstand as she is accused of stealing an apple: 'Excuse me, ma'am, could I have a minute of your time? Have you got a pencil?')

The final outcome of what has been termed in the trades 'gorilla warfare' between Universal and Dino De Laurentiis has seen De Laurentiis emerge victorious. It now seems doubtful that the Universal version will be made, although we're sure to be greeted by the Paramount version at Christmastime, complete with its man-in-an-ape-suit and ludicrous mechanical robot. De Laurentiis has invested huge sums in a 40-foot mechanical Kong which will actually be placed in the streets of New York and, according to press flacks, atop the World Trade Centre! If it all sounds ridiculous – it is. At a cost of over $15 million, all we can expect to see is something on the level of Herman Cohen's *Konga*. The De Laurentiis version is a shameful waste of talent, time and money that could go toward the production of new and unique fantasy films that could thrill today's audiences as *King Kong* once did in 1933. That, and only that, would fulfil the legacy of *King Kong* and the imaginations of the men who created it.

HIS MAJESTY, *KING KONG* – VIII
THE USURPERS OF THE THRONE

By Donald F. Glut

No studio had yet been able by the mid-seventies to secure the rights from RKO General to remake *King Kong*. Hammer Films had tried to buy them in 1970 but were refused. Though RKO would license other studios to make sequels or new adventures with the huge anthropoid, the original King Kong story was to remain unique. Surprisingly RKO reconsidered four years later; and by 1975 it seemed as if everyone was planning a remake of the classic.

Filmmaker Steve Barkett and model animator Jim Danforth were perhaps the first persons actively to pursue the remake rights for *King Kong* in 1974 after meeting with RKO's Daniel O'Shea. It was O'Shea's job to negotiate the sale of RKO's old properties. But their project was drowned by the publicity amassed by two giant studios, Universal and Paramount, when in 1975 they both announced their own remakes of *King Kong*. What followed was gorilla warfare.

The *King Kong* remake controversy originated in the spring of 1975, when the American Broadcasting Company's Michael Eisner saw Bette Midler in a *Kong* spoof in the musical show *Clams on the Half Shell*. Eisner, conceiving a rock musical version of *King Kong* with Midler as Ann Darrow, relayed his idea to a seemingly uninterested Sid Sheinberg, head of MCA (which owns Universal). Eisner then suggested a *King Kong* remake to Paramount Pictures chairman Barry Diller. Diller was seeking the participation of Italian film mogul Dino De Laurentis while Sheinberg was looking for a producer at Universal, each without the other knowing. The world became *King Kong* conscious when both studios announced that they had the rights to remake the famous film.

Already there was consternation among the cult of devotees that had grown about the original *King Kong*. 'Don't Rape the Ape!' became a slogan among fans at science fiction and film conventions who did not want their beloved classic tampered with; the memories of the Toho Kong efforts had left permanent scars. There was no real artistic reason to remake *King Kong*, the original being perfect in its own right. The fear existed that neither studio would make the film utilising the talents of a model animator like Ray Harryhausen or Jim Danforth. Many fans hoped that neither Universal nor Paramount would eventually secure the coveted rights.

Universal's claim to have bought the rights was based on an alleged verbal deal made between O'Shea and MCA lawyer Arnold Shane. But De Laurentiis and RKO had signed a mutual agreement. Soon both studios were in a legal battle to make their respective picture and each was suing the other.

While the legal battle raged, advertisements began to appear in January 1976 depicting a new King Kong straddling the twin towers of New York's World Trade Centre, a girl clutched in one paw, the other hand battling jet planes. The poster boasted that there was only *one* new *King Kong* – Paramount's – and that it would premiere in theatres by the following Christmas. A coupon accompanied the colour poster offering a copy free of charge; Paramount was deluged with poster requests.

Paramount's *King Kong* poster aroused new anxiety for the fans who held so dear the original. Soon television news broadcasts showed ape-suited protestors carrying

picket signs across the observation deck of the Empire State Building, insisting that Kong not perish atop the World Trade Centre in the new version but where he had fallen in 1933. De Laurentiis was setting his version of *King Kong* in the 1970s and the old Empire State Building simply was not tall enough to meet his demands. Universal's remake would be set during the thirties when the Empire State Building was still the tallest structure in New York. There was some discussion of the two studios joining their resources and making *King Kong* as a combined effort, but Paramount and Universal were both adamant in keeping their stories within their selected time periods. The fight would not end by amalgamating.

Further complications arose after an investigation into the copyright of the original *King Kong*. A question existed as to whether or not the copyright on the picture had ever been properly renewed. One thing was certain, however: the original story version of *King Kong*, published prior to the film's release, had lapsed into the public domain.

Universal Pictures announced that its version, entitled *The Legend of King Kong*, would be based upon the story rather than the movie. Other producers also seized upon this revelation. Producer Roger Corman of New World Films announced his own remake; another was rumoured to be originating in Japan; one more *King Kong* was to be shot in Korea in a three-dimensional process. Corman quickly abandoned his own *King Kong* project. Pressure by Paramount necessitated the changing of the Korean film's title to *Ape*. Soon the trade papers announced the forthcoming *Kongorilla*, *Queen Kong*, *Queen Kong: The Illegitimate Son of You Know Who* and Italian filmmaker Mario Bava's *Baby Kong*. Both *Ape* and the shorter-titled *Queen Kong* began shooting during the war between Paramount and Universal.

The final court decision was that Dino De Laurentis and Paramount owned the rights to remake the movie *King Kong* and could begin immediately. At first Paramount used the title *King Kong: The Legend Reborn*. Universal agreed to postpone its story-based

134

version *The Legend of King Kong* for eighteen months and, meanwhile, settle for eleven percent of Paramount's profits on their remake. De Laurentis had already announced two sequels, *The Bionic Kong* (capitalising on the popularity of *The Six Million Dollar Man* and *The Bionic Woman*, two Universal television successes) and *King Kong in Africa*. Gradually, with Paramount's *King Kong* before the cameras, interest in *The Legend of King Kong* waned at Universal.

Of the two major remakes, *The Legend of King Kong* was the most promising. The picture was to utilise the studio's gimmick 'Sensurround', which had made its bow in the spectacular *Earthquake* (1975). Peter Falk was intended to play Carl Denham with Ann Darrow tentatively to be portrayed by Susan Blakley. (Fay Wray herself was to appear in a cameo.) The music was to be the original score written by Max Steiner for the 1933 movie. At first most of the gorilla scenes were to be enacted by an actor in a gorilla costume (test footage having been shot of ape-suited Bob Burns, his gorilla head made by Rick Baker, going through actions on a miniature jungle set) while the dinosaurs, and Kong during his battles with the dinosaurs, would he brought to the screen through stop motion. Jim Danforth, perhaps the finest three-dimensional animator in the motion picture industry and twice an Academy Award nominee (for his work in *The Seven Faces of Dr. Lao*, 1964, and *When Dinosaurs Ruled the Earth*, 1970) was put on salary at Universal. 'I saw no reason to remake King Kong,' Danforth told me. 'But I felt the Universal script to be far superior to Paramount's.' Eventually the decision would be made not to use a gorilla-suited actor and to create all the monster effects through animation.

Since *The Legend of King Kong* was to be based on the *King Kong* story instead of the 1933 movie, Danforth was instructed to design a new set of prehistoric creatures for Universal's picture. Bo Goldman's screenplay also made the legally-required changes though he retained the period setting and flavour of the original *King Kong*.

Carl Denham is now an unlikeable, greedy showman who thinks nothing of risking the life of his motion picture star, Ann Darrow. On Skull Island he and his crew encounter such monsters as a huge lizard-like creature, giant dragonflies and carnivorous beetles that devour the carcasses of animals. Instead of battling a tyrannosaurus Kong now saves Ann from a herbivorous ceratopsian dinosaur, a Danforth invention he, dubbed 'triclonius', somewhat resembling the familiar triceratops. Kong then carries Ann to his cave and shares his food with her, after which he kills a huge arthropod and drives away a leathery-winged pterosaur. After Kong is overpowered on Skull Island, the doors of the Great Wall become the raft that brings him to New York. In the city Kong wrecks a steam shovel (replacing the elevated train) and finally meets his demise atop the traditional Empire State Building. Still hoping to get some spectacular footage of Ann in the grip of Kong, the unscrupulous Denham is killed while grinding his camera.

The Korean *Ape* (also known as *A*P*E*) which went into production after De Laurentiis began lensing his *King Kong*, was made on an incredibly low budget, most of which seemingly went into the colour film and stereo equipment. The picture was directed by Paul Leder and starred Rod Arrants as a journalist and Joanna DeVarona as a young starlet. The picture was made by the Lee Ming Film Corporation and picked up for American release by Jack H. Harris (who released *Schlock*) and Worldwide Entertainment Corporation.

The producers of *Ape* originally sought Rick Baker, already working in the Paramount *King Kong*, to build the ape suit. Baker deliberately quoted them a low bid, knowing their financial limitations. His price proved too expensive still and *Ape* utilised instead a standard gorilla outfit sold by the Don Post Studios.

The Ape is another oversized gorilla who stomps through some cheap miniature sets (no optical effects were used because of their interference with the 3-D process), wrecking a boat and a native village, and then fighting a giant shark (an attempt to capitalise on the shark craze instigated by Universal's *Jaws* in 1975). Of course, the simian falls in love with the starlet, who is on location shooting a movie on his turf. The journalist, her boyfriend, tries to save her with the aid of the Korean and American armies. The Ape fights off some toy tanks and helicopters before dying from the countless bullet wounds. 'He was too big for a world as small as ours,' says the journalist, comforting his girlfriend before the final fade-out.

Paramount Pictures felt that *Ape* infringed on their *King Kong* rights. The advertising for *Ape* flashed in big letters, 'Not to be confused with *King Kong*.' Paramount won its injunction against the picture and Harris altered his advertising. The court case had already given *Ape* a wealth of free publicity. The picture was completed in time to beat the release of the De Laurentiis *King Kong*.

Queen Kong: The Illegitimate Son of You Know Who was to be a Harlequin Productions spoof, produced and directed by David Winters from a script by Batman creator Bob Kane. This Queen Kong is, said Winters, 'a homosexual gorilla who falls in love with the Bruce Cabot character'.

The official story from Paramount Pictures was that Dino De Laurentiis had been inspired to make his *King Kong* after spotting a poster from the original film on his daughter's wall. *Schlock*'s John Landis claims to have suggested the *Kong* property to De Laurentiis after the latter expressed interest in making a movie about a giant space monster. Whatever the real origin of Paramount's *King Kong*, the picture remains as one of the true fiascos in the genre, a film that in the opinion of this writer should never have been made.

Dino De Laurentiis was determined to make his *King Kong* a grand scale epic, far surpassing in quality the 1933 *King Kong*. '"No one cry when Jaws die," Dino says, his voice rising in passion . . . . "But when the monkey die, people gonna cry. Intellectuals gonna love Konk; even film buffs who love the first Konk gonna love ours. Why? Because I no give them crap. I no spend two, three million to do quick business. I spend 24 million on my Konk. I give them quality."' (Schickel, Richard, 'Here Comes King Kong', *Time* vol. 108, no. seventeen [October 25, 1976], pp 70).

But fans of the original *King Kong* were doubtful that De Laurentiis would give them the promised quality. The picture was originally budgeted at an incredible $16 million; but before the project had reached completion that figure had escalated to nearly $25 million. Soon the news broke that the new Kong would be played by an actor in a gorilla suit, arousing visions in many film buffs of another Konga or Japanese version of the King. Further disappointment arose with the leak that the new *King Kong* would be so 'streamlined' that all the dinosaurs, so much an integral part of the original, had been dropped from the remake's cast list.

Lorenzo Semple, Jr. hastily turned out a screenplay for *King Kong*, updated with the obligatory profanities and minus all giant residents of Skull Island save Kong himself and a giant snake. The names of the characters had been changed from the original. Dwan, the Ann Darrow character of the new version, was given such inspired dialogue as, 'You goddamn chauvinist pig ape, what are you waiting for? If you're gonna eat me, *eat me*!'

On a televised press conference, De Laurentiis unveiled his stars. Though Barbra Streisand, Cher Bono and Goldie Hawn had all been considered for the female lead, the part went to a newcomer, New York fashion model Jessica Lange. Jeff Bridges was to play Jack Prescott (the Driscoll counterpart), a vertebrate palaeontologist, while Charles

Baby Kong, one of numerous intended Kong rip-off projects that never saw the light of day – planned, in this case, by Italian horror maestro Mario Bava.

Grodin would play the Denham-inspired Fred Wilson.

King Kong himself was not so easily cast. One thing was certain, however: the animation process for which most Kong devotees had been praying would not be used. De Laurentiis wanted to make his *Kong* big – both on screen and in front of the cameras. This bigness was originally to be manifested in an ape-suited actor. But when a notice appeared in *Variety* asking for 'ape-like' black actors to test for the role of Kong, the production was immediately lambasted by civil rights groups. De Laurentiis then countered with the announcement that his King Kong would be played by a life-sized mechanical robot, a concept that seemed impossible considering the actions a realistic Kong would have to perform on screen.

When an aircraft company informed De Laurentiis that they could build such a robot given two years' time, he went elsewhere for the artificial beast's construction. *King Kong* had already been booked into a thousand theatres across the United States with a premiere date of Christmas Eve, 1976. Italian special effects expert Carlo Rambaldi told De Laurentiis that he could build the monster right on the lot of MGM (where much of *King Kong* was being lensed) in time to perform his stunts before the cameras. The robot would be 42 feet high.

But even as the King Kong mechanical giant was under construction, De Laurentiis was employing 25-year-old Rick Baker to develop a gorilla costume in the event that the mechanical version should suffer a mishap. Baker had designed the apeman outfit for *Schlock* and two-headed gorilla suit for *The Thing with Two Heads* (1972); his hand had already doubled for King Kong in a television commercial. He had won an Emmy award for aging makeup applied to actress Cicely Tyson in the television drama *The Autobiography of Miss Jane Pittman*. A long time enthusiast of authentic and screen gorillas, Baker looked forward to creating the most realistic movie gorilla of all. 'King Kong offered the one chance to do a really perfect gorilla suit,' Baker later said. 'With the money and the time it could have been outstanding. Unfortunately, it wasn't. There were compromises and enforced deadlines. A once in a lifetime opportunity was lost.' (Kilday, Gregg, 'The Making of a Movie Prop: Kicking the Kong Around', *Los Angeles Times* [December 30, 1976], p. 10).

Originally, De Laurentiis had wanted his Kong to be not a gorilla but a manlike missing link. Baker refused to build anything other than a gorilla suit with the producer meeting him halfway, agreeing to a creature with 'the body of a gorilla and the mind of a man'. Soon both Baker and Rambaldi were competing with one another to design the best

Kong suit. Baker's was a simian masterpiece, complete with extension arms and articulated fingers, while Rambaldi adhered to the concept of an anthropomorphic missing link. When the director of the picture, John Guillermin (who had acquired the *King Kong* job as a result of directing another special effects epic, *The Towering Inferno*, in 1975) saw both ape suits, he declared Baker's version the winner.

Meanwhile, the giant mechanical Kong was beset by problems. Somehow the creature acquired two right hands during the process of its construction. Glen Robinson (who won Oscars for his special effects in *The Towering Inferno* and *The Hindenburg*), supervisor of mechanical effects, oversaw the robot's construction. The giant was given 'life' by a hydraulic system, worked by a staff of technicians at a control panel with almost 70 hydraulic levers. Once completed, television news broadcasts were featuring the robot and tantalising viewers without showing them too much. 'He is fully functional,' said Rambaldi, 'the first such creature conceived by Hollywood. His arms can move in sixteen different positions. He can walk and turn at the waist. His eyes and mouth move. He is a very human monster, terrifying when aroused but with the soul of a romantic lover.' The finished mechanical monster cost between two and three million dollars and proved to be a diamond mine of publicity. Unfortunately the thing did *not* perform as its designers had anticipated. The two functional hands designed by Rambaldi, also hydraulically powered and equipped with safety devices to ensure that Jessica Lange would not be crushed in Kong's grip, were quite impressive. But it was soon obvious that the 42 foot-tall robot would not be able to perform in most of the scenes requiring a full-bodied Kong. It was time to call upon Rick Baker.

Baker was finally given the job to play King Kong in *most* of the scenes (Bill Shepard enacting the scenes wherein Kong battles the serpent, is trapped in a pit and takes fantastic leaps), wearing a gorilla suit designed by both himself and Rambaldi. It was Rambaldi who designed the seven mechanised masks for the suit worn by Baker. Activated at a distance, the heads could register 30 different expressions. These facial movements were indeed marvellous; yet none of the masks really matched up with the less realistic features of the giant King Kong robot. All the more reason, then, for the ape suit to dominate the screen action. The robot itself was relegated to a few dark long shots lasting such a short time that most viewers did not have time to compare it with the costume. Nevertheless the publicity proclaimed that King Kong was being portrayed in the remake by a life-sized mechanical prop. Baker's credit in the film's end titles was reduced to '. . . a special contribution', all the glory for Kong's creation being heaped upon Rambaldi and his technicians.

Baker (officially referred to as the 'miniature' Kong) wanted to play the part like a real gorilla, walking on all fours. But De Laurentiis was still determined to humanise his ape. Director Guillermin demonstrated the gait and upright posture that he wanted to see in Kong and Baker had no choice but to comply. Furthermore, De Laurentiis wanted his Kong to be more of a romantic character than a fierce monster. Though Baker played the part as best he could under the circumstances, the new Kong emerged as a rather weary old character – and quite bored, probably from lack of monsters to fight on Skull Island. (In *King Kong's* early stages of production, Paramount came to Jim Danforth to invent a scene wherein Kong fights some kind of prehistoric beast. Danforth was to select the animal and then animate the scene. After reading the script of *King Kong*, however, Danforth refused to be associated with the Paramount version.) The movie became a love story rather than a fantasy, adventure or horror film.

The new *King Kong* follows an oil company expedition headed by Fred Wilson to an uncharted island perpetually blanketed by fog. Wilson hopes to make the greatest oil find in history for his employers, the Petrox Oil Company. Stowing away aboard Wilson's vessel, the *SS Petrox Explorer*, palaeontologist Jack Prescott comes forth with reports of a huge beast associated with the island as early as the year 1605. No one believes him.

Dwan is discovered unconscious in a rubber lifeboat. Reviving on board the *Explorer*, she explains that she was a starlet aboard her future director's yacht. Had she been in the cabin with him watching a print of *Deep Throat*, she too would have been killed when the yacht exploded.

The story progresses as per the 1933 *King Kong*, with the discovery of the wall and the interruption of the native ceremony. Later, Dwan is kidnapped from the *Explorer*, drugged and dressed in native attire to become the replacement 'Bride of Kong'. Dwan revives to scream at her first glimpse of the giant gorilla.

Kong's initial appearance is hardly exciting. At first we see his face in extreme close-up. When he finally grasps her (the full-sized mechanical hand) there seems to be little menace despite his towering height. Kong merely stands there, holding his blonde bride. Then, after roaring his approval, Kong disappears into the jungle.

Little happens on the island as Prescott, Wilson and members of the *Explorer* crew set off to rescue Dwan. Most of the footage seems to have been devoted to Kong holding Dwan, exploring her with his fingers and registering the gamut of the very impressive mechanised facial expressions. Dwan, during these scenes, supplies such dialogue as: 'I can't stand heights! Honest to God, I can't! When I was ten years old and taken up the Empire State Building, I got sick in the elevator!' And, 'I'm a Libra. What are you? Don't tell me. You're an Aries! Of course, you are! I knew it!'

Only one of these moments actually shone out in the film. Dwan falls into a mud puddle, after which Kong holds her under a waterfall, then puffs out his cheeks to blow her dry (a feat no real gorilla could perform). Amazingly, the scenes with only human actors are generally more interesting than those featuring Kong. Scenes that should have been exciting, such as Kong shaking the men off the log and into the 'bottomless' ravine and Kong reaching down to grasp the hiding Prescott, are slow, dull, as if Guillermin knew how to handle people but not giant apes. The Skull Island sets are also dull and unconvincing, obvious studio mock-ups. (Many of the exteriors for the Skull Island scenes were shot on Kauai, one of the Hawaiian Islands.)

In his volcano crater lair, Kong battles an enormous snake (an obvious mechanical prop), apparently the only other monster on the island, while Prescott absconds with Dwan. Wilson, meanwhile, learning that the oil on the island requires another 10,000 years to be of any use to Petrox, decides to bring Kong back to the United States instead as a kind of monstrous living commercial. Kong bursts through the gates of the Great Wall; but instead of channelling his wrath against the native village, the ape immediately stumbles into a pit especially prepared with chloroform.

The romantic implications of the Kong/woman relationship are stronger in the 1976 *King Kong*. On board ship, deprived of his miniature bride, Kong nearly bursts free of the huge tank which contains him. Wilson threatens to have the beast destroyed rather than lose his ship, but Dwan, feeling strong affection toward the ape now, manages to quiet down the monster. (What happened aboard ship in the original *King Kong* was left to the viewer's imagination.)

There is no build-up to Kong's escape from Shea Stadium. A quick cut shows Dwan descending via helicopter to race up the glamourised reproduction of the island's sacrificial pillar, behind which is a red, white and blue mock-up of the Great Wall. After a few words from Wilson, King Kong, wearing a silly crown on his head, tears himself free of his cage, manages to single out Wilson from the crowd and crush him to death underfoot. Only during Kong's escape was the full-sized robot used, and then in such distant quick cuts that the average viewer was not aware of the difference between mechanical prop and ape-suited actor. (Less than a minute of actual footage of the ape robot appears in the final cut.*) The differences were obvious, however, to anyone bothering to compare the giant and 'miniature' Kongs.

I was an extra during the shooting of the stadium scenes. After hours of retakes, during which the Kong robot remained hidden behind the Petrox Wall and while master of ceremonies Bob Hastings kept reminding everyone that the star of this picture was a mechanical marvel over 40 feet tall, the giant Kong finally made his appearance. He did not walk out; he was *rolled* into view with cables supporting him under the arms. When the crowd demanded that Kong *move*, Hastings explained that one of the cables had broken down earlier that day but that the monster would definitely move the following night.

Writer Bill Warren, who had been one of the crowd on a subsequent evening, reported: 'The thing was holding parts of its cage in its hands, and our first action, after a half-hour wait, was to slowly edge off the bleachers and out of the arena. The robot then went as berserk as it could, waving its feet, turning its head and snarling, and lowering its arms to drop the pieces of cage. Large cranes then ran into the scene, and workmen picked up the parts and handed them back to the robot for a retake while a minor comic hired for the occasion blathered on about the robot, how it cost a million bucks (I've heard three million from people in a position to know), how it was the electronic wonder of the age. I thought for all that wonder they could have taught it to pick up things when it drops them, but that was just a passing idea. Not once did the comic mention that most of the time on the screen, you won't be seeing this electronic marvel, you'll be seeing one of two guys in a monkey suit . . . . The robot broke down frequently, and as the comic muttered on about its supreme wonderfulness, one of the technicians on the film grumbled, "Wish to hell the thing worked!" (Warren, Bill, 'Model Animation? What'sa dat?,' *Cinefantastique* vol. five, no. three [winter 1977], p. 34.)

De Laurentiis' attempt to create a totally sympathetic Kong fully emerges during the last part of the film. Dangerous though he may be, Kong is not a particularly formidable monster. He hides behind miniature buildings rather than lash out at man and his machines. Somehow he does manage to wreck the *one* elevated train in which Dwan and Prescott are fleeing. Later on, Kong manages to abduct Dwan from the one tiny bar in all of New York where she is having a much-needed drink.

Prescott wants to save Kong and preserve his species by returning him to Skull Island. But once Kong climbs with Dwan to the top of the World Trade Centre, the Mayor (played by John Agar) orders his squadron of helicopters to open fire. The final scenes do not duplicate the original poster showing a defiant Kong, one leg atop each of the towers. Kong is literally dwarfed by the structure and must take an enormous leap to reach the safety of the second tower once the helicopters begin to shoot at him. There is no classic image of the raging beast fighting to the end while perched at the city's highest point. The helicopters merely swoop down at him like exterminators come to eliminate a rooftop pest.

Dwan begs Kong not to set her down. 'No, Kong. Pick me up. They'll kill you!' The strange love between them reaches its peak as Kong faces the fire power of the helicopters, which splatter his chest and back with gore. Instead of immediately plunging to the city street, Kong lies atop the tower roof. When Dwan finally reaches out to touch him, he undramatically drops off the side, making his descent off screen.

The original publicity promised that the full-sized robot Kong would perform these

*'I'm a Libra. What are you? Don't tell me. You're an Aries!' Jessica Lang,
the new girl in the hairy paw, gets ditsy with Ko*

scenes on top the actual World Trade Centre. The excuse for the scene being done in the studio and in miniature was that the robot was too heavy to be safely lifted above the streets of New York. A full-sized styrofoam mock-up of Kong was assembled at the base of the World Trade Centre for the final shots in the picture, however. Crowding around the dummy were 30,000 curious unpaid extras, there to witness the demise of King Kong.

Just prior to the film's release, Dino De Laurentiis sought an Academy Award for his robot. Naturally the Academy of Motion Picture Arts and Sciences was not about to award an Oscar to a mechanical contrivance. It was then that De Laurentiis admitted that most of the scenes were performed by the very non-mechanical Rick Baker, who certainly would receive an Academy Award. KNX Radio carried the story on a news broadcast.

Nevertheless, when *King Kong* opened on schedule in colour, wide screen and stereophonic sound, millions of people had already been swept up by the publicity over the robot's alleged performance. Supposedly knowledgeable critics were still writing extensively about the robot's incredible abilities and participation in the film. Regardless of what might have been said later about Rick Baker and the gorilla suit, the publicity had worked its miracle. People were thoroughly convinced that the robot had done most of the picture if not all of it.

The new *King Kong* left many viewers unsatisfied and wondering where the $25 million budget had gone. Even without the original RKO picture as a comparison, Paramount's *King Kong* presented nothing that had not already been explored on the screen in 'giant monster' films for decades. In my opinion the new *King Kong* appears to be no more than an incredibly expensive Godzilla film and leaves no doubt that there is still only one *King Kong*.

Before completing *King Kong*, Dino De Laurentiis announced yet another sequel title, the obvious *Son of Kong*. Before its release, scenes from his *King Kong* were incorporated into the television specials *The Big Party* and *Life Goes to the Movies*. Behind-the-scenes colour footage of people crowding around the full-sized Kong mock-up at the base of the World Trade Centre was given the title *The King Is Dead!* and made available to home movie collectors.

*A number of out-takes from this sequence and behind-the-scenes shots showing the robot in its slow-moving action appeared in 'King Kong: Fact or Fantasy', a 1977 episode of the documentary television series *Wide World of Adventure*.

RETURN OF THE URBAN GORILLA
THE TWO *KONGS*: A COMPARATIVE REVIEW
By Kenneth Thompson

By Definition, *I* is the classic original, *II* the imitative upstart. But though a tremendous rooter for *I* I can't (as some of my friends and colleagues tended to expect) get hot under the collar about the presence of *II*. The situation seems to me analogous to jazzed-up renditions of Bach which tend to give considerable if ephemeral pleasure without in the least disturbing the Bach originals which remain steadfastly unaffected. Without quite being able to share the enthusiasm of one or two *Films Illustrated* colleagues, I do feel that *II* is far from being the dire disaster that some fans of *I* were confidently predicting.

The tripartite structure of *I* is faithfully followed by *II*: (a) the introduction and build-up; (b) the island sequences; (c) the New York sequences.

A fundamental difference in the two films is that *II* dispenses entirely with the original characters. Otherwise they are furthest apart in (a), to such an extent that *II* has almost nothing in common with its predecessor, offering an entirely new story line. The two share a slow opening and leisurely build-up, but *II* is more lethargic, not merely because the film has been made at a considerably greater length, so that it's something like 50 minutes before Kong makes his debut, but equally because it lacks the mystery and cumulative effect of *I*. An oil company's expedition to investigate possible oil deposits off a fog-shrouded island is an ineffective substitute for an expedition headed by a fearless and intrepid film-maker of the 'bring 'em back alive' school searching in unknown waters to photograph nobody knows what.

The first real point of contact between the two films comes with the arrival at Skull Island, which in *I* is imaginative but phoney, in *II* naturalistic and beautiful (superby photographed, too). The landing and first encounter with the Kong-worshipping natives is most effectively done in *II*, which duplicates the conception of the enormous wall with its gigantic gate but recreates it on a bigger and more effective scale – though surprisingly eschewing the big gong, replacing it with a disappointing pair of wooden trumpets which apparently don't work. The preparation of the bride for Kong is a more picturesque affair in *II*; but the abduction of the heroine, somewhat simply accomplished in *I*, becomes ridiculously easy in *II*.

Early on, Charles Grodin as oilman expedition-leader Fred Wilson, and Jeff Bridges as stowaway zoologist Jack Prescott, were hazy but at any rate discernible counterparts to Robert Armstrong as film-maker Carl Denham and Bruce Cabot as mariner right-hand man. But though the characters are important and well-defined throughout (a), they take a back seat after Kong has entered into the proceedings. Not so the heroine Dwan. Though Kong upstages everyone else, Dwan (as played by Jessica Lange) is far from eclipsed. She is a pole apart from Ann Darrow (as played by Fay Wray). Whereas Ann was demure, unglamorous and unsophisticated, Dwan is the reverse. Whereas Ann, following her abduction by Kong, was consistently scared and gave vent to her fright in the succession of screams which won such renown and acclaim for Miss Wray as to immortalise her in film history, Dwan lets loose only a casual scream or two, quickly becomes reconciled to the situation and even counter-attacks with aggressive diatribe ('You goddam chauvinist pig ape!').

In *I*, Kong disturbingly kept changing in size and mien, and his locomotion was distinctly on the jerky side. The gorilla in *II* is intrinsically superior in every respect, his size remains constant, he does not have startling changes of countenance, and he moves with fluent ease. But this state of affairs is as unsurprising as it was predictable. Dash it all, some appreciable advance must have been made in 43 years of special effects. Kong *II* is magnificent even if he can't displace Kong *I* in the affections of those who have enjoyed Willis O'Brien's creation over the years.

Much of the island sequences in *II* are impressive, but one misses the sundry encounters with stegosaurus, brontosaurus and pterodactyl, particularly the use by Kong *I* of boxing tactics and his jaw-breaking victory over tyrannosaurus rex. Kong *I* was presented with more than a dash of humour, and moreover had a chest-thumping pride in his own prowess. Kong *II*, for all his magnificence, is a much more taciturn and intense fellow. And the going is easy: he is not called upon to combat a succession of diverse dinosaurs, having only an encounter with a giant slithery snake. This encounter is basically copied from *I* and the log-rolling sequence is quite an exact copy.

It is possible to dislike the way *II* owes much of its inspiration and ideas to *I* yet at the same time makes fun of it. Dwan's 'chauvinist pig ape' remark is one instance. There are others. Dwan mentions her horoscope as predicting that she will cross the water 'to meet the biggest person in my life.' Again, when the searchers are pursuing Kong across the island, somebody remarks, 'Who the hell do you think went through there – some guy in an ape suit?' This element of ridicule seems rather cheap, the more so because in its later phases *II* tends to take itself very seriously.

The even more spectacular recreations by *II* of *I*'s big set-pieces in the island sequences are topped by the scene in which Kong breaks through the wall-door into the native village. This scene was terrific in *I*, breathtaking in *II* where it is, to my mind, the highlight of the film.

Unlike *I* there is a bridge passage in *II* connecting the island with the New York sequences. After Kong has been overcome (by chloroform, instead of Denham's gas bombs), *II* has an additional and sometimes quite bizarre sequence set on the tanker which is transporting the giant ape which is confined to a hold.

With the possible exception of the scene in which Kong busts up the overhead railway (which *II* copies practically shot for shot and then adds a bit of its own), the New York scenes in *II* seem to me a disappointment. In *I*, Kong is placed on exhibition on the vast stage of a large theatre, in *II* he is much less effectively displayed at a circus in a park. Kong's escape from his fetters and the crowd panic which ensues are less effectively staged than in the original film.

But perhaps the real disappointment of *II* is the mess it makes of the famous climactic sequence. The now-familiar poster for *II* has falsely prepared us for the new version's finale (in fact it's decidedly a cheat). For though we know that the World Trade Centre substitutes for the Empire State Building, and that old biplanes have understandably been replaced by contemporary aircraft, nothing else is as per poster prediction.

Kong does not stand with left leg on one of the twin towers, right leg on the other; no fighters take part in the attack, only helicopters; and, worst of all, the blue sky and sunshine is but an optical illusion. For some unaccountable reason, the producers' confidence seems to have deserted them, and in fact the finale (indeed, most of the New York sequences) takes place at night. Decidedly, I submit, the Empire State and the biplanes reign supreme.

One can now only speculate what might have happened had Universal's projected remake in more faithful, un-updated style materialised. Meantime, *II* is a version for the seventies with some visual magnificence and the most attractive Miss Lange to commend it.

THEY KILLED *KING KONG*

by Robert F. Willson Jr.

In a famous essay about the 1933 film (*Dissident*, Spring 1960), X. J. Kennedy asked, 'Who Killed King Kong?' The question led Kennedy to a conclusion about the movie's major sociological implication: that we identify with Kong's primal personality and secretly desire to crumple buildings and subway cars in a civilisation which has become too complicated for us. When the ape dies something within us is squelched, forcing us to accept our modern conformity, our readymade suits, schedules, and social values. We are regularly drawn to *King Kong* showings on late night TV primarily because, as Kennedy puts it, our little deaths occur in such prosaic settings: 'It is not for us to bring to a momentary standstill the civilisation in which we move. King Kong does this for us. And so we kill him

again and again . . . while the ape in us expires from day to day, obscure, in desperation.'

Despite the obvious ingenuousness of the 1933 *Kong*, Kennedy's point about its fascination perceptive. The attitude it reveals toward American society is, however, is significantly different from the one revealed in Dino De Laurentiis' remake. In the original a movie producer named Denham (played by Robert Armstrong) sets out to make a jungle adventure following the 'Beauty and the Beast' story line. For his heroine he searches the streets of Depression-struck New York until he finds Ann Darrow (Fay Wray), a down-and-out working girl whom he catches in the act of stealing an apple from a fruit stand. Off they sail, with Bruce Cabot and others in tow, to find their pot of gold.

This opening sequence establishes some critical facts about the film's point of view. What motivates director, starlet, and male lead is the American dream – the hope of attaining fame and fortune through one daring act of entrepreneurship. When the dream turns into a nightmare and Kong emerges as a marauding destroyer of the very symbols of civilisation the princpals had sought after, we in the audience are meant to feel something akin to the horror of films in the Frankenstein genre. There we blame the atheistic curiosity of a mad scientist; in *Kong* we reluctantly blame the overzealous Horatio Alger for letting his ambition get out of hand. In psychological terms *Kong* acts as an instrument of revenge; a kind of purge figure, whose massive strength and accompanying innocence we may identify with but whose moral duty of humbling man and his works we must accept. As Kennedy's essay urges, we engage in the ritual re-killing to remind ourselves of our vulnerability.

In the recent remake, Kong and American society are perceived and presented in a radically different way. Denham has become a cartoon-strip caricature, an oil company junior executive (played by Charles Grodin) who lusts after what he believes are rich oil deposits on Kong's island. He is certainly not treated as a resourceful Horatio Alger; his ambition is, after all, the same as that of the corporation he works for. When he doesn't find liquid gold but the giant ape instead he decides to bring back his black 'prize' and use it as an advertising gimmick for the products of Petrox Corp. Inc. Now when Kong

145

breaks loose in New York City we are invited to seek a scapegoat beyond our own greed or ambition: the corporate monster. Grodin's character is only an extension of the system, and director Guillermin indulges in a cheap, theatrical trick by arranging for Kong not just to step on his persecutor but to grind him into the dirt of Shea Stadium with a gleeful smile on his face. As in the original, Kong acts as a purge figure, but his power is easily overcome by the forces of a corrupt system that keeps us oppressed. Entrepreneurship is after all a dead item in 1977.

My claim about the film's social statement and about Kong's role in making that statement is reinforced by some not so subtle changes in the script of the earlier version. For example, Kong climbs not the Empire State Building (seen as something of a positive symbol in the 1933 film) but the World Trade Centre. The building reminds the ape of the twin peaks on his native island, and, with Dwan in hand, he hopes to regain the peace he knew before the oil company representatives came to disrupt his life. To have the ape make the mistake is far-fetched enough, but to attempt an ironic touch by humbling him at the foot of big business' main headquarters is beneath art. In addition the machines that destoy Kong – helicopter gunships – are presented as blatant reminders of the most recent testing ground for the products of the military-industrial complex: Vietnam. As if to strongly underscore the ape's essential essence, his identity as victim and not menace, the sequence in which he is murdered is made especially bloody. When the bullets rip into the body we can't help recalling My Lai and similar massacres of Vietnamese innocents. By means of such touches the film never allows its to forget that they, the conglomerate killers, destroyed King Kong, dooming him from the moment they removed him from his ecosystem on the island. And, by implication, these same killers will 'destroy' us should we dare to challenge their profit margins and tax loopholes. America of the seventies is too cynical to take Kong seriously, while thirties America, reeling from a devastating depression, was only too willing to accept a fantasy in which civilisation is brought to a halt. For this reason the 1933 version impresses by its innocence, by its respect for Kong's gift of sheer destructiveness unqualified by strong human emotions. The society for which the film was made took its economic plight seriously – it had already been humbled by Mr. Hoover's policies – yet it could seek escape with the same seriousness by embracing a film that depicted panic in a realistic way. Guillermin's remake, on the other hand, is high camp, treating both the civilization and the ape's threat with detachment and only mock-seriousness. Like children, the thirties audience did not know what to fear, but it knew fear; for us we have seen the worst – atomic bombs, mass murder, Arab oil boycotts – and by comparison Kong is a teddy bear.

The situation that best illustrates this change in approach and style is the 'love affair' between Kong and the beautiful Dwan. In the 1933 version Fay Wray longs for stardom and three squares by making the director's jungle epic. When she is offered up to Kong by frightened natives as a particularly enticing sacrifice, the film implies that all the preceding Mrs. Kongs, black and white, have been devoured. Fay has genuine reason to scream her head off, which she does quite effectively almost from start to finish. But in the remake our advanced zoological knowledge is called into play; we are reminded by the script writers that apes (even great ones) are herbivorous. The film's heroine (played by Jessica Lange) is therefore in no immediate danger, even though she understandably suspects the ape's intentions, since she is not aware of the beast's dietary preferences. While the less sophisticated thirties audience could readily accept the horror of Kong as flesh eater, the modern audience could not be deceived on this question. We are also ecology-minded, so director Guillermin makes us respond with justifiable horror to the

Make-up effects artist Rick Baker as Kong, wearing his own ape suit. Baker's ape was a impressive creation – though markedly different to his animatronic counterpar

gassing technique by which Kong is subdued. As he passes out in a pit filled with anaes-thetising fog, he raises one hand above the cloud in a momentary but futile gesture of defiance. Such touches only serve to create overwhelming sympathy for the ape and nothing but contempt for his captors. That contempt is spoken by a young anthropologist stowaway (Jeff Bridges), whose biting wit and long hair are supposed to qualify him as the only sensitive defender of Kong and as Dwan's romantic interest. Instead of the neutral or directly opposed stance of Fay Wray and Bruce Cabot in the original, Lange and Bridges are portrayed as Kong's only friends, willing to sacrifice their affections for one another in order to save the ape.

Guillermin's enlightened approach does not necessarily require that Kong should be loved, but it does melodramatise the story considerably. There are good guys and bad guys in the film, and most of the human characters suffer by comparison with Kong. In the original the ape is not given so many humanising touches, nor do we observe so many changes of mood in his personality. During the remake's long wooing scene atop Kong's mountain, he treats Dwan as a child would treat a Barbie doll, bathing and fondling her with curiosity. Only when he tries to undress her does his glance appear to take on the dimensions of an aroused rapist. Still Dwan's charge that he is a 'goddamned male-chauvinist-pig ape' sounds only embarrassingly humorous in the context: their markedly different dimensions prevent anything like a forced affair. Nonetheless the mere fact that the two communicate on even the most basic level of emotion requires a drastic shift in the audience's perception of the ape-hero. His stature as a menace is considerably reduced, and the sympathy factor is considerably increased.

The remake also takes a markedly different approach to the character of the film's heroine. In the original we at no time have the sense that Fay Wray wants to *save* her pursuer. Her only true love is Bruce Cabot, with whom she is finally, happily, united. Director Armstrong's last words, as the bewildered citizenry and news-hungry reporters gather around the fallen carcass, are: 'That's your story, boys – it was Beauty killed the Beast!' While the line sounds curiously like a rationalisation for his own blunder, Armstrong's words underscore the ape's tragic fall and Fay Wray's type as romantic heroine.

In the remake, on the other hand, Dwan emerges as a Marilyn Monroe-like starlet. She is found by the Petrox crew, floating in a rubber raft and garbed in a revealing I. Magnin gown. It seems that she is the sole survivor of an explosion aboard the yacht of a Hollywood producer who had been promising her a 'big part' in his next spectacular. The producer's morals, however, are dubious; he and other companions were below decks watching *Deep Throat* when the explosion occurred. The heroine of Guillermin's version is thus introduced as a kooky but basically sweet virgin whose aversion to porn has apparently 'saved' her for a marriage with the film's other virgin, Kong. They make an intriguing, if incongruous, couple.

When Kong takes his bride to his cave she at first screams uncontrollably, then turns to verbal abuse, and finally inquires about his sign. Campiness aside, the one-sided dialogue is clearly designed to establish a courtship ritual, in which Dwan and hairy husband gradually come to know each other better, as if they had just met at a Hollywood party. Aboard ship, on the way back to New York, Dwan pulls away from an embrace with anthropologist Bridges in order to run (or, more precisely, drop) to Kong's side and placate him when he threatens to tear the ship apart in the role of a jealous spouse. Her loyalty and devotion strike everyone as remarkable but admirable. And, in the final sequence atop the World Trade Centre, Dwan begs Kong to hold her close so that the gunships will not fire on him. Guillermin appears to want to convince us that the two are genuinely in love, probably because he has taken care to show how much they have in common.

Kong's assault on the elevated subway train, an iconic moment from the original film, recreated in a poster for the 1976 remake.

Both are movie stars, freaks, the subjects of snapshots and media attention. Both are admired more for their bodies than their brains; they are expected to act as symbols rather than as 'real' beings. Both are denied genuine love and happiness by an exploitative society. In the end Kong's death is depicted both as a massacre *and* a suicide, suggesting that the ape decides he does not want to live any longer in our corrupt and violent world. Bullets are his sleeping pills. And as the crowd gathers around the hairy hulk, Dwan finds herself at the centre of the publicity whirlwind, carried away both physically and metaphorically to the fame she had been seeking from the beginning. To achieve this fame she uses Kong and at the same time foregoes true happiness as an anthropologist professor's wife. While the original united Fay and her man the remake frustrates this formula in order to state that hero and heroine are simply victims of a system that sullies all innocence and destroys what it doesn't understand. Fantasy has become melodrama; romance is turned to the uses of satire. The attempt is an embarrassing failure.

For the review of the original *King Kong* in its March 3, 1933 edition, the *New York Times* ran this caption: 'A Fantastic Film in Which a Monstrous Ape Uses Automobiles for Missiles and Climbs a Skyscraper.' This description may reduce the movie to its barest spectacular details, but it also points up the joyous and healthy state in which the thirties audience could indulge its escapist and, if X. J. Kennedy is right, disruptive desires. Kong *was* larger than life. For all its technical advances, its satiric purpose, and its zoological wisdom (i.e., apes eat grapes, not people), the remake manages to somehow cut the ape-hero down to size. By giving him a range of emotional responses that would be the envy of an Actors' Studio graduate, De Laurentiis and Guillermin leave us with the unmistakable impression that Kong is a jealous husband who went berserk and tried to hold his wife hostage until she agreed to leave her lover and return to him. Do we need to be reminded, especially in a film using such a successful fantasy formula, that those things always end in suicide?

HIS MAJESTY, *KING KONG* – IX

By Donald F. Glut

The Anglo/Italian production of *Queen Kong* was still not completed as Paramount's epic played its thousand theatres. *Queen Kong* was produced by Dexter Films at Shepperton studios in Great Britain. Unlike the Paramount film, this was an outright spoof with no pretentions of outranking the RKO original. The picture, directed by Frank Agrama, is a reverse on the old Kong story. Luce Habit (Rula Lenska), a female movie-maker, wants to shoot a film with her star Ray Fay (Robin Askwith). In the remote village of Lazangawheretheydothekonga, Luce discovers the huge female gorilla Queen Kong, who runs rampant once she is brought back to London in pursuit of her beloved Ray Fay. In one sequence the ape dreams that she is a normal sized anthropoid dancing with Ray. The climax of *Queen Kong* occurs atop the Post Office Tower. Advance poster artwork for the picture depicted Queen Kong fighting off planes, a nude Ray Fay in one hand and a huge bra in the other.

Like *Ape*, *Queen Kong* incurred legal problems, this time from both De Laurentiis and RKO, who sued on the grounds that it marked an infringement of copyright and that its terrible script would be detrimental to the reputation of Paramount's *King Kong*. Yet even closer to the De Laurentiis picture was a Chinese film released in 1977 long after the furore over the giant ape had subsided. The Shaw Brothers of Hong Kong got into the King Kong act with *Mighty Peking Man*, virtually a remake of Paramount's remake. Evelyne Kraft played the huge monster's human bride.

Another 1977 picture that made use of the famous ape (here called King Dong) was titled *The Winner of 10 Academy Awards*. It was released in colour by Spectrum Films. Chuck Vincent directed. Yet another attempt to cash in on the Kong mania of the seventies was the retitling of *Tarz and Jane and Boy and Cheetah*, an 'X' rated Tarzan spoof of 1975 which was directed by Itsa Fine and released in colour by Fine Productions. In 1977 the picture was recirculated as *Ping Pong*, but its cheap ape suit appeared no taller than the actor wearing it. That same year *King Kung Fu* and the announced titles *Attack of the Giant Apes*, *The Return of King Kong* (Chinese), *The New King Kong* and *Kong Island* left little doubt as to their source of inspiration.

The original *King Kong* was in its first year of release when already it was being spoofed in another form of animation, the cartoon. No less than four cartoon parodies of *King Kong* were released in 1933. *King Klunk* was a Pooch the Pup short for Universal Pictures, directed by Walter Lantz and William Nolan. Pooch ventures to a prehistoric island where the ape King Klunk falls in love with his girlfriend, then battles a dinosaur which emerges from the water, for her safety. Klunk is then brought to the city for a re-enactment of Kong's Empire State Building demise. *Parade of the Wooden Soldiers* (Paramount), directed by Dave Fleischer, spoofed Kong as toys come to life. Mickey

Queen Kong (1976) was suppressed for 25 years due to an injunction by De Laurentiis Productions. This British comedy is now notable as by far the worst of the Kong rip-offs.

Mouse had his own King Kong misadventure in the Walt Disney cartoon *The Pet Shop* (United Artists). A caged gorilla in Mickey's pet shop falls in love with Minnie Mouse, surely as strange a relationship as Kong had with Ann Darrow. Inspired by a picture of Kong on the Empire State Building, the gorilla carries Minnie to the top of a bird cage (simulating the skyscraper's dirigible mooring mast). Mickey and a squadron of the shop's birds defeat the ape and save Minnie. (Hollywood Film Enterprises' home movie edition of this cartoon was re-titled *Mickey the Gorilla Tamer*.) Bob Clampett brought the giant ape Ping Pong to life from a picture on a magazine cover in the 1933 Warner Brothers cartoon *I Like Mountain Music*.

Clampett brought another giant gorilla to life, this time off a box of animal crackers, in the Warner Brothers colour cartoon *Goofy Groceries* (1940). Another giant gorilla breaks loose at a circus to fight the mighty Superman in the Paramount colour cartoon *Terror on the Midway* (1941), directed by Dave Fleischer. King Kong made cameo appearances in other colour cartoons, including the British Beatles' feature *Yellow Submarine* (United Artists, 1968), directed by George Dunning; *The Family That Dwelt Apart*, a Canadian cartoon of the middle 1970s, based on E. B. White's story in the *New Yorker*; the titles of *The Strongest Man in the World* (Walt Disney Productions, 1975) – a sequel to *Now You See Him, Now You Don't* directed by Vincent McVeety – and the titles of *The Pink Panther Strikes Again* (United Artists, 1976), animated by Richard Williams; and *Basketball Jones* (1976), by St. Johns and Talmadge.

Amateur filmmakers have also used the King Kong character for their own special effects movies. During the 1960s, Jon Berg, now a professional puppet animator, brought a gorilla to life in some very impressive stop-motion colour footage. In 1965 Steve Kaplan went into production on *Kong!*, an amateur version of the RKO picture, recreating its key scenes. An amateur production titled *Son of Kong Returns* surfaced in 1965. The author shot four amateur films featuring giant gorillas in prehistoric settings: *The Earth Before Man* (1957) in colour, with a prehistoric ape vs. woolly rhinoceros; *The Time Monsters* (1959), in colour, in which a giant ape battles a Ceratosaurus and is observed on a time machine screen; *Tor, King of Beasts* (1962), in which Carl Denham finds the giant ape Tor on a lost plateau in this amateur version of *King Kong*; and *Son of Tor* (1964), partly in colour, an amateur *Son of Kong*, co-starring Godzilla and other famous movie monsters. (Tor also appeared in *Frankenstein in the Lost World*, a novel by myself first published in Germany as *Frankenstein bei den Dinosauriern*, Vampir Horror-Roman, 1976. Atop a prehistoric plateau somewhere in Africa, Tor, King of Beasts, captures the female assistant of the scientist seeking to destroy the Frankenstein Monster. Tor and his lost world are destroyed during a traditional volcanic eruption.)

THE APE GOES EAST

By Pete Tombs

The footfalls of the mighty Kong continued to reverberate around the world for many years after beauty killed the beast. There were a number of semi-sequels (official and otherwise) and a good few movies 'inspired by' (if we are being kind) Cooper and Schoedsack's original. However, the 1933 film's classic status, its near perfect special effects, click-tight scenario and, above all, the huge affection in which it was held by succeeding generations of moviegoers made the chances of an outright remake an unlikely prospect. Until 1975, when Dino de Laurentiis had the unfortunate idea of 'updating' the original giant monster movie. The story of that production and its fallout is told elsewhere in the present volume. However, one of the effects of the worldwide advance publicity for Dino's folly was that exploitation producers the world over began to look at the idea of pipping him to the post. Their plan was to mine box office gold by taking advantage of the huge publicity the remake was garnering, even in pre-production.

There had already been a number of *Kong*-influenced Asian movies. The two Japanese Toho productions are well known and generally worthwhile additions. India also heard the call of the great Kong. The prolific (and copyright careless) studios of Bombay's Bollywood had already released two 'King Kong' movies – but both the 1962 *King Kong*, although directed by special effects master Babubhai Mistri, and the 1965 *Tarzan and King Kong* are actually in the tradition of the Italian 'muscle man' movies rather than sci-fi fantasy. Giant creatures are more often to be found in the country's popular mythological films, feeding off the public's huge appetite for retellings of the epic sagas of the Ramayana and the Mahabharata.

The most *Kong*-like is the monkey king Hanuman, who can be found in numerous Indian films right from the early days of silent cinema down to the latest CGI super-productions. He also featured in a 1974 Thai/Japanese co-production, *The Six Ultra Brothers versus the Monster Army*. Here he takes on a band of evil crooks who steal the head of a huge stone Buddha. Along the way, the giant Monkey God also saves Earth from being burned to a crisp by the sun and unites with the Ultramen to defeat a bevy of evil creatures from outer space.

The many scenes of building stomping and the giant Hanuman (or more accurately, a man in a Hanuman suit) striking terror and wonder into the human population definitely put this one in the 'influenced by *Kong*' category.

A more remote *Kong* influence can be found in the 1991 Hindi language production *Ajooba Kudrat Ka* ('A Miracle of Nature'). Produced by Bombay's infamous Ramsay Brothers team – the Indian equivalent of US exploitation greats like Roger Corman – the film, set in the Himalayan mountains, is a kind of giant Yeti/Kong hybrid with a few touches of *Mighty Joe Young* thrown in. Most viewers will get as far as the song and dance number with the cutesy-pie little girl singing, 'Yeti, I love you' before deciding this film is one giant footprint too far.

It was the legend of the Yeti, the giant snowman of the Himalayas, that seemed to inspire the Hong Kong-based Shaw Brothers in their attempt to steal a march on De Laurentiis' *Kong*. Variously titled *Goliathon*, *The Mighty Peking Man* and *Colossus of Congo*, the film went into production only months after the announcement of Paramount's remake in 1976. However, special effects problems and difficult location shooting in India delayed the film's completion by more than a year. It was finally released in August 1977 – well after the De Laurentiis spectacular had premiered.

The film was directed by Ho Meng Hua, a Shaw contract director since the late 1950s. Born in 1923, the veteran director had worked in all the popular genres then offered by the Shaws, but had shown himself particularly adept at horror (*Black Magic 1* and *2*, *The Oily Maniac*) and exotic martial arts (*The Flying Guillotine*, *The Vengeful Beauty*).

The all important special effects were handled by two Japanese teams. The first were contracted for a three month period, but had to leave when the shooting schedule overran. The replacement team – which included Koichi Kawakita, who later worked on the nineties *Godzilla* revivals – then had to match effects work that was already in the can; causing more difficulty for the overstretched production.

Mighty Peking Man finally came in at more than HK$6 million, a large budget for a

KING KONG COMETH!

Hong Kong film. Due to losing the race with Paramount, box office returns were poor, but the film has since garnered a certain cachet among seekers of the exotic and the unlikely. And it certainly is both of those.

It begins with a very effectively staged earthquake high in the Himalayas. Stories subsequently leak out about a giant ape-like creature disturbed by the tremor. Known as Mighty Peking Man (presumably Mighty Himalayan Man didn't have the same ring for local audiences), he becomes a subject of much interest in the media. An unscrupulous Hong Kong businessman puts together a team to locate the monster ape and bring him back to HK, where he will be exhibited in a huge stadium to sell-out crowds.

Johnny Feng is recruited to head the expedition. An intrepid explorer with a broken heart (he lost his girl to his suave younger brother), Johnny fearlessly leads the team through a series of perilous adventures. An elephant charge, tiger attacks and dangerous climbs up sheer rock faces all take their toll on both men and morale. Finally, while Johnny is asleep one night, the team abandon him. He carries on alone, determined to find the monster. His fervent hope is that the subsequent media fame will bring his fickle girlfriend back to him. Menaced by the giant ape, Johnny is saved in the nick of time by a beautiful blonde white girl wearing the skimpiest of animal skin bikinis. She seems to have a rapport with the creature that she calls 'Utam'.

Johnny discovers that, as a young girl, she was the only survivor of a light plane crash that killed both her parents. Growing up in the wild, she has learned how to communicate with and control the animals that live there – including Utam, for whom she has developed a special affection.

The blonde Samantha is played by Swiss-born Evelyne Kraft. She was a popular actress in European exploitation movies during the 1970s and went on to make the *Charlie's Angels*-style *Deadly Angels* for Shaw Brothers. Director Ho recalls how her freewheeling European ways shocked the local Hong Kong crew when she stripped to the buff for her wardrobe sessions. He makes good use of her sinuous body at the film's conclusion when he has her racing through the crowded streets of Hong Kong in her tiny tattered bikini, constantly on the verge of (and sometimes actually) exposing a stray nipple or two.

Her role in *Mighty Peking Man* was as a kind of female Tarzan. It's an idea at least as old as *The Jungle Princess* (1936) starring the iconic Dorothy Lamour. Popular with the public, the idea of the sexy jungle girl was kept alive via serials such as *Nyoka the Jungle Girl*, TV shows like *Sheena, Queen of the Jungle* and in movies like the German *Liane* series. Ironically, a 1968 Italian variation – *Eva, la Venere Salvaggia* – was later retitled *King of Kong Island* to also cash in on the De Laurentiis movie.

Up in the mountains, Johnny and Samantha inevitably fall in love. He persuades her to return to 'civilisation' with him and they take the giant ape along. Reunited with his slimy business partner, Lu Tiem, Johnny allows Utam to be chained up and exhibited as an exotic curiosity to a crowd of gawking yahoos in the local sports stadium. While Johnny enjoys a liaison with his former girlfriend, the devious Lu Tiem decides to put the make on Samantha. Rather foolishly, he does this within full sight of Utam – who inevitably goes berserk, breaks free of his chains and lumbers off to save her, stomping half of a miniaturised Hong Kong on the way.

The finale is the familiar *Kong* climax of total mobilisation as army and air force hunt down and destroy the confused and lovelorn ape. He is lured to the top of a tall building where giant petrol tanks are exploded, killing him as he attempts to snatch toy helicopters out of the air.

Two endings were shot for the film. The happy ending sees Samantha survive. In the

US release, she dies from friendly fire, cradled in Johnny's arms as Utam burns in the flames. Welcome to civilisation, Sam.

For all its schlocky content, the film moves at a pace brisk enough to avoid tedium and is efficiently directed. Considering the drawn-out production, and the fact that Ho had to work on three other films at the same time, it's remarkable that anything coherent survived. The Shaw Brothers were a potent force in filmdom at this point and the production values are high. The model work and miniatures are generally excellent, and there are some enjoyably camp moments provided by the kitschy romantic interludes set to ersatz seventies soft soul music. The film was re-released theatrically in 1999 by Quentin Tarantino's Rolling Thunder distribution outfit to generally favourable reviews.

A much sadder spectacle is presented by the other Asian Kong clone that attempted to steal a march on Paramount's big budget remake. This was the 1976 South Korean production known in the West as *APE*. On the posters it was spelled out *A*P*E* in an attempt to link it in the public's mind with the similarly billed *M*A*S*H*. The distant connection was that both were set in Korea, and involved military operations of some sort. (Altman's film had also just been released on video – one of the first major films to be available in the new format.)

Unlike Japan, South Korea is not known for its giant monster movies. However, there had been a number of them from the early 1960s into the 1970s. The most famous was the 1967 production *Yongary*, a variation on the theme of *Godzilla*, which was released in the US as *Yongary: Monster from the Deep*. In the same year came the much more obscure *Monster Wangmagwi*. Interestingly, this one has a definite *Kong* influence. Its titular creature is a kind of giant apelike robot that is sent to earth by evil aliens who use it to destroy Seoul. The monster captures a young bride in her wedding gown and carries her in the palm of its huge hand as it goes about its work of destruction. There are even suggestions of a sexual interest by the robot monster in the young woman.

Despite these and a few other examples, giant monster movies never really caught on in South Korea. The lack of special effects expertise and the superiority of the easily available Japanese productions made them a risky proposition. However, this did not stop ambitious Korean companies from attempting them. The chance of a foreign sale made them even more attractive, and so the Lee Ming and Kuk Dong companies combined with American director Paul Leder to make a film that marked a new low in international co-production.

Plotwise at least, *APE* is pretty much a *Kong* clone. So much so that Paramount sued. And won. The film's advertising had to be altered to remove *Kong* references. However, there are still several lines of dialogue that link the two pictures: 'If you bump into him, ask him if his name is King Kong,' the leading lady says, on being told that a giant marauding ape is heading her way. Presumably Paramount's executives, on finally seeing the film, decided another court case would only result in extra publicity for a movie already destined for an early grave. However, once again, as with *Mighty Peking Man*, *APE* survived the years and has now been elevated to the overcrowded pantheon of movies that are 'so bad they're good'.

In fact, *APE* is so bad it's bloody appalling. Its main point of interest, apart from its primitive 3D effects, is that it's one of the thankfully few films that show no evidence of talent whatsoever – either in front of or behind the camera. No doubt many of its faults can be put down to the poverty row budget. The film's producers apparently wanted to hire Rick Baker to make the monkey suit. Fresh off the Paramount pic, Baker quoted them a cut price rate – but it was still too much, and they finally bought a secondhand gorilla costume from Hollywood mask specialist Don Post. Frankly, it looks as though the moths got to it first. Then there's the fact that the actor hired to fill the suit seemed entirely clueless as to how a giant ape might actually move. The net result is a feature-length man-in-a-monkey-suit joke that's even more laughable than John Landis's intentional spoof, *Schlock!*. The final nail in the film's coffin is the appearance of a plastic cow, about four inches high, plonked into the middle of a field so that *APE* can step over it. And let's not mention the appalling model work that would shame an 8mm amateur production.

The story begins abruptly on board a ship taking the giant ape ('36 feet tall!') to the US – specifically Disneyland. The ape breaks free and wades into the water, heading for the coast. On the way he grapples with a large plastic shark (*Jaws* reference anyone?). Once on dry land, he then proceeds to stomp all over some very frail (and fake) looking miniature houses. Miraculously, everything he stomps on seems to burst into flames. He heads for Seoul. Cue running, screaming streams of massed Korean extras fleeing the doomed city. Then the ape changes direction ('He's headed for the hills!'). Cue running, screaming extras surging back into town. Of course, it's the same extras and the same running – only the film is flipped to change the direction of the flow.

An American starlet arrives in Seoul to make a movie. A former boyfriend, now a journalist based in Korea, interviews her and their romance starts anew. Needless to say, she soon catches the eye of the mighty ape and is dragged off to his lair. 'Be gentle with me, big fella,' she purrs as she lays back in his giant simian hand. It's one of the last lines of dialogue she utters, as the remainder of the film consists of her doing little more than screaming her head off.

The Korean and US army unite to fight the monster. He has now taken up residence atop a high hill, where he appears to be executing some strange dance steps as bullets and missiles are pumped into him. Tearfully he sets the girl free and resigns himself to his fate. He expires in the usual Kong-like fashion, as a miniature tank fires bullets and toy helicopters buzz through the smoke on not so invisible wires.

The American journo comforts his actress girl-

1990s poster for The Mighty Peking Man *(1977). Made by Hong Kong's Shaw Brothers, it gained cult status when re-released by Quentin Tarantino's Rolling Thunder Pictures.*

Held in the hands of the Mighty Peking Man, Evelyne Kraft evokes both Jessica Lange and Fay Wray.

friend with the immortal line: 'He was just too big for a world as small as ours.'

Paul Leder, the film's director, entered show business as a singer and actor on the New York stage after World War Two. He later graduated to writing and producing, before hitting the director's chair with *The Marigold Man* in 1970. Most of his extensive filmography consists of micro-budgeted exploitation pics, some of which (*My Friends Need Killing*, for example) have acquired a certain reputation. He died in 1996 and is probably best remembered today as the father of Mimi Leder, one of the very few women to make it to the top of the tree as a Hollywood director.

At least Leder doesn't appear to have taken *APE* too seriously. The film has a number of rib-nudging moments that assure us he knew he was dealing in crap. One of the better ones is the ape giving a one-finger salute to a crashing helicopter as it hits a mountain side. Leder's own cameo as the director of the film within the film is also enjoyable. When his blonde starlet complains that the rape scene they are shooting is getting a little too energetic, Leder exhorts the lead actor to 'rape her more gently'.

Whatever his other faults, Leder worked super fast and the film was completed before the De Laurentiis epic. It was picked up for US release by exploitation specialist Jack H. Harris. Famous for his astute marketing of *The Blob*, a 1958 monster movie favourite, Harris gave *APE* a typical huckster's launch. It was released with several different titles, and presumably several different cuts. *Attack of the Giant Horny Gorilla*, *Hideous Mutant* and *Super Kong* were just a few of the many names attached to this insignificant piece of celluloid. The story is that prints were sent to theatres with no title cards. That way it could be promoted as anything the exhibitor thought he could get away with – even as *King Kong*.

On a dollar-spent-to-dollar-earned ratio, this micro-budgeted Korean *Kong* was undoubtedly far more profitable than the De Laurentiis remake. That's exploitation, folks! Or more accurately, APESploitation.

HIS MAJESTY, *KING KONG* – X
KING KONG LIVES

By Donald F. Glut

Before the original *King Kong* was released in 1933, the story was run in an issue of the pulp publication *Mystery Magazine*. It was this *King Kong* that had lapsed into the public domain and fed the controversies surrounding the *King Kong* remakes of the 1970s. *King Kong* was directed toward a more general audience and consequently omitted many of the film's monster sequences. Editor Forrest J. Ackerman wrote in the missing scenes when he reprinted *King Kong* in his magazine *Famous Monsters of Filmland*, issues no. 25 (October 1963), 26 (January 1964) and 27 (March 1964). They became part of the magazine's three-part series, *The Kong of Kongs*.

The actual novel of *King Kong* was written by Delos W. Lovelace and published in 1932 by Grosset and Dunlap. There were some differences, such as Denham's final lines ('It was Beauty. As always, Beauty killed the Beast') to the police sergeant while looking down at the dead ape from the parapet of the Empire State Building. In 1976, in the midst of the Kong-mania aroused by Dino De Laurentiis' remake, at least four reprints of the novel were in the book stores, including *The Illustrated King Kong* from Grosset and Dunlap. That year Grosset and Dunlap also issued a simplified version of the story *King Kong; A Picture Book*.

Mark of the Beast, a mid-1960s novel by John E. Miller, published in England by Badger Books, had a scientist create an enormous ape in his laboratory. The cover depicted a gorilla, obviously patterned physically after Kong, rampaging through a metropolis. William Rotsler's novel *To the Land of the Electric Angel* (Ballantine Books, 1976) featured a King Kong robot, eight stories high, who snatches up a woman and then battles fighter planes until its destruction in a futuristic Roman style arena. Rotsler wrote the story long before De Laurentiis announced his own anthropoid robot.

My Side (Collier Books), 'by King Kong as told to Walter Wager', was the huge ape's supposed autobiography, loaded with obvious jokes and anachronisms. *Kong* reveals that he was born on February 29, 1912, to a gorilla father and human mother. He was named Stan Kong and grew to a height of nearly 132 feet. The narrator goes on to tell how the natives on his island were actually a shipwrecked *Porgy and Bess* stock company. When the ship finally came with its motion picture crew, Captain Englehorn was actually a Nazi and Ann Darrow was in reality an American undercover agent hunting down Communist spies. Kong, according to *Kong*, had been tricked by Denham into appearing in the RKO movie under the pretext that he was to essay the role of King Lear. And only the destructive scenes in New York were performed by O'Brien's miniature dummy. Years after the completion of *King Kong*, the ape went on to star in his Japanese outing with Godzilla, enter politics and finally retire.

Robert Bloch's short story *The Plot Is the Thing* (1966) climaxed with the protagonist's being dragged off to become Kong's 'bride'. *Fay Was a Darn Nice Girl*, published in 1969 by the *New York Times* was writer Arnold M. Auerbach's alleged interview with the retired King Kong on his island home. Kong explains how he and not an animated miniature starred in *King Kong* and that only his death scenes were simulated with a model. That same year the *New York Times* printed *Portnoy's Mother's Complaint*, by Russell Baker. Mrs. Portnoy identifies with Fay Wray, whom she resembled in her youth, and sees her husband as Kong. Philip José Farmer's delightful *After King Kong Fell*, first published in *Omega* (Walker and Co., 1973), reveals that *King Kong* was based on actual events. Written with an obvious love for the picture, the story is about a man who was a child in the theatre the night that Kong escaped. Kong's appearance in New York arouses the interest of two unidentified superheroes of the 1930s, obviously Doc Savage and the Shadow. The protagonist of the story had grieved over Kong's death – and also for his beloved aunt who, with her lover, had been crushed beneath the monster's corpse. The story also described the lawsuits that resulted from Kong's rampage, revealed how the ape apparently did have sex with Ann Darrow and told how Denham, after another voyage to Skull Island, was slain by the witch doctor who had lost his towering god. A *King Kong* limerick by Gene Gallatin appeared in *Famous Monsters of Filmland* no. 102 (October 1973).

Gallery magazine published a satire *Queen Kong* in 1975. Brandon French demonstrated his abilities to imitate the styles of various writers in his retelling of the *King Kong* plotline, *King Kong: As it might be told by Joseph Conrad, Charlotte Bronte, Ernest Hemmingway [sic], Jonathan Swift, Samuel Robertson, and William Faulkner in a celestial story conference.* A collection of Kong type stories *The Rivals of King Kong*, edited by Michel Parry, was set for publication by Corgi Books in 1977. (Following *The Rivals of King Kong* will probably be *The Rivals of the Wolf Man* and *The Rivals of Godzilla*.)

The best of the many non-fiction books about the mighty ape was *The Making of King Kong* (A. S. Barnes and Co., 1975), by Orville Goldner (a technician on the original *King Kong*) and George E. Turner. The book covered virtually every aspect of the RKO classic's production. The text was supplemented by over 160 photographs and pieces of artwork and remains a real credit to its authors and a lasting tribute to the film.

The Making of King Kong was followed by a deluge of Kong-related non-fiction books once the Paramount and Universal remakes became big news. *Ape: The Kingdom of Kong* (Lorrimer Publishing, 1975), which is also known under the title *Ape: Monster of the Movies*, treated movie simians in general. *The Girl in the Hairy Paw* (Avon Books, 1976), edited by Ronald Gottesman and Harry Geduld, *King Kong Story* (1976), a French book edited by René Chateau, and *The King Kong Story* (Phoebus Publishing Co., 1977), by Jeremy Pascall contained articles, stories, book covers, comic strip pages and other Kong manifestations. Two different Japanese books, each titled *King Kong*, were similar ventures. *The Creation of King Kong* (Pocket Books, 1976), by Bruce Bahrenburg, appeared in bookstores just before the release of the Paramount *King Kong* to extol the questionable virtues of the remake. And *King Kong* the Semple script of

This early 1933 issue of Mystery *magazine features a pulp adaptation of* King Kong, *now long out of copyright.*

that film, was published by Ace Books in 1977.

Grosset & Dunlap published the Kong-inspired *Giant Apes Colouring Book* and *Giant Apes Activity and Games Book* in 1976, both illustrated by Tony Tallarico. Periodicals dedicated to Kong also rode with the publicity of the remake film, among them *Kong News* (a newsletter sent out by Paramount while its *King Kong* was in production), *Kong* (Countryside Communications, 1976), *King Kong! The Monster That Made History* poster magazine (Sportscene Publishers, 1977), *King of the Monsters* (Cousins Publications, 1977) and a Japanese *King Kong* magazine. *King Kong* a musical stage play that premiered in South Africa and then moved to London in 1961, was not about the famed gorilla. It was a biography of the Zulu boxer Ezekiel Dhlamini who was known as 'King Kong'. The more traditional Kong did, however, appear several times on stage, though not with impact of his Carl Denham booking. Philip Morris used an ape-suited actor called King Kong in his stage show *Macabro expectáculo* which played in Mexico. Maureen Stapleton played a character who fantasizes being carried off by Kong in *The Secret Affairs of Mildred Wild*, a play by Paul Zindel presented in 1972 at New York's Ambassador Theatre. The highlight of the musical *Clams on the Half Shell* (1975) at New York's Minskoff Theatre was a scene with Bette Midler sitting and singing in Kong's giant hand, with the Empire State Building sinking in the background, simulating their ascent.

King Kong's roars were first broadcast over the radio on the night of February 10, 1933, in a special presentation written by Russell Birdwell, edited by H. N. Swanson and heard over the National Broadcasting Company. Besides providing listeners with interviews with Cooper and O'Brien, the show presented capsulized scenes from the upcoming motion picture *King Kong*. In the 1970s, Kong also was the basis for the 'King Cub' radio commercials for Datsun automobiles and some Arctic Circle stores commercials.

Kong's television appearances were more numerous. He has been seen in various incarnations on *Super Circus* (Gnik Gnok), *The Tonight Show*, *Sinister Cinema*, *Sonny and Cher*, *Horror Theatre* (Kong's son Ping Pong), Bob Clampett's *Time for Beany* (Ping Pong, played on various occasions by George Barrows and Walker Edmiston), *The Ghost Busters* (Bob Burns as Tracy, the ape's head made by Rick Baker; Forrest Tucker as Tracy's human partner Kong), Japan's *Kikaider* (superhero vs. the missile-firing Blue Kong, a type of combination ape-bulldog monster), *Saturday Night*, *Fright Night* (Los Angeles), *The 49th Annual Academy Awards*, *Donny and Marie*, the special *Halleluja, Horrorwood*, and cartoon series like *Frankenstein, Jr.* and *The Underdog Show*.

RKO licensed its simian superstar to Videocraft International in 1966 for a series of King Kong colour cartoons for television's children's market on the ABC network. The show premiered as an hour-long 'movie' titled *King Kong* which loosely followed the plotline of the 1933 film. Dr. Nelson, a scientist, and his two children discover Kong on Mondo Island. Kong proves to be an amiable oaf, who saves the family from an attacking carnivorous dinosaur. As per the RKO movie, Kong is finally brought back to New York where he climbs the Empire State Building. This time, however, he climbs back down, surviving into a string of fantastic adventures on the series. Kong's major adversary in these cartoons was the insidious Dr. Who, who managed to materialise as a flesh and blood character in the feature-length movie *Kingu Kongu no Gyakushu*.

Another of television's giant ape cartoon shows was *The Great Grape Ape*, produced by Hanna-Barbera Productions. The hero, a huge purple ape wearing a jacket and baseball cap, blunders through his misadventures, somehow managing to defeat the villains. In one episode the Grape Ape substitutes for the malfunctioning, forty-foot-tall 'Tonzilla' gorilla robot that a scientist built to star in a new monster movie. The robot's inventor

rebuilds his creation and has it capture the picture's female star, while Grape Ape goes off to rescue her. There was some merchandising on this character, including a comic book *The Great Grape Ape* (September 1975) from Charlton Publications.

The finest King Kong footage ever made for television appeared in a Volkswagen 411 commercial made by David Allen. The commercial, titled *King Kong*, depicts the mighty ape (animated model) battling the airplanes in the famous Empire State Building sequence. The only real difference between this and the 1933 footage is that the commercial was shot in colour. Instead of falling to his death, Kong grabs one of the planes, tucks it under a hairy arm and climbs back to the street. After tossing the craft into the trunk of a huge Volkswagen 411, Kong and his miniature 'date' (played by Vickie Riskin, the daughter of Fay Wray) drive off as the ape waves goodbye through an open window.

Dave Allen shot some test footage, quite similar to that which appeared in the Volkswagen commercial, at Cascade Pictures in 1970 when Hammer Films was investigating the possibilities in remaking *King Kong*. 'I made it as a portfolio piece,' Allen said to me. 'I quite keenly enjoyed doing it. I wouldn't have done it if I weren't so overly enthusiastic about the original *King Kong*.' When the Hammer project was shot down like Kong himself, Allen cut his footage into a Cascade sample film that went out to various advertising agencies. The Volkswagen people, realizing that 1930s nostalgia was viable in America at the time, were interested in using Kong to promote their product. A number of production companies, thinking in terms of a gorilla-suited actor, bid for the Volkswagen project. When Volkswagen executives viewed Allen's sample in the Cascade reel, their decision had been made.

One close-up, showing Kong's hand working the shift, required a non-animated Kong. Gorilla impersonators George Barrows and Janos Prohaska were both considered for the job but the part eventually went to Rick Baker, years before the Paramount remake. Allen animated his foot-high Kong model with affection. *King Kong* was enthusiastically received by the viewers, but dismally by the advertising agency. The agency people felt that it conveyed a false impression of the Volkswagen 411's actual size. They also feared that viewers might believe that apes drove their automobiles. When an executive's daughter was literally frightened by the commercial, that only contributed to its being quickly pulled from the network programming. Fortunately at least some of

'Ping Pong!' makes 'em hear for the hills in issue six of Mad *(August-September 1953).* Mad, *then in comic-book format, has since produced numerous Kong parodies.*

Kong's appreciators were able to see this priceless piece of film.

Less imaginative television commercials utilizing King Kong were made for Gatorade, Dodge, Datsun (King Kab), Ford (Bob Burns as Kong), Kitty Salmon, the Woolworth stores, Ames Home Loan (Kong smashing a window and then turning to face the airplanes) and Yale Auto Loans.

A *King Kong* comic strip was serialised in French newspapers in 1948, but the story-line did not follow the 1933 motion picture. Western Publishing Company (Gold Key) issued its own *King Kong* comic book in 1968. The story was based on the Grosset and Dunlap novel and the artwork, though fine in its own right, bore little resemblance to actual characters or scenes from the motion picture. (In 1977 a giant-sized reprint of this book was issued by Western.) Years before, Western (then under the Dell Comics banner) featured a King Kong-influenced story in *Turok, Son of Stone* no. 6 (December-February 1957). 'The Giant Ape' was about a Kong-sized gorilla ruling a mesa desired by a tribe of cave people in a prehistoric valley of America's South-west. Weakened by a poisoned arrow, the gorilla falls off a cliff. Western's *Underdog* comic book featured 'King Gong' in its tenth issue (December 1976), a villainous mechanical giant ape who falls off the Umpire State Building upon sighting the heroine standing in the street.

One of the earliest (and best) comic book lampoons of *King Kong* was 'Ping Pong!' in the sixth issue of *Mad* (August-September 1953), published by EC (Entertaining Comics). Drawn by Bill Elder, the excellent satire climaxes with Pong's transport to New York, where the unimpressed population is larger than he. When *Mad* changed from colour comic book to the more sophisticated black and white magazine format, it frequently made use of the King Kong character. In particular, *Mad* no. 94 (April 1965) featured 'Son of Mighty Joe Kong', written by Dick de Bartolo and drawn by Mort Drucker. James Garner, Doris Day and Dick Van Dyke are characters who find the titled ape in the African jungle and bring him to New York to star in his own Broadway dance routine. It is Doris Day (as Rae Faye) who climbs the Empire State Building when Kong refuses to marry her. She jumps; but Kong, signing an autograph, fails to catch her. *Mad* finally spoofed the De Laurentiis *King Kong* in its 192nd issue (July 1977) with 'King Korn', written by Dick de Bartolo and illustrated by Harry North.

National Periodical Publications (DC Comics) has contributed to Kong's mythology. 'The Gorilla Boss of Gotham City!' was featured in *Batman* no. 75 (February-March 1953). The brain of executed criminal George 'Boss' Dyke is transplanted into the head of the world's biggest gorilla. The gigantic monster creates a wave of crime and destruction. The story included the necessary scene of the giant ape, with the apparent figure of Batman tucked under one arm, ascending a television tower to confront an attacking Batplane.

The Boy of Steel met his own Kong-like adversary in the Superboy story 'Kingorilla!' in *Adventure Comics* no.196 (January 1954). Kingorilla guards a giant Oriental idol in a lost jungle and tries to devour Superboy before the flying hero, apparently refusing to be another Fay Wray, knocks him unconscious.

National introduced its own Konglike continuing character in *Superman* no. 127 (February 1959). 'Titano the Super-Ape!' told of a chimpanzee named Toto who is sent into space in an artificial satellite. When Toto is bathed in the radiation of two colliding meteors, one uranium and the other kryptonite, he becomes a giant chimp upon returning to Earth. The ape, now called Titano, has also acquired kryptonite-vision which makes him a deadly threat to the Man of Steel. Superman finally hurls Titano into the prehistoric past to live among creatures his own size.

Titano had mysteriously become a giant gorilla when he returned in another story titled 'Titano the Super-Ape', in *Superman* no. 138 (July 1960). Titano is brought back to the twentieth century by a time-transporter, where he climbs the Daily Planet Building to suggest yet another Empire State Building image. Both 'Titano the Super Ape!' tales were drawn by Wayne Boring. More allusions to King Kong were made in 'Krypto Battles Titano!' in *Superman* no. 147 (August 1961). Titano battles three tyrannosaurs simultaneously before making friends with Superman's super-dog. An unusual digression from the Titano stories occurred in the *Tales of the Bizarro World* series in *Adventure Comics* no. 295 (April 1962). 'The Kookie Super-Ape!' was illustrated by John Forte. It introduced a 'Bizarro' duplicate of Titano (created from lifeless matter by means of a duplicator ray focused on the original ape) who becomes a professional wrestler. The Japanese film *Kingu Kongu tai Gojira* received some spoofing in 'Jimmy Olsen's Monster Movie!' which Curt Swan illustrated for *Superman's Pal, Jimmy Olsen* no. 84 (April 1965). Newspaper reporter Olsen transports both Titano and the fire-breathing Flame Dragon of Krypton to battle each other for a new horror film.

'The Super Gorilla from Krypton', drawn by Wayne Boring for the *Superman* strip in *Action Comics* no. 238 (March 1958), featured King Krypton, a huge gorilla with the Man of Steel's powers. But the ape finally reveals himself as a scientist from Superman's home world, changed into a gorilla by a backfiring evolution machine. The Man of Steel himself aped the famous RKO character in 'When Superman Was King Kong!' in *Superman* no. 226 (May 1970), drawn by Curt Swan. Clark Kent is affected by red kryptonite, which always affects him unpredictably, while attending a screening of *King Kong*. Bursting from his Kent disguise, Superman shoots up to become a growling giant, even carrying girlfriend Lois Lane to the top of the suspiciously familiar Metro Building to battle some

'Son of Mighty Joe Kong' is the obvious generic title of this April 1965 Mad *magazine parody, with cover boy Alfred E. Neuman switching positions with the Great Ape.*

fighter planes. He falls to the street unharmed and, after creating more havoc, regains his normal size. It is Titano, snatched from his current domain, a planet of giants, who dons Superman's costume to allow both a normal-sized Kent and the 'Man' of Steel to appear briefly together.

National spoofed the 1933 movie with 'King Klonk, the Killer Gorilla' in *The Adventures of Jerry Lewis* no. 85 (January-February 1965), written by Arnold Drake and drawn by Bob Oksner. After falling in love with Lewis, Klonk is floated by four blimps from his jungle home to the United States where, after performing a number of demeaning show business routines, he goes berserk. Klonk combats a squad of ape-suited policemen before floating back home. *Kamandi, The Last Boy on Earth* no. 7 (July 1973), written, drawn, and edited by Jack Kirby, was a tribute to *King Kong* with the titled young hero substituting for Ann Darrow. Kamandi is captured by the future world's animal-men and tied to a stake and offered to an enormous talking gorilla called Tiny. The ape regards Kamandi as a toy and, after reviving from a temporary shot from a chemical shell, seeks him out in the city, then carries him to the top of a skyscraper for a re-enactment, complete with biplanes, of the obligatory Empire State Building climax. 'Kongzilla!' was a parody of two movie monsters, written by George Evans and drawn by Frank Robbins, and published in the first issue of *Plop!* (September-October 1973). Kongzilla, a huge apelike monster with a reptile's hind legs and tail, stalks a young newlywed couple through the city streets. But it is the husband instead of the wife that Kongzilla finally abducts, proving to be a female of this monstrous species. In the winter of 1976, National reprinted several of their gorilla stories including 'The Super-Gorilla from Krypton' and 'The Gorilla Boss of Gotham City!' in the first issue of *Super-Heroes Battle Super-Gorillas*.

The Marvel Comics Group changed the *King Kong* theme somewhat, though its inspiration was quite evident, in 'I Discovered Gorgilla! The Monster of Midnight Mountain!' in *Tales to Astonish* no. 12 (October 1960). Gorgilla is a huge apelike missing link with a long furry tail. When the explorers who think to capture the brute are saved by Gorgilla from an attacking tyrannosaurus they let him remain in his lost world. But Gorgilla himself made the journey to civilization in 'Gorgilla Strikes Again!' in *Tales to Astonish* no. 18 (April 1961). Stowing away aboard a ship, Gorgilla reaches New York, hides within the city's sewers and bursts free through the playing field of Yankee Stadium (most likely an inadvertent enactment of a scene originally planned for the 1933 *King Kong*) Gorgilla's rampage through the city is climaxed with a climb up, not the Empire State Building, but the Statue of Liberty from which he is shot by a bazooka. Both Gorgilla tales were drawn by Jack Kirby.

Marvel's *Nick Fury, Agent of SHIELD* no. 2 (July 1968) featured a giant robot Kong, a prop for an intended motion picture, which battles a real tyrannosaurus on a prehistoric island. Jim Steranko both wrote and illustrated the story. Another *King Kong* spoof appeared in *Not Brand Echh* no. 11 (December 1968). 'King Konk', by writer Roy Thomas and artist Tom Sutton, brought the giant gorilla to civilization where he battles parodies of Marvel's comic book heroes. Finally he leaps from the Empire State Building into the East River to swim back home. Thomas and artist Gil Kane paid tribute to *King Kong* in 'Walk the Savage Land!' in *The Amazing Spider-Man* no. 103 (December 1971). Newspaper publisher J. Jonah Jameson leads an expedition to a prehistoric realm to get a photo story on a legendary monster called Gog. Jameson brings along blonde and beautiful Gwen Stacy to give his story sex appeal. He sounds the gong which brings the orange, scaly Gog out of the jungle. Gog carries off Gwen and is soon combating a tyrannosaurus in the follow-up issue's (January 1972) story, 'Beauty and the Brute', in which the creature is revealed as a being from another planet. Gog's final stand on this world was high above New York, each foot straddling a tower of the World Trade Centre (three years before Paramount's *King Kong*), in 'Gog Cometh!' The story was published in the *Kazar* strip in the 18th issue (June 1973) of *Astonishing Tales*, written by Mike Friedrich and drawn by Dan Adkins.

'Death Is a Golden Gorilla!' was another Kong tribute by Roy Thomas, illustrated by George Perez for *Fantastic Four* no. 171 (June 1976). A gigantic auric gorilla emerges from a crashed space-ship and is soon crashing its way through New York. A bystander makes a timely comment: 'I thought this was just a publicity stunt for one of those *new movies* about *King Kong*!' This time the ape (named Gorr) ascends the Baxter Building, headquarters of the superhero group, the Fantastic Four. Defeated by the heroes, Gorr shrinks to normal gorilla size before toppling from the roof and being saved from death on the pavement by the Fantastic Four.

Crazy, Marvel's black and white humour magazine, featured another movie spoof, 'Kink Konk', in issue no. 19 (August 1976), written by Len Herman. Ernie Colon adapted some photographs from the 1933 movie to augment his artwork. Konk falls from his familiar skyscraper perch, being unaccustomed to the shoes he is wearing ('. . . 'twas booties that killed the beast!'). After the release of the Paramount *King Kong*, 'New TV Spinoffs for King Kong' was featured in *Crazy* no. 24 (April 1977). Kong is shown in parodies of currently popular television shows in this satire by Jim Simon, Jayson Wechter and artist Murad Gumen. 'Kink Konk Goes on Television', by Len Herman and artist Alan Kupperberg in *Crazy* no. 26 (June 1977), had the ape lampooning various popular television programmes. He finally climbs the 'Neelson Tower Building' to reach the top in the ratings, only to be shot down by critics.

Other comics publishers also realised the potential in graphically portraying Kong-like characters. Radio Comics' *Adventures of the Fly* no. 10 (January 1961) included 'The World of the Giant Gorillas!' Superheroes the Fly and the Black Hood find a tribe of Kong-type apes living in a prehistoric world in an Indian jungle. These apes, however, possess nearly human intelligence through a quirk of evolution. One ape rescues the heroes from a brontosaur. The Fly returns the favour by summoning a swarm of prehistoric insects to save the gorillas from an ambushing herd of tyrannosaurs. A series called *Mytek the Mighty*, about a Kong-like gorilla robot, was featured in issues of the British comic paper *Valiant* (Fleetway Publications) in 1965. Mytek was built by Professor Boyce in the shape of the Akari apegod in order to pacify that warlike Central African tribe. As might be expected, the robot falls under the control of a would-be tyrant.

America's Best Comics, published by the American Broadcasting Company in 1967, featured a story based on the 'King Kong' television cartoon series. Simply titled 'King Kong', it brought the good-natured gorilla to the city where he saves it from some wild animals that had escaped from a circus. *The Friendly Ghost Casper* no. 129 (May 1960), from Harvey Comics, presented 'So This Is Ding Dong?' With good witch Wendy clutched in one paw, Ding Dong climbs the Empire State Building until his angry father, Bing Bong, orders him down. 'Sacrifice!' was a *King Kong* spoof written by John Simons and drawn by Steve Hickman for *The Monster Times* no. 7 (April 26, 1972). Kong carries Ann Darrow to his skull-shaped lair and disrobes her. Then, before a perplexed Ann, he complacently eats the clothes. A comic-strip version of 'King Kong vs. Godzilla' appeared in *England's Legend Horror Classics* (1975). Jules Feiffer depicted Richard M. Nixon as Kong destroying the Government in his 'Feiffer' strip for the April 25, 1974, issue of *The Village Voice*. And numerous newspaper comic strips either spoofed or referred to the King while the De Laurentiis *King Kong* was still in the news.

Major Magazines' *Cracked* no. 139 (January 197[7]) featured 'The Men Behind Kong', about the people who constantly groom the big ape to maintain his public image. 'King Kung' in the next issue of *Cracked* (March 1977) spoofed the De Laurentiis picture with John Severin on the art. *Cracked* no. 141 (May 1977) followed with 'King Kong's Boyhood', with the baby ape growing up in Africa, finding life difficult due to his increasing size and inevitably entering the movies.

Sick no. 112 (October 1976), from Charlton Publications, reviewed the mythical book *Loves of Kong*, which was supposed to be the ape's autobiography. 'King Dong (or Monkey Business in the Bush)', in the third issue of Cousins Publications' *Goose* had the giant ape exposed as a costumed basketball player. Nevertheless his captured bride bears him two healthy infant gorillas. Wallace Wood's beautifully rendered Sally Forth comic strip, published in *The Overseas Weekly*, spoofed the old fashioned horror films from November 1976 through February 1977. The lovely heroine encountered various incarnations of Lawrence Talbot (whose lycanthropic form Ms. Forth mistook for a 'doggie'), the Mummy, Frankenstein's Monster, Dracula and a huge Kong-like gorilla. The evil Captain Meno exchanges Sally's mind with that of the ape and soon the thinking, talking anthropoid is pursuing a growling naked woman through New York's streets. Finally the Ape with Sally's mind chases the woman with the ape's mind up the Empire State Building to be attacked by biplanes from an antique airplane show.

One of the most unusual Kong-inspired graphic story projects occurred at Warren Publishing Company. Publisher James Warren had acquired an unpublished painting by illustrator Frank Frazetta depicting a Kong-sized nude woman atop the Empire State

Building, fighting off biplanes while holding a miniature gorilla in one hand. Sixteen of *Eerie* Magazine's writers and artists were then challenged to create a story based on this painting and including the Frazetta scene. *Eerie* no. 81 (February, 1977) was graced with the Frazetta painting on its cover while seven of the stories inspired by it were published inside. Two of these tales were especially related to the original *King Kong* plotline.

The first, 'The Bride of Congo', written by Bill Dubay and drawn by Carmine Infantino, begins at the conclusion of the 1933 motion picture. Amy La Bido (the Ann Darrow character) yet moons for the huge ape Congo, even after her marriage to Chuck Gauntlet (substituted for Jack Driscoll). Chuck unsuccessfully tries to impress Amy by dressing up in a gorilla suit. When Amy learns that Kong, though weak and battered, had survived the Empire State Building fall, she gives him a transfusion of her rare (type o-gargantua) blood which restores him to health. But some of Congo's blood enters Amy's veins and causes her to grow to the ape's size. With her gorilla-suited husband in one hand, she goes on to live the scene depicted on the Frazetta painting, until Congo himself ascends to fetch her. Congo and Amy return to his domain on 'Noggin' Island where she bears him a healthy hairless ape. 'The Giant Ape Suit', by writer Roger McKenzie and artist Luis Bermejo, revealed that the thirty-foot-tall gorilla that fell from the Empire State Building in 1933 was actually a robot invented and controlled by one Edgar Cooper. Over thirty years later, a scoundrel named Reicher discovers Cooper's other robot creation, a giant mechanical woman. Working the female automaton from within, Reicher hopes to loot New York until Cooper, inside the dilapidated ape robot, pursues him up the Empire State Building, where both of them are destroyed.

International Insanity no. 5 (March 1977) not only featured a pinup of a 'nude' Kong, but also the story 'A Date with Kong', by Judy Brown and Frank Cirocco. The most popular girl in school is escorted to her prom by a smaller-than-usual Kong who falls from a rooftop after slipping on a banana peel.

The sheet music from the original *King Kong* was published during the film's initial release. (The selections were 'The Forgotten Island', 'A Boat in the Fog', 'Aboriginal Sacrifice Dance' and 'King Kong March'.) Max Steiner's score, condensed into the 'King Kong Suite', became part of Jack Shaidlin's album *50 Years of Movie Music* (Decca) in the early 1960s. More selections from *King Kong* were featured on *Max Steiner: The RKO Years* (Max Steiner Music Society) and *Now, Voyager* (RCA,1973), the latter by Charles Gerbhardt and the National Philharmonic Orchestra. (The selections appeared under

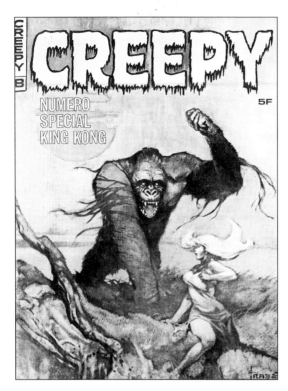

the titles 'The Forgotten Island', 'Natives', 'Sacrificial Dance', 'The Gate of Kong' and 'Kong in New York'.) *King Kong* (United Artists Records, 1975), by LeRoy Holmes, presented the entire Steiner score, unfortunately with limited orchestration. (The individual cuts were now called 'Main Title', 'At the Ship's Rail/Mysterious Seas', 'The Last Port of Call', 'Approaching Kong's Island/ Love Theme', 'Jungle Dance/Anne [sic] Is Offered to Kong', 'Rescue Team Follows Kong and Meets Brontosaur', 'And That Children, Is Why There Is No 6th Avenue "L" Today' and 'Death on the Empire State'.)

A fully orchestrated *King Kong* soundtrack album, authorised by Steiner's estate, was performed by England's National Philharmonic Orchestra conducted by Fred Steiner and issued in 1977 by Entr-acte Recording Society. (The cuts were listed as 'Main Title; A Boat in the Fog', 'The Forgotten Island; Jungle Dance', 'The Sea at Night', 'Aboriginal Sacrifice Dance', 'The Entrance of Kong', 'The Bronte; Log Sequence', 'Cryptic Shadows', 'Kong; The Cave', 'Sailors Waiting', 'The Return of Kong', 'King Kong Theatre March', and 'Kong Escapes; Aeroplanes; Finale'.) *King Kong*, a soundtrack album of John Barry's music from the Paramount remake film, was issued by the Dino De Laurentiis Corporation in 1976. (Included on the album were 'The Opening', 'Maybe My Luck Has Changed', 'Arrival on the island', 'Sacrifice – Hail to the King', 'Arthusa', 'Full Moon Domain – Beauty is a Beast', 'Break-out to Captivity', 'Incomprehensible Captivity', 'Kong Hits the Big Apple', 'Blackout in New York or How About Buying Me a Drink', 'Climb to Skull Island', 'The End is at Hand' and 'The End'.) The theme music from the Paramount *King Kong* was also issued on a single recording in a new disco version. Todd Matshikiza's music and Pat Williams' lyrics from the play about Ezekiel Dhlamini were made available on another *King Kong* (Decca) album.

There were more frivolous King Kong records. 'I Go Ape' (RCA) was a late 1950s rock 'n' roll record using the King written and recorded by Neil Sedaka. 'King Kong Stomp' was featured on the album *Dracula's Greatest Hits* in the mid-1960s. 'Science Fiction/Double Feature', on *The Rocky Horror Show* and *The Rocky Horror Picture Show* albums of the mid-1970s' used the character. In 1956 Bobby Pickett released his own 'King Kong' (Polydor) record tribute to the 1933 film. In a cut also titled 'King Kong' the mighty ape fights a giant sea monster off the coast of Japan, on the album *Sounds of Terror*. A Bob Newhart comedy album from Warner Brothers Records featured the monologue 'The Night Watchman', in which the titled character's first night on the job at the Empire State Building coincides with Kong's famous climb.

A serious attempt at presenting the Kong story in the fashion of radio drama was the album *King Kong* (Golden Records), produced about 1965. Adapted by Cherney Berg and directed by Daniel Ocko, the story was presented in two parts, 'Journey to the Island' and 'The Capture, Triumph and Death of King Kong'. Ocko played Captain Englehorn (who was the narrator), Nat Pollen played Driscoll, Ralph Bell was Denham and Elaine Host played 'Anne'. The changes from the original *King Kong* plotline included Denham and Driscoll getting into a fistfight en route to Kong's island, his battling a palaeoscincus (actually an armoured herbivore instead of the flesh-eater described on the record) in place of the tyrannosaurus and Driscoll and Anne getting married by Englehorn aboard his ship. The recording may have been played over some stations as a radio play.

That *King Kong* has achieved mythical status is reinforced by the fact that his image is recognisable to millions of persons throughout the world. His giant-sized image (twelve feet tall) can be viewed in amusement parks and wax museums thanks to a model made available through Hollywood's Don Post Studios. Another attraction, called 'Kong, eighth Wonder of the World', graces a New Jersey Amusement Park; and there is even a King Kong Memorial dominated by a life-sized reproduction of the character. Kong's image has appeared in advertising for a King Con fantasy films convention, for Moore Fabrics, Ronrico rum, Artists Entertainment Complex, Libbey-Owens-Ford glass, Potrazebie, Inc. (Brooklyn Heights pottery studio), American Express, a Cincinnati delicatessen (Kosherilla), American Sound Company (Ampzilla), Strathmore paper products, the Fort Worth *Star-Telegram*, Steak & Brew (New York), Mother's Cookies, Darco East (Cleveland), *The Monster Times*, Dave Bromberg's *Wanted Dead or Alive* (Columbia) record album, Datsun (King Kab), and the television show, *Fernwood 2 Night*.

In addition to all the other King Kong merchandise that had been appearing in stores for years, a new plethora of Kong-related products was unleashed in 1976 and 1977 in association with the Paramount remake. These included King Kong Viewmaster reels from the GAF Corporation, Slurpees, posters, keychains (containing horsehair from the giant Kong robot), iron-on transfers, T-shirts, Sedgefield Jeans, Schrafft's chocolate and peanut butter candy, a china bust from Jim Beam bourbon (including a King Kong cocktail), Halloween costumes and other paraphernalia. In Los Angeles both a King Kong restaurant and a King Kong Klub opened about the same time as De Laurentiis' movie. Certainly 1977 was the Year of the Ape.

As Carl Denham said in 1933, Kong was a 'King and a God'. But the mighty Kong found his Skull Mountain throne threatened by an upstart from prehistory. This usurper arose from the waters off the shores of Japan and announced his presence with a blast of his destructive radioactive breath. The world would soon recognise him as the new King of the Monsters.

KING KONG LIVES:
IS IT MONKEY SEQUEL, MONKEY DO?
By Will Murray

King Kong isn't giving interviews today. The 60-foot ape lies stretched out on a hospital green platform on Soundstage Four, his barrel chest cut open. Electrodes run from his sleeping head. His wrists and ankles are manacled and a vicious circular bone saw is suspended over his open chest.

Grips sleep at his feet, giving new meaning to the phrase, 'Monkey see, monkey do.' And in a corner of the set, the god of Skull Island's own anatomically-correct rubber and silicon heart sits on a plastic tarpaulin. Beside it hangs a three-foot-tall device known to cast and crew as the Jarvik 7000 mechanical heart.

Director John Guillermin is waving a green flag in front of the glass-enclosed press booth, which is set high above the Atlantic Institute set. Star Brian Kerwin, almost unrecognisable in a group of extras, is reacting to Guillermin's suggested scene.

Guillermin shakes the flag, which represents the Jarvik 7000 suspended over Kong's gaping chest, and the press surges to the glass. Then, a camera flashes. Others follow.

Guillermin calls cut. 'No flashes!' he barks. 'And stop smiling back there.'

'Monkey see, monkey do' seems to be the operative phrase on this set. John Guillermin isn't giving interviews, either.

'He's feisty,' explains production designer Peter Murton, who was asked to join this film after working with Guillermin on *Sheena*. 'But he's one of the most professional and organised directors I've ever worked with. You don't mind people being difficult if they're right. I've never known him to insist on a downright bad decision. He listens. He's not dogmatic.'

Murton is discussing the secrets behind the giant Kong of *King Kong Lives!* Essentially, it is a sophisticated inflatable doll with crawlspaces inside for crew members to manually operate certain breathing features.

'You can make it mechanical,' Murton explains, 'and it *looks* mechanical. It's a funny thing. You can spend thousands of dollars, but there is that little out-of-sync thing with a human hand on it that's much more *convincing*.'

Murton is alluding to the multi-million dollar Kong robot built by Carlo (*E.T.*) Rambaldi for Dino De Laurentiis' 1976 remake, which was also directed by Guillermin. That Kong appeared in only one brief scene due to an insurmountable technical problem: it didn't work. This inflatable Kong is a descendant of the Rambaldi robot.

'We're using the same face mold for Kong, as it was ten years ago,' Murton reveals. 'So, *never* throw anything away!'

In fact, this Kong is twins. With the Kong head in place, he's King Kong. With the alternate head, he becomes a she: Lady Kong. And therein lies the plot to Dino De Laurentiis' sequel, *King Kong Lives!*

King Kong has lain in an incurable coma for ten years. But with the modern strides in artificial heart transplantation, it becomes feasible to instal a mechanical ticker in Kong's barrel chest. There's just one hitch.The operation is impossible without a transfusion of Kong blood.

Enter Lady Kong. She's discovered in Borneo by a not-so-intrepid adventurer named Hank Mitchell, played by Brian (*Murphy's Romance*) Kerwin. Lady Kong is brought to the States for the operation performed by Dr. Amy Franklin, a role essayed by Linda (*Terminator*) Hamilton. Kerwin and Hamilton share *one* of the film's love stories.

'We start out at odds with each other,' Kerwin notes. 'She doesn't like me. I don't like her. I don't like the way she wants to treat my ape. She doesn't like the way I want to treat her ape. We are forced to work together because the two apes escape. In order to keep the Army from killing them, we have to pool our resources and go off into the mountains to find the apes on our own.'

Contrary to what one might expect, Linda Hamilton is *not* playing the Fay

Wray/Jessica Lange role. Brian Kerwin is. But he's playing his interspecies romance opposite *Lady* Kong.

'I like it,' Kerwin says. 'I hope it does for me what it did for Jessica Lange. The best character in any monster movie is being the monster's *friend*. And it's fun riding in the hand. I'm the *only* one who gets to do it.'

This is a fact that relieves Linda Hamilton no end. 'I'm happy that I don't have to get picked up by the monkey and become the object of his *desire*,' she admits. 'I *save* Kong. And it's nice to play someone who is not hysterical and dramatic and intense *all* the time.'

Hamilton is not concerned about working in a sequel to a remake that wasn't a critical success or a box office bonanza.

'I feel very good that I'm involved in a Kong movie, because it's a legend,' she reasons. 'And there's no way it will ever *not* be a legend. Whether it fails or not, it's *still* a Kong film.'

John Ashton, who as Sgt. Taggart chased Eddie Murphy in *Beverly Hills Cop*, shares Hamilton's attitude, although he expresses himself differently. 'It's a special effects movie,' Ashton counters. 'And King Kong's the star of it. Acting is really secondary. You just play it as *straight* as you can and let it all develop from there.'

Ashton plays Colonel Nevitt. According to everyone else on the set, he's the villain. But Ashton doesn't see it quite that way.

'He's just a guy who's an Army colonel assigned to capture King Kong and Lady Kong. When King Kong starts kicking over all his tanks and jeeps, he gets carried away with his assignment. Instead of capturing him, he wants to *kill* him. I consider him a guy who's only doing his job. He just gets a little *overzealous*.'

At one point, the big ape got a little overzealous and almost squished Ashton for real. 'We had some shots in Tennessee with helicopters hovering over us at about ten feet,' Ashton relates. 'There were three of them and their props were almost touching each other. They lift Lady Kong. I was standing right next to her and she weighs five tons. Instead of swinging one way, she started coming *at* me! I'm playing this macho colonel and suddenly, I said, "I'm out of here, man!" *That* was scary.'

In *King Kong Lives!*, the various Kongs are not always played by giant furry airbags. There will be no stop-motion animation used in this film because of time constraints, but there will be some miniatures on miniature sets. For the most part, however, King Kong will be played by a man in a suit.

You can't keep a Great Ape down – even after he's been riddled with bullets and fallen from the Twin Towers. In King Kong Lives, *he's revived by a handy artificial heart.*

Special effects master Carlo Rambaldi's workshop is easy to find. Although tucked away hidden in a far corner of the De Laurentiis Entertainment Group's Wilmington, North Carolina lot, you can't miss it. A giant ape's arm reaches out of the half-open corrugated door. You have to squeeze past it to enter.

Inside, Kong's prop arm terminates abruptly. The rest of him, not to the same scale, lies inside the hangarlike interior. A working head sits on a pedestal. A headless apeskin hangs on a hook. Another skin is being dressed by a craftsgirl.

Peter (*Greystoke*) Elliott, whose official title is primate choreographer, is explaining the problems of being King Kong.

'The biggest problems are conceptual,' Elliott observes. 'Kong is a *fantasy* animal. So, we're trying to lose the man in the suit, but have an ape that's *not* an ape and *not* a man. It's finding that fine balance. Kong tends to walk upright more often than a real gorilla or most other primates. Strangely enough, the *biggest* thing is hiding our leg length.'

The other critical elements involved in the Kong suit are the mechanical heads designed by Rambaldi to convey a range of emotions. Rambaldi demonstrates one of his creations, the Lady Kong head, which sits on a pedestal, hooked up to four sets of waist-high levers set on a common base.

Rambaldi strips the skin from the head to reveal the complex wires and rubber muscles that lie under the face.

'Everybody sees the external face,' he notes, 'but 90 percent of the work is inside.'

Replacing the mask, Rambaldi takes a lever in hand, and Lady Kong's lip curls. 'This lever moves this muscle by the cable. This lever is one detail of the mask. Of course, we must combine different expressions,' he explains. Working several levers at once,

Rambaldi brings Lady Kong's face to simian life in an eye-blinking, snout-wrinkling snarl.

'We need seven people to move everything,' Rambaldi adds. 'The seven must coordinate the movement to get anger or surprise.'

According to Rambaldi, no serious thought was given to resurrecting the Kong robot. Building a new, fully functional version was feasible, but not practical.

'With modern technology, it's possible to make a giant Kong,' Rambaldi says, 'but I'm afraid the movie will cost $200 million and three years of shooting.'

Later, Peter Elliott is going through a battle scene between Kongs and US Army. This is the second attempt to film this difficult shot. The day before, when Kong collapsed in a hail of automatic weapons fire, the blood squibs sewn into his suit worked *too* well, and the cast, crew and entire set were drenched in a sanguinary storm. It has taken a full day to clean up.

Amid the smell of incense and bee-smoke, they're trying it again. A miniature barn has been set on a raised stage. Kong looks realistic except for the cables leading out of his hairy rump to the battery of controllers.

On cue, Kong falls, and the Kong crew begin working the levers. Kong's face contorts realistically. Rambaldi seems satisfied with the rehearsal. They're ready to shoot. But a technician manning a spot high above the soundstage calls down that he has a minor problem. Within minutes, he announces the problem is no longer minor. It will be hours before the stubborn scene can be reshot.

It's on days like this that filmmakers wonder if it's all worth it. And walking through the back lot, where among discarded props from other De Laurentiis non-hits like *Maximum Overdrive* and *Year of the Dragon*, the stripped aluminum skeleton of the multi-million dollar Kong robot from 1976 lies cannibalised and useless, you have to wonder yourself.

Not Martha (*Cat's Eye*) Schumacher, however. She's the producer and she's as sure as steel that *King Kong Lives!* will be worth all the bucks and the backache.

'Kong has gotten a lot of air time on television,' she points out. 'In newspapers, there are always jokes about King Kong. People still appreciate Kong. He's a legend. He'll never die. Whether he's dead in a film, he'll never die in our storytelling.'

There's a strange sense of *deja vu* hanging over *King Kong Lives!* It's exactly ten years since Dino De Laurentiis announced his original *Kong* remake for a Christmas 1976 release. Now, with many of the same creative people behind it, they are rushing to meet another self-imposed Christmas release date. An inevitable question comes up: why a sequel and why *now*?

'I think John and Dino have been sleeping with the idea for eight years,' Schumacher says, 'wondering when the time would be right. Successful filmmaking is satisfying an audience. Let's keep them satisfied with a wonderful story. That's what *King Kong Lives!* is. The legend is *back*. He *lives*.'

Is this a fantasy/adventure, or, as some cast members suggest, a romantic comedy about a pair of giant monkeys?

Schumacher pauses for a long, thoughtful moment. 'It combines *all four* into a charming story,' she says at last. 'There is humour. There is adventure. There is hard emotion and also a love story, too. This is not a rip-off of a sequel. It's a *serious* picture. It's not a *joke*.'

KING KONG LIVES

Reviewed by Roger Ebert

Nobody gets thrilled in the movies anymore. They've seen it all.

King Kong is a gorilla that stands 50 feet high, and everybody takes him for granted. Four redneck hunters chase him into the woods, for example, and set off some dynamite to trap him under tons of rocks, and then they tease him with burning logs. If these hunters were sensitive and thoughtful like the folks in the National Rifle Association ads, they wouldn't tease Kong, they'd regard him with a sense of quiet awe and reverence, after setting off the dynamite.

Or take the head of the research institute. He's in charge of a project to supply Kong with an artificial heart. When he's informed that the operation is impossible because of Kong's low blood plasma level, he explodes: 'That heart cost $17 million!' In real life, he would have cackled, '. . . and now we're going to need another huge injection of government research funds to study gorilla blood!' The problem with everyone in *King Kong Lives!* is that they're in a boring movie, and they know they're in a boring movie, and they just can't stir themselves to make an effort. Even the lowliest extras in a 1950s' B picture would have been able to scream better and roll their eyes more than the actors in this film. They act like they've used Kong's tranquiliser gun for target practice on themselves.

The picture's big news: Kong did not die after being machinegunned and falling from the top of the World Trade Centre. (I guessed that from the last picture, in which Kong looked remarkably intact after arriving at street level.) The injured Kong was carted to a university research centre outside Atlanta, where he has lain in a coma for the last decade, awaiting an artificial heart.

Anyway, wouldn't you know, just when things look darkest for Kong, a big-game hunter discovers a female Kong in the jungles of Borneo, and transports her to research headquarters for a transfusion that will make it possible to implant Kong's artificial heart.

After the operation, romance blooms between the two creatures, who break their shackles and escape into the woods, where the Army attempts to shoot them down, while the female heart specialist and the big game hunter (who have taken to sharing sleeping bags) use computers to monitor the big fella's condition.

Every movie like this has at least one amazing line of dialogue. I especially liked it when the heroine cried to the Army troops: 'Don't shoot the female! She's gone into labour!' This moment was especially amazing since the two Kongs had mated for the first time only three days earlier. With a turnaround time like that, it's remarkable that there isn't a little Kong in every one of the holiday movies.

RACIAL IMAGERY IN *KING KONG*

By Bruce M. Tyler

As popular culture, the King Kong films reflect Americans' fascination with racial imagery, sex, and violence. The films also deal with the themes of barbarism versus civilisation, of beauty and the beast. Kong can be said to symbolise Blacks in America, and all three Kong films – the 1933, 1976, and 1986 versions – reflect the dominant racial practices and values of their times.

Each Kong film has presented a progressively more liberal system of racial values. Thus, the films can be viewed as historical documents mirroring changes in American society and culture.

In the 1933 version, Kong represented Blacks running amok in America. By climbing to the top of the Empire State Building, Kong challenged white power, science, and technology, for the Empire State was at that time the tallest building in the world and perhaps the greatest structural achievement of science. And in capturing a white woman and taking her with him, Kong threatened white civilisation's greatest prize.

Some commentators have interpreted the 1933 version as a symbolic attack on Franklin D. Roosevelt's New Deal programme and on his tacit support of integration. Whether consciously or not, whether politically inspired or not, *King Kong* reinforced the racial status quo and played upon white fears of Blacks. The 1933 film came during a time of major race riots; it came in the midst of the notorious Scottsboro, Alabama, rape trial.

The producers of the 1976 version of *King Kong* made the racial imagery explicit by advertising for a 'well-built' Black man to play Kong. The NAACP protested, and the advertisement was withdrawn. Here, too, Kong grabbed a white woman and climbed atop the tallest building in the world – this time the World Trade Centre, 110 storey high. Once again, Kong challenged white science, white technology, and threatened white womanhood. Once again, Kong was cast in the role of the super-Black, the super-rapist, the revolutionary wreaking havoc on white civilisation.

King Kong Lives, released in 1986, is the most liberal Kong film ever, reflecting the present climate of opinion on race relations. But even though the racial messages are subtle, they are still quite evident. For example, Lady Kong's arrival in Atlanta brings a crowd out, and a Black boy waves a Confederate flag, alerting the viewer to the race theory guiding the film's plot – the race war. Even though Lady Kong and King Kong are in Atlanta, the heart of the 'liberal' or 'new' South, the message is: King Kong versus the Ku Klux Klan.

The army is mobilised to protect the lives and property of private citizens, presumably only whites because few Blacks appear in the film. Every military man is a Southerner, including the commanding officer, Colonel Nevitt (John Ashton), who can't wait to blow Kong to smithereens, and does so at the cost of his own life. A group of hard-drinking white hillbillies form a lynch mob to go after Kong. One says, 'I want that ape's head on the hood of my pickup truck!'

On the other hand, racial liberalism is symbolised in the film by Dr. Amy Franklin (Linda Hamilton), who performs a heart transplant on Kong. She does everything she can, even risking her life, to save Kong from the military. Hank Mitchell (Brian Kerwin), who had brought Lady Kong to Atlanta, risks his life to save both her and King Kong and emerges a humanitarian concerned not only with the physical welfare of the Kongs, but with their dignity as well.

KING OF KONGS?

KINGDOM KONG

By Jeff Giles

Peter Jackson, Fran Walsh and Philippa Boyens are indisputably different people, but it is tempting sometimes to think of them as three voices in one person's head. One voice is exuberant (Boyens), one hilariously bleak (Walsh) and one eternally steady and focused (Jackson). It's late Friday night at Jackson and Walsh's house on a bay outside Wellington, New Zealand. The couple's children are in bed, and there are no scenes to shoot tomorrow, so they're lingering over dinner with Boyens, who wrote the *Lord of the Rings* movies with them, as well as their latest epic picture, *King Kong*. The wine has been poured – more than once. The conversation has become giddy. 'What was the question you asked about the possibility of failure?' Jackson says, attempting to steer the talk toward solid ground. Walsh laughs: 'It's more than the *possibility*. It's the *inevitability*!' Now Jackson laughs. He tries again: 'To live the rest of your life trying to top *Lord of the Rings* would be a foolish and unsatisfying thing to do. So you set your sights on making a thoroughly entertaining movie so that people are not disappointed. It is highly unlikely *King Kong* will ever make more money than *Lord of the Rings*.' Boyens can't stand all this levelheadedness another second. She leans forward. 'Hello?' she says. '*For the record*, *Kong* is going to kick *Lord of the Rings*' ass! It will!' Jackson and Walsh look at her fondly. Then, virtually in unison, they say, 'That's the wine talking.'

All told, the *Rings* trilogy won seventeen Oscars, grossed nearly $3 billion worldwide and made Jackson a superstar director, even as he apologised for looking like a hobbit. (He's since lost 25 pounds, shed his glasses and, at Walsh's urging, begun wearing a somewhat broader palette of colours.) Jackson has wanted to remake *King Kong* since he was thirteen – the 1933 original, with the luminous Fay Wray, is so close to his heart that it couldn't be removed without life-threatening surgery. In 2003 Universal Pictures' Stacey Snider offered him, Walsh and Boyens an extraordinary $20 million advance to write, direct and produce.

Earlier this fall, Jackson invited *Newsweek* to be the first to visit the set of *King Kong*, which is due in theatres next December. His remake takes place in the thirties and is being shot in New Zealand – Weta Digital is building old New York on computer with a fanatical accuracy, using original blueprints and historical records. The movie stars Jack Black (as the obsessive movie director Carl Denham), Naomi Watts (as leading lady Ann Darrow) and Adrien Brody (as Jack Driscoll, in Jackson's version a playwright in the Arthur Miller mode, who's been cajoled into writing Denham's screenplay). Andy Serkis, whose acting was the basis for the digital Gollum, will 'play' Kong, whose prehistoric island is breached by Denham as he hunts for one of the planet's dwindling mysteries. Serkis hasn't begun working with Watts yet. Judging from the menacing grunts and body language he summoned up for a reporter with a moment's notice, he is going to scare

The classic battle to the death from King Kong *(1933). New Zealand fantasy film director Peter Jackson intends to pay homage, by having Kong fight not one but three t-rexes.*

177

the crap out of her.

Jackson hopes to bring the Kong myth to a generation that's allergic to black-and-white movies, confuses *King Kong* with *Godzilla* and never saw the original, just the campy seventies remake. 'I'm 26, and the only thing I knew about Kong was that he got on the Empire State Building and was shot down by planes,' says Colin Hanks, who plays Denham's long-suffering assistant, a new character. 'I watched some of the Jessica Lange version. It's painfully obvious that it's a guy in a monkey suit. I mean, he's literally walking around, looking in windows and going, "Where's Jessica Lange?"'

One morning on the set, Black stands behind an antique hand-cranked Bell & Howell movie camera that's been perched on a nearly full-scale steamer ship on the lot. It's a clear, windy day. Crew members are on an adjacent hill watching the airport so that takeoffs and landings don't ruin the takes: planes fly so low over the lot that you can see the kangaroos painted on their tails. In this scene Black's character, Denham, is filming his own stars, capturing some edgy flirtation between Ann Darrow and her smooth co-star Bruce Baxter. Watts and Kyle Chandler, who plays Baxter, nail the thirties-style inflections in dialogue taken straight from the original. He tells her women are trouble. She stiffens: 'Well, is *that* a nice thing to say!' He retreats: 'Aw, you're all right. But women – they just can't help being a bother. Made that way, I guess.'

Black, playing director to the hilt, eventually calls cut and ad-libs some effusions. 'Wonderful,' he says. 'Does somebody have a hankie, because you are *steaming up* the screen with *true-to-life* emotions! If we could just do one more for luck' – this is a Jacksonism, and there are suppressed smiles all around – 'and let's bring it down a little in the eyes.' Apparently, that's another Jacksonism. The director comes out from inside the ship, headphones around his neck, laughing and telling Black, 'At least you're learning!' Later, Black explains: 'My main job on this movie is not hamming it up too much. My natural tendency is to clown, so, yeah, he has told me on a few occasions, "You need to relax the eyes."' *King Kong* has just begun filming, and it's touching to see the cast and crew make their first overtures at friendship. Told the filmmakers clearly love him, Black replies, 'They love me? How do you know that?' He purses his lips and thinks. 'Well, they *may* love me, but I totally love them twice as much.'

The original *King Kong* is many times greater than the sum of its parts, and whether or not Jackson's remake ever achieves anything like its permanence, it can certainly improve on some things – the animation of Kong, for starters. (The early computer rendering of the gorilla will give you a sense of the realism and ferocity Jackson's after.) It can redress the dated, if not racist, portrayal of the islanders who watch Kong get dragged off in chains. As for the performances in the original, Brody puts it best: 'Fay Wray was fantastic, but [otherwise] the acting is pretty atrocious in parts of it.' Jackson, Walsh, Boyens and Watts met Wray in New York after the Oscars. The director videotaped her briefly, and everyone remembers how Wray, 96, instantly transformed into a movie star, tilting her head and looking beautiful. 'I thought, "My God, I'm actually filming Fay Wray,"' says Jackson. Wray died five months later. 'Pete was devastated,' says Boyens. 'He was in love with her.' She smiles. 'While he was filming Fay, I said to Fran, "Uh-oh, get the camera off him – he's gone geek."'

After dinner at Jackson and Walsh's house, everyone wanders up to the director's den, which, with its Civil War soldiers, its *Lord of the Rings* figures, its movie books and its big flat-screen TV, looks like the room of an independently wealthy twelve-year-old. Jackson shows off some collectibles from the original *Kong*. He has a Kong, made of lead and fake fur and smaller than the palm of your hand, that was used for the shot where the gorilla falls from the Empire State, banging ignominiously against the building on his way down. Also a brontosaurus, three feet long, its skin worn away to reveal a metal frame wrapped with rubber, cotton and thread. 'This is the one that eats the sailor in the tree,' he says. He picks up a model of the top of the Empire State Building, a bit roughly constructed out of cardboard and painted silver: 'That's what I made when I was thirteen.'

Everyone slumps down onto couches, and after prompting from Boyens, Jackson does something unexpected. He plays an 'animatic' – an animated version of a scene made for planning purposes – of the last nine minutes of his movie. In other words: Kong's final stand atop the Empire State, and his fall. The animation is no-frills. The score is a patchwork. And yet the sequence, far different from the original in its choreography and emotional depth, is stunning. Even the sound of biplanes sputtering toward the gorilla is heartbreaking, because you know that Kong is not a villain – and you know what's coming. After the sequence ends, nobody talks. Then Walsh, ordinarily that funny, bleak voice in the head, speaks up. 'People always ask Pete, "Why do you want to remake *King Kong*?"' she says. '*That's* why.'

The Kong and I
Peter Jackson has long been fascinated by 1933's *King Kong*.
1970: Jackson, nine, sees the classic film for the first time.
1974: Tries to remake it at thirteen.
1976: Desperate to see the remake with Jessica Lange – and certain there will be a giant line for tickets – he arrives at theatre at 8 a.m. He waits three hours alone.
1996: Launches ill-fated attempt to remake *Kong* for Universal.
2003: Signs on with Universal again.
2004: Sweeps Oscars with *Rings*, meets Fay Wray, stands atop Empire State Building.

KIWI KONG COMETH!
By Paul A. Woods

Peter Jackson is not making any specious attempt to give the audience a new, 're-imagined' *Kong* for our times, but has placed the narrative faithfully back in the Great Depression – February 1933, to be exact, when the original *King Kong* became a huge hit among the disaffected and desperate Manhattanites whose city he physically assaults (expressing their joyously destructive wish-fulfilment).

As the director now observes of his 1996 plans to remake *Kong*, 'Our first script was sort of *Indiana Jones*-ish and rather flippant.' In the '96 screenplay, Carl Denham's latest picture is to be *Indonesia . . . Hell Hole of the World*, a Third World travelogue-cum-exploitation picture in the vein of *Grass* and *Chang*. (The film's narrator is scheduled to be Denham's buddy 'Ernie' Hemingway – the pugnacious author having been something of a Coop-styled adventurer himself.) Other strands of the Denham-Cooper analogy may still make the final cut – such as Denham refusing to make a big deal out of the fact that his cameraman lost a limb while filming mating bears, insisting, 'Pain is temporary. Film is forever.' (Think of Robert Armstrong as Denham in 1933 – 'I'd have got a swell picture of a charging rhino, but the cameraman got scared' – and Cooper and Schoedsack's personal risk-taking in their travelogue films.)

Rather than trying to make modish changes, the Jackson *Kong* (which started shooting in early September 2004) is following the dramatic structure of the original film, and

Jack Driscoll (Bruce Cabot) is ostensibly the hero of the original Kong. *Fay Wray disliked wom-
aniser Cabot, parodied in Jackson's* King Kong *as actor Bruce Baxter.*

the personae of its main characters. Jackson and his co-screenwriters, Fran Walsh and
Philippa Boyens, are playing up the ruthlessness of Carl Denham, making him a colder
fish than the admirably devil-may-care maverick portrayed by Armstrong.

Jack Black makes Denham into a pipe-smoking cherub, standing all of five foot four
with his moptop hair tucked under a 1930-style wig. 'People do seem surprised at that
casting, which I can understand,' Jackson also conceded to *Empire*. 'We did a little bit of
thinking. "Okay, it's the thirties, what say we model our Denham on the young Orson
Welles?" Like Welles, Denham is a genius with an obsessiveness and recklessness that is
eventually going to lead to tears. Then we thought of Jack.'

Jackson has found an actor who resembles the young Welles circa the infamous *War
of the Worlds* radio scare, and whose mischievous qualities may counter Denham's hard-
assed aspect. The director is also acutely aware of *Kong*'s origins as a film made by film-
maker-adventurers about themselves – the clapperboard used on the deck of the *Venture*
in his remake reads 'A Denham Picture', reminding the more attentive that this is a film
about the (abortive) making of a film.

Ann Darrow, whose beauty lures the savage beast to his doom, is Naomi Watts, the
blonde Australian who first turned heads in David Lynch's hypnotically cryptic *Mulholland
Drive* (2001). Although the ability to deliver lung-bursting screams is still paramount, Ms.
Watts insists that co-writers Walsh and Boyens shared her concern that Ann be something
more than a swooning heroine in distress. 'Who a woman was in the 1930s is very different from the way a woman is today,' she told *Empire*. 'Even though we're playing it in that
period, we've still got to relate to her. You see her backstory, a lot more about who she is,

why she can survive and what makes her loyal to Kong,' she confirms.

Such loyalty was entirely absent from the original, where Fay Wray displayed only abject terror. As director Jackson emphasises, 'Kong is a very old and brutal gorilla, and he's never before felt a single bit of empathy for another living creature.' But, as with Jessica Lange in the '76 remake, and the version of Ann who appears in the jokier, pastiche-laden '96 screenplay, some form of emotional connection will be made.

In one section of the '96 screenplay, Jackson drew upon the same influences that inspired Willis O'Brien to create his painted Skull Island backdrop:

The vegetation is THICK, the JUNGLE DARK. ANCIENT GNARLED TREES twist out of the ground, thick LICHEN and long MOSSES hang from branches and TANGLED VINES. STEAM RISES from festering SWAMPS . . . DEEPER into the island, the steam is VOLCANIC – hissing out of FISSURES and BUBBLING MUD POOLS. The way light and contrast play on the landscape is reminiscent of the etchings of 19th century artist Gustave Doré.

Celebrated illustrator Doré had a cinematic sensibility that pre-dated the birth of cinema itself. Environment lent a realistic perspective and physicality to his mythical human figures, his most dramatic drawings and etchings showing his characters at war with their hostile worlds. The ship of Doré's Ancient Mariner drifts ghostly through a perilous waterway beset by jagged cliffs, like the passage of Poseidon in *Jason and the Argonauts* (1963); *Witches Dancing on a Sabbath* uncannily resembles a sabbat from a black and white horror movie, its influence seen in that occult classic of the silent era, *Haxan* (1922); his subterranean foothills for Milton's *Paradise Lost* are awash with serpents, dragons and other less distinct primordial reptiles. These creatures that ooze out of the crevices of Hell foreshadow those that emanated from O'Brien's psyche.

Jackson's Skull Island is an elaborately designed piece of Hollywood primitivism. As the *Venture* first approaches it out of the fog, the crew are met by the faces of giant stone gods, like those of Easter Island. Throughout production, the *Kong is King!* website ran a commendably geeky series of video production diaries, wherein Jackson, his cast and crew took their core audience on a nuts-and-bolts tour through shooting the remake. 'We've got to create the fog that they're sailing through and the whole ocean voyage, the water simulations,' said VFX supervisor Joe Letteri of the environments artificially created by his team, including a digital version of the *Venture* itself.

In the concept art by Jeremy Bennett, the swamp where the crew are attacked on their raft by the brontosaur is bordered by huge, looming, Doré-inspired trees that block out the sunlight.

In the tradition of the Hollywood epic, there are also giant sets, particularly the Great Wall that Kong eventually breaks through. 'As in the original film, I wanted the wall to have been built by the hand of some ancient civilisation,' explains Jackson. 'And of course the people who occupy Skull Island today are not the people who built this. The people who built these structures have long since disappeared, for whatever reason – something to do with dinosaurs and big gorillas, I suspect.'

As for the other main setting, 'We're creating thousands of extras for New York,' said Joe Letteri, 'we're creating cars and vehicles, taxis, trams, L-trains [elevated trains, like the one Kong punches out], really anything you expect see in a city, we're building it.'

'A lot of people are thinking that New York in New Zealand is kind of a crazy notion,' admitted Jackson, 'why don't we go to New York and shoot it for real? But of course the reality is that shooting modern-day New York as 1933 is almost impossible . . . So what we're doing is we're building a backlot in the Hutt Valley.'

KING KONG COMETH!

This genteel district of Wellington found itself improbably transformed. 'We built a theatre district which was at the lower end of the set,' describes the director. 'We're doing Times Square, we're doing Harold Square, which is where Macy's is, it's New York compressed into two blocks.'

Field research also entailed a trip to the Big Apple itself, unrecognisable from the era of the Great Depression. 'I really wanted to look at the top of the Empire State Building,' said Jackson in the production diaries, his hair blowing about the top of the grand urban monument like that of a wild Skull Island native, 'and I wanted Naomi to look at it too, because in the movie that's where she's going to be at the end.'

This painstakingly literal approach to fantasy was applied to the creation of the city itself. 'There is considerable difference between present New York and 1933 New York,' acknowledged digital building supervisor Chris White. 'A lot of what we see is the amount of high-rise buildings that have been added to the city. The skyline of 1933 is a lot different to what we see today.

Conceptual artist Jeremy Bennett described his colour palette of dark greys and dark brownstone buildings as 'a lot different from what I saw and experienced, it's a lot grimier and dirtier, smoggier . . . It's not a New York that Mayor Giuliani would want to portray to the world . . . . When I think of New York, I think of steam coming out of the sidewalk, this grimy, depressed look.'

('Well everybody knows why there's steam coming out of these sewers in New York,' quipped Jackson, playing on an urban monster myth. 'It's the huge alligators that are breeding under the streets.')

Jackson's extension of the original Cooper/Schoedsack universe is highly referential, if subtly played. 'It has that wonderful mixture of emotion and fantasy,' he says of the 1933 original. 'It's all that we are trying to capture with this film.' *Ain't It Cool News*, the fanboy website that champions Jackson's films, reports that the set of Denham's cabin has authentic vintage photos on the wall of elephants being lifted onto a ship via a large crane (a reference to *Chang*?), while a mocked-up newspaper has a headline reading, 'Gas Bombs Used To Rob Banks' – the very same devices with which Denham incapacitates Kong. Film geek Jackson is also said to use rare 1933 artefacts from his own collection, including a native spear which appears on a wall in one sequence, and the original SS *Venture* life ring, while director of FX photography Alex Funke pointed out that Denham's camera in their remake is the very same one used in the original.

Also among the props is a 'spicy' 1930s pulp magazine titled *Stolen Sweets*, with an alluring Fay Wray-type figure on the cover. But the references extend far beyond such detail, as if Jackson has used the original *Kong* as a template for his film to both pay tribute and justify its own existence. Everything that was taken for granted because it was what the audience themselves were experiencing – the Depression, unemployment – is now made overt. Ann is no longer just a hard-luck case who gets lucky, but an out-of-work actress. When Denham is seen in a diner trying to persuade the hungry Ann to join his production, she tells him about her last job: 'That's a tough audience,' he acknowledges, 'if you don't kill 'em first, they'll kill you.'

'We wanted to keep it true to that thirties style of filmmaking,' verifies costume designer Terry Ryan. 'And because it embraces so many areas that the original hadn't, like vaudeville, burlesque, it tries to show the very dark side of New York.' The weird world of Depression-era vaudeville is briefly glimpsed in a scene featuring jugglers and acrobats, plus a big fat lady and a tiny little woman boxing on stage. ('Give it more muscle,' Jackson shouted jokingly at the monitor, 'we want bleeding noses.')

Meanwhile, out on the freezing February streets, unrest is growing. The area

Bombs away: Merian C. Cooper and a brunette Fay Wray pose with the gas bombs that capture Kong both in the original and in the 2005 remake.

where the 'House of Unemployment' and the Salvation Army soup kitchen are situated has become an urban shanty town called 'Hooverville', after President Herbert Hoover, and looks like a bombed-out tenement from the London Blitz. People down on their luck build shabby placards reading, 'Down With Hoover', and the more revolutionary legend, 'Land To The People'. An extra, playing a cop boasts, 'We show them the nightstick, they generally behave themselves.' There are even some little street urchins and black people in the New York street scenes, more accurately reflecting NYC's social and ethnic mix than the original film (where the only blacks incongruously lived on an uncharted island southwest of Sumatra).

In the production diaries, Jackson proudly shows off one of his most treasured *Kong* artefacts to Jack Black: the original Edgar Wallace *Kong* script. 'Did you get the first draft on ebay?' asks Black with beady-eyed curiosity. When Jackson guardedly answers, 'Uhh, I got the first draft from somewhere else,' Black cracks up with laughter at the suggestion that his director's obsessiveness will stop at nothing.

Also in the production diaries, Jackson responded to the question, 'Why did you decide to do your remake in the 1930s, and not in modern times?': 'The main answer is that I wanted to do the sequence with Kong fighting the biplanes on top of the Empire State Building,' confirmed the director, illustrated by his collection of model World War One aircraft – and an animatic showing a dark Kong on the Manhattan skyline. 'I think the other reason is it's the last age of exploration, if you like. It's the last time period in which there could be those blank spots on the atlas.'

Even the SS *Venture* is placed in more direct danger than in the original film, in the form of a violent storm. And the sequence where a driven Denham confesses to Driscoll that their destination is Skull Island – 'The last remnant of a dead civilisation. It's gonna vanish, Jack. This island is sinking. It's going to disappear from the face of the earth . . .' – seems to be derived from *Son of Kong*, where both the island and the title character meet a watery grave.

Despite his use of modern technology, Jackson insists, 'I'm wanting the film to be deliberately old-fashioned, a mysterious escapist film like the ones I used to love as a kid.

KING KONG COMETH!

The Tarzan movies or the ones with a forgotten world full of dinosaurs.' Expressing bemusement at the high-tech sci-fi strain in most modern fantasy (with the notable exception of his own Tolkien adaptations), the monstermeister stressed, 'I want a throwback to scary natives and island monsters.'

Reacting against the heresy of the De Laurentiis remake, where the nearest thing to a dinosaur is a single giant serpent, the director aimed to be as palaentologically correct as possible. During one respite from filming, Jackson reminisced to the video camera:

'In the original movie, you may remember, the sailors were shooting at a brontosaur – I think it may have been the only carnivorous brontosaur in the world. There's this wonderful scene of the brontosaur tipping the raft into the swamp, and staggering out of it after the sailors. The original brontosaur from 1933 still survives and is very close by,' he intimated, before producing the original Marcel Delgado model from his collection like the middle-aged fanboy he is. Threadbare and shedding its stuffing, the model is clearly a cherished piece of history.

'There are actually a couple of shots at the beginning of the brontosaur scene that were done with a mechanical brontosaur head rising out of the water. It wasn't stop-motion animation,' Jackson elaborates. Naturally, he owns the original mechanical model of the dinosaur's head too. 'You can actually recognise its little head from the original film. Of course, the irony is today that we don't have miniature dinosaurs anymore, they're all gonna be computer-generated.'

And then, of course, there are the things that lurk at the bottom of the chasm where the sailors fall to their deaths – in this case, wetas, the word taken not from an acronym but from the name of an insect indigenous to New Zealand. 'Mix a scorpion, a centipede, a tapeworm and a lobster together and imagine the creature . . . attacking the *Venture*,' observed *Ain't It Cool* of the CGI beast termed 'the swamp monster'. It so happens that this description also fits the insect that's far from exotic to many NZ households, and which plays a deadly role in Jackson's realisation of the 'spider scene' – the infamous excised sequence of the 1933 original. This time, one assumes, the director will have no need to excise the spider scene because 'it slows down the action'.

'Peter Jackson is making a modern day $200 million Ray Harryhausen film,' said *Ain't It Cool*'s Quint, paying tribute to the veteran stop-motion animator who made his own pilgrimage to his fan Jackson's set. 'The much publicised dinos are just the tip of the iceberg.'

By far the most demanding of the computer simulations will be Kong himself – a gradual CGI construction that evolved slowly throughout the shoot, only completed during post-production. As Jackson correctly (if regretfully) surmises, the malevolent toy that was the original Kong would invite less terror today than derision, to a technically jaded generation that expects its imaginary beasts to look *real* rather than awe-inspiring. (Even the 1933 *Variety* review stressed that Kong's jerky animated movements required suspension of disbelief. But audiences of the Great Depression had not witnessed an endless stream of sterile technological miracles. In their need to escape from the mundane terror of poverty, they were more likely to *work with the film* and enter a world of dark fantasy.)

As Jackson says of his own reliance on computer graphics, 'There's not even any need today to build a giant robot hand, like the first version or the Dino film in the seventies.' But still, his tall, dark leading man would be incarnated by a real actor behind the CGI.

The distinctive features of Anglo-Iraqi performer Andy Serkis, formerly the flesh-and-blood figure behind Gollum in the *Rings* films, were disguised behind a black motion capture suit with an artificial bulge around the belly that made his shape resemble a gorilla. Serkis would also, as Naomi Watts explained, provide 'a pair of eyes for me to look at,' rather than a blue screen.

'I'm lit up like a Christmas tree,' he observed of the approximately 60 markers dotted all over his body. 'That data is fed into the computer, and what it does is record it. So if there's a movement, all those cameras will pick up that movement.'

All his movements were projected onto the CGI-created Kong. The actor describes himself as 'puppeteering that character', working in 'a very experimental space'. Ms. Watts claimed to be 'completely transported when I look at him,' while Serkis, unconsciously evoking the potency of the original *Kong*, observed, 'Just because we can't touch each other doesn't mean we can't get inside each other's heads.' With Fran Walsh and Philippa Boyens present on set, scenes were rewritten as Kong's character developed throughout filming, with the help of his human counterpart.

Wearing a strange helmet device with a mike that helped simulate a gorilla's growl, Serkis struck anthropoid poses and movements with the eerie authenticity of an actor permitted to study silverback gorillas at London Zoo, and the 'gorillas in the mist' in their native Rwanda, at close quarters – to the extent of being able to vocalise the apes' varying emotions and moods, catalysing Ms. Watts' reactions with simian noises and threatening growls. In the manner of the extensive research behind Tim Burton's otherwise disappointingly 're-imagined' *Planet of the Apes* (2001), Serkis compares how 'in the 1933 version Kong was bipedal, standing up on two feet. Now we all know that gorillas are quadruped and it takes a lot of effort to get up on two feet.'

As director Jackson confirms, 'With modern technology there is a reason to do it: You can do a photo-realistic gorilla.' But the actor at least seems to recognise how Kong properly occupies a world of gods and monsters, rather than mere apes and monkeys. 'If you do it totally real,' he conceded to *Empire*, 'it might not have the dramatic impact.'

'He's not gonna be sweet and cuddly,' enthused Jack Black. 'He's a fucking carnivore, as in, *eats flesh*!' Which brings to mind the still strangely shocking scenes of Kong chewing on a Skull Island native in his mouth, or biting the head from some luckless joe in New York City. (These scenes could always be seen in the largely uncensored British prints, which, unlike in the US, were not recalled for cuts on re-release – though the almost pristine prints of the film in circulation since the 1990s make the violence much clearer.)

It certainly pays off on the promise of the '96 screenplay's more intense moments:
A NATIVE loses his balance and topples off! He THUDS INTO THE GROUND at KONG'S FEET . . . KONG quickly scoops him up and BITES HIS HEAD OFF in a PG 13 kinda way!
The SURVIVING NATIVES scatter! KONG rampages after them, STOMPING ON THEM and BITING THEIR HEADS OFF . . . in a scene that not only gets a PG 13, but is PRAISED by the MPAA for its sensitivity!

However, Serkis had something to say about Kong's depiction as a carnivorous gorilla. 'I'm very keen for Kong to remain a vegetarian,' he insisted. 'He doesn't eat people; he just kills them.' For the sake of authenticity, it seems that biting off heads is acceptable – as long as the big ape doesn't *chew* on them.

Jackson has also aimed to standardise Kong's height, describing him as 'a 25-foot gorilla on the loose' in the 1996 screenplay and later placing his proportionate height at around 30 feet for the film. As revealed by the trailer, both his dimensions and his animal characteristics are mightily impressive. But still, such a literal frame of reference seems a little unfaithful to the Cooper/O'Brien conception.

That the original Kong varies from a mere eighteen to a full fifty feet when on the rampage in New York – via way of the classic poster that shows him towering disproportionately over the skyscrapers of NYC, hundreds of feet tall – is part of what makes this cinematic shaggy ape story into a surrealistic archetype. And besides, the trailer for

Jackson's film offers no explanation of how a 30-foot tall anthropoid can comfortably hold a grown woman, approximately five and a half feet tall, in the palm of his hand. (By this writer's inexpert calculation, Kong would have to be around 60 feet tall for the proportions to make sense.) Sometimes, perhaps, fantasy and realism are best kept apart.

Andy Serkis also took on the human role of Lumpy, the tattooed, chainsmoking cook of the *Venture* who never takes the cheroot out of his mouth. Jackson's film has increased the number of original characters, Lumpy now assisted in the catering by Choy, played by Lobo Chan – an echo of Chinese cook Charley in the original film. Other expansions include the subdivision of male romantic interest/hero Jack Driscoll into two characters: Driscoll himself – now a playwright slumming it in Hollywood, author of a Broadway comedy called *Cry Havoc!*, and played by the distinctly European-looking Adrien Brody – and Bruce Baxter, Denham's leading man, portrayed by Kyle Chandler. Both his name and his pomaded black hair are knowing references to Bruce Cabot, who

The original version of Kong's last stand: the biplanes move in on him, state-of-the-art military technology back then, period pieces now . . .

played Driscoll in the original film. Like Cabot, Baxter is a self-styled ladies' man who, in a nice piece of intertextual reference, leaves Ann Darrow cold the same way in which the actor Cabot failed to impress Fay Wray.

('Fay Wray adored Cooper, Robert Armstrong, and most everyone connected with the making of the picture . . . with one notable exception,' writes *Kong* expert Steve Vertlieb, who interviewed Miss Wray in her later years. 'She detested Bruce Cabot and said that she found him crude and offensive. While she remained ladylike at all times in her comments to me, she hinted that he had tried to put the moves on her. She didn't encourage or appreciate his advances.')

Denham also has a cameraman named Preston, played by Colin Hanks (son of Tom), while Brit juvenile star Jamie Bell, the dancing prodigy of *Billy Elliott*, appears as a cabin boy named Jamie, who indulges in a little period hoofing with vaudeville trouper Ann.

On 29 June, 2005, the first trailer for the uncompleted *King Kong* was premiered at cinemas as support to another remake, Spielberg's post-9/11, nuclear-family-in-peril revision of *War of the Worlds*. Confounding all expectations that it would hold back any 'money shots' of Kong, maybe teasing with a dark shadow and a loud roar in the way that the 1933 trailers did, director Jackson opted to put his wares on display.

'One of the key decisions was how much, or how little, to show of Kong,' confided the filmmaker. 'We really felt strongly that we really did want to show Kong, because *King Kong* has so much more to offer – its story, its themes and its characters – than what our gorilla looks like.'

Brave words, by which his film may ultimately be judged. As for the trailer itself, it offers a guide as to how Jackson has embellished his classic source material:

The trailer opens in the shadow of the Empire State Building, with nattily 1930s-attired Carl Denham telling his assistant, Preston, 'I want the crew on the ship within the hour . . . Tell them the studio are pressuring us for an early departure.'

'It's not ethical!' protests Preston.

'What are they gonna do, sue me?' bites back Denham. 'They'll have to get in line.' (Jackson's Denham is, it seems, already a target of litigation – unlike the Robert

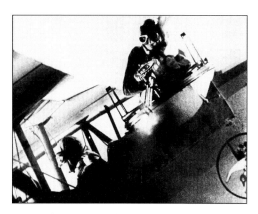 

. . . and open fire. The pilot and gunner are Merian C. Cooper and Ernest B. Schoedsack. Peter Jackson is said to be emulating Cooper's wish to 'kill the sonofabitch' himself.

Armstrong original who only fell from grace in the aftermath of Kong's rampage, in Son of Kong.*) 'I'm not gonna let 'em kill my film!' As they cross the street to take a yellow cab, Denham soberly warns, 'We have three hours to find a new leading lady or we're finished.'*

Denham speaks in voiceover: 'There are thousands of actresses out of work in this city.' He watches with fascination as beautiful blonde Ann Darrow, down on her luck, steals an apple from a sidewalk vendor. 'Somewhere out there is a woman born to play this role,' intones Denham. A close-up on anxious, bonneted Ann dissolves into the SS Venture *at quayside.*

Denham's voiceover continues: 'A woman who will journey into the heart of the unknown. Towards a fateful meeting that changes everything.' Ann and Jack Driscoll first set eyes on each other aboard the ship, in a scene pregnant with romantic cliché.

The Universal Pictures logo appears, followed by a cut to a montage of seafaring shots. 'I've come into possession of a map,' continues Denham, as the camera closes in upon it. 'An uncharted island.' Cut away to three death's head skulls lined up in a row – then back to a concerned Ann and Jack. 'To a place that was thought to exist only in myth.'

'*Whoa! There's a wall ahead!*' *young Jimmy calls down from the crow's nest. They brace for impact as the* Venture *runs into a sea wall – the ship already running into more physical danger than in the 1933 version.*

'*Up until now,*' *continues Denham's voiceover, to shots of a mist-wreathed Skull Island.* '*That's where I'm going to shoot my picture!*' *he promises in a dramatic whisper, as the camera tracks toward it.*

'*You're feeling uneasy, Ann.*' *Denham gives direction on the island, as the crew watch and cameraman Herb shoots the scene. The screen cuts back and forth to the island's native tribe, more dusky than black, a lost sub-Pacific race.* '*The feeling's washing over you.*' *Cut to the menacing painted face of a tribal elder.* ('*In the rain his skin is as deeply black as a pool of oil, his stringy hair clinging to his head,*' *as* Ain't It Cool *describes a face-painted tribesman who fits much the same description.) One dark-skinned young girl raises her arm aloft as if offering herself, heavy-eyed and seemingly drugged – she is obviously the bridal sacrifice to Kong.*

'*Scream, Ann! Scream for your life!*' *Ann shrieks, hitting the higher registers in the style of Fay Wray, emoting in exactly the way that Miss Wray did when Robert Armstrong put her through her paces. She receives a guttural reply in kind that emanates from the bedrock of the island, the hum of insects and the chirruping of exotic birds suddenly overwhelmed by a distant, deep roar. The camera rapidly backtracks from a giant cave as the island's bestial monarch is heard for the first time.*

Jackson himself applied a similar directorial technique to 'the scene where Ann realises that Kong has a curiosity about her, and that curiosity may be the one thing that keeps her alive.' He directed Naomi Watts to play to thin air, and the sound of Kong's guttural grunts:

'Throws her down. She lands, he's suspicious. She looks dead, and he prods! Another prod! He's not sure, he sniffs, sniffing. *One last big prod!*'

Then, in the manner of Denham urging Ann to 'scream for your life!', he intensified his directions: '*You're terrified, you're gonna die!* His rage is building, he's gonna kill you! He's getting angrier, *he's gonna kill you!*'

'*FROM ACADEMY AWARD-WINNING DIRECTOR PETER JACKSON,*' *reads the legend. It's nighttime on the island, as we hear the banshee wail of the scary shaman-witch-doctor. Ann is a prisoner of the native tribe, her arms bent brutally up her back. The indigenous young bride of Kong, who has been given a respite, stares impassively at her. Cut to the* Venture *crew – led by an anxious Jack and Lumpy the cook, looking desperately for Ann.* '*Miss Darrow!*' *shouts Jimmy.* '*By the wall!*' *comes the distant shout of the man who first spots her – manacled by her wrists atop an elevated stone platform, lit with torch fire. All throughout this montage of scenes, Howard Shore's theme music builds threateningly to a percussive climax, redolent of the ominousness of* Jaws *and the repetitive orchestral theme for the original Japanese* Godzilla.

Close-up on the eyes of Kong, flickering open – ancient, contemplative, expressive, and authentically simian. We see the hyperventilating but fascinated face of Denham, as he watches Kong reach out to take the unconscious Ann, and the anxiety and horror of Jack as he locks and loads on his rifle.

'Kong is basically the last of his own species,' Andy Serkis explained the symbiosis of beauty and beast to *Empire*. 'He knows that once he dies, his species is gone. So the drive to find a mate is unbelievably powerful. That comes out in a frustrated aggression. He connects that the bride sacrifices are female and he is male, but he is overcome by this intolerable rage because he can't mate with them . . .'

We see the verdant flora and untamed landscape of Skull Island in the daylight, as

Jack leads the search party in the first of a frenetic montage of scenes:

The crew are rapidly pursued by an araptosaur that emerges from the swamp. One crewman fires his rifle at a small velociraptor. Ann runs for her life, while the crew run for theirs from a bevy of seamless CGI brontosaurs, Denham running with an old tripod camera on his shoulder.

Denham flails frantically against a vast mass of giant predatory insects (including wetas). Cut to Ann and Jack embracing – then to Kong in New York City, throwing a vintage yellow cab through the air. It smashes to pieces as an hysterical crowd run hither and thither in different directions.

The portion of the 1990s screenplay that reads, 'KONG BOUNDS AFTER THE CAB, running on FOURS with incredible speed' has been faithfully retained. Kong also remains the authentically simian creature (though somewhat darker) described in Jackson and Walsh's '96 script:

. . . a 25 foot SILVER-BACK GORILLA. His fur is MATTED, ANCIENT SCARS mark his body – evidence of life and death struggles with unknown beasts. His face is AGED – SILVER HAIR predominant. He is resting on his KNUCKLES . . .

A relatively youthful, kick-ass Captain Englehorn opens fire on the dinosaurs with tommy guns. (Jackson has provided the crew of the Venture *with enough heavy-duty firearms to mow the primordial reptiles down – though it doesn't prevent just as many of them meeting a bitter end as in the first film.)One sailor delivers a well-aimed kick at the jaw of a velociraptor. Ann falls from a tree, to be caught by Kong as a tyrannosaurus rex advances, trying to bite the terrified woman out of his grasp with a snap of its jaw.*

Jack frantically pursues Kong and Ann through the streets of Manhattan, jumping over a snowpile as Kong leaps through the air, landing on a vegetable truck.

Shocked Ann is gripped by the arms by uniformed guards at the King Kong presentation on Broadway. Lumpy frantically reaches to a comrade falling from a log into a ravine. One crewman is sucked underwater by an amphibious dinosaur. Jimmy howls with despair. Ann and Jack run for it.

Ann is confronted by a growling t-rex, when Kong suddenly leaps in to protect her, his huge, impossibly agile legs thudding against the ground. The silverback gorilla becomes a monster for the only time in the trailer, as he gives a menacing, open-mouthed roar, then closes his jaw with an audible crack of bone.

First showcased in December 2004, by an arresting piece of conceptual art in *Newsweek* that showed Kong fighting the tyrannosaur, the fight sequence will run in the completed film at seven minutes long. As seen in animatics displayed in the production diaries, the t-rexes have a lopingly organic walk equal to anything in *Jurassic Park*. As described by Quint of *Ain't It Cool*, who viewed a six-minute animatic cut, it begins with a lone Ann wandering across a group of prehistoric crocodiles, and hiding behind a tree. Just as it seems they're about to close in on her hiding place, they're yanked out of frame in a cacophony of screams and growls.

Her saviour is a tyrannosaurus rex – but the king of dinosaurs is also about to claim her as its own. As it gives chase, the flesh of its original prey falls from his mouth, Ann staying a few steps ahead until, at the end of the protracted chase sequence, she's trapped at the edge of a chasm with nowhere to run to.

Enter Kong. He picks her up and holds her aloft with one hand, fighting off the t-rex with the other. It's here that Jackson doubles up on O'Brien's classic sequence, with the entrance of the second t-rex. Also unlike the O'Brien original, the great ape goes at it like a total-combat streetfighter, rather than the humanoid dirty boxer of 1933. As Kong saves Ann from his jaws by interposing his bicep, he roars with pain as the dinosaur rips a lump of flesh from his arm. The great ape drops her, but she's saved from her fall by his foot. With both fists free, he tears into the reptiles, beating them hands down until the arrival of yet a third t-rex forces Ann to run for her life again.

Ann and Kong both fall over a cliff, but she manages to save herself by catching hold of a vine. She nearly ends in the jaws of one of the tyrannosaurs, however, leading Kong to abandon a fight down below and make a frantic climb up the cliff face. This is the cue for Kong to crash back into frame as seen in the trailer, and the *mano-a-mano* sequence that most closely pays tribute to the t-rex clash in the original film – but it's apparently less of a contest this time, Kong mercilessly ripping into the solitary dinosaur until, in an iconic scene that resonates down the decades, he wiggles the reptile's slack jaw to make sure it's dead.

Even with some of Ann's flight from terror still playing against blue screen, and many of the digital effects still unfinished, the last three minutes of this sequence drew rapturous cheers and applause when previewed at the San Diego Comic-Con on 16 July 2005, two weeks after the trailer previewed in theatres.

As this book goes to press, *King Kong* is undoubtedly the movie marketing event of the decade, in a manner that may be out of proportion to its significance as a film. (However good it is, it can only ever be a remake of a classic film from an earlier time – one that didn't need action figures or Happy Meals to make its impact.)

Universal have released a poster that shows a growling, quadruped Kong sitting atop the Empire State Building, beset by Helldiver biplanes. As obsessive Kong fan Jackson explains, 'They're the American naval plane of the early 1930s, and they are the same aircraft as they use in the original film.' As the Helldiver is 'an extinct aircraft . . . you can't even buy a plastic model kit,' research of the original factory drawings was required at the Smithsonian Institute before Jackson could place Jim Dietz, a favourite World War One artist of his, at the helm of one of the biplanes.

Rumours that Jackson himself would take the bit part of the gunner who finally brings down Kong are as yet unconfirmed. But it's highly likely that the Kiwi director, who has a habit of making brief appearances in his own films, will be unable to resist placing himself in the same position that Merian C. Cooper and Ernest B. Schoedsack once did, when Cooper insisted, 'Let's kill the sonofabitch ourselves!'

And yet, it remains to be seen whether Jackson's interpretation will retain all the mythic qualities of the character. When speaking to two of the *Kong* purists who contributed to this book, Steve Vertlieb and Paul Mandell, it was striking that each writer made the same objection to the Kong glimpsed in the trailer: 'He's a *gorilla* . . . he looks just like the ape in the remake of *Mighty Joe Young*.'

Which may well appease today's youth audience, with their insistence on apparent realism in all things – particularly in fantasy, it seems. But our contributors are from an earlier generation of 'film geeks' who were in many ways easier to please, and yet more demanding in terms of imaginative input.

The Kong that roars at the t-rex that threatens Ann Darrow in the Jackson trailer is a formidable beast. But King Kong, as has been stated in these pages, is not merely a giant gorilla. His malevolent, fanged teddy-bear visage is no one's idea of anthropoid authenticity – and yet, laughable as Cooper and O'Brien's conception may appear to oversophisticated modern audiences, he remains an archetypal monster of the imagination to anyone who (like Jackson) first encountered him at a sufficiently impressionable age.

Peter Jackson's Kong can certainly walk the simian walk, and possesses a subterranean growl that rises from the pit of his stomach like a volcano ejecting lava from Hell.

In remaking King Kong *for a modern audience, Peter Jackson has promised to recreate the famous lost scene where the sailors (centre) cling on for dear life as the spiders close in.*

But it's a moot point as to whether he will ever supplant O'Brien's little stop-motion behemoth in the popular imagination.

At an early press conference for the remake, Jack Black was asked by Japanese journalist Riebo Shibasaki, from *Cut* magazine, whether he was aware of the Toho movie *King Kong vs. Godzilla*. 'King Kong – the king of all monsters,' came the contemplative response. 'Even better than Godzilla. He's smarter and stronger than Godzilla. Godzilla's a stupid lizard.'

As the press laughed at his pop-culture chauvinism, Black hit upon what makes the great ape such an iconic beast: the personification of animalistic male rage. 'King Kong is almost a man. A giant man. *Sasquatch!*'

ACKNOWLEDGEMENTS

This book would not exist were it not for the goodwill, enthusiasm and expert knowledge of the following contributors: Steve Vertlieb, Kevin Brownlow, Lawrence French, Danny Peary.

Special thanks to Paul Mandell for his contributions and advice.

The following articles appear by courtesy of their respective copyright holders: 'Introduction' by Paul A. Woods. Copyright © 2005 by Plexus Publishing Limited. 'Missing Links: The Jungle Origins of *King Kong*' by Gerald Peary, from *The Girl in the Hairy Paw*, edited by Ronald Gottesman and Harry Geduld, Avon Books, 1976. This revised version copyright © 2004 by Gerald Peary. *Chang* by Kevin Brownlow, from *The War, the West and the Wilderness*, Alfred A. Knopf, 1979. Copyright © 1979 by Kevin Brownlow. 'His Majesty, *King Kong*' by Donald F. Glut, from *Classic Movie Monsters*, Scarecrow Press, 1978. Copyright © 1978 by Donald F. Glut. *The Lost World* and 'The King of Kongs' by Denis Gifford, from *A Pictorial History of Horror Movies*, Hamlyn, 1973. Copyright © 2005 by the Estate of Denis Gifford. '*The Lost World*: Merely Misplaced?' by Scott MacQueen, from *American Cinematographer*, June 1992. Copyright © 1992 by Scott MacQueen. 'Restoration: *The Lost World*' by Lokke Heiss, from *Cinefantastique*, May 1998. Copyright © 1998 by Lokke Heiss. 'The Men Who Saved *King Kong*' by Steve Vertlieb, from *The Monster Times* issue three, March 1972. This is the second part of an article that ran over two issues of *The Monster Times*, edited into a longer form for *The Girl in the Hairy Paw*, edited by Ronald Gottesman and Harry Geduld, Avon Books, 1976. Copyright © 1972 by Steve Vertlieb. 'Interview with Ray Harryhausen' by Lawrence French. Copyright © 2005 by Lawrence French. *King Kong* by Danny Peary, from *Cult Movies*, Vermilion, 1982. Copyright © 1982 by Danny Peary. 'Beauties and Beasts: The Eroticism of *King Kong*' by Steve Vertlieb. Copyright © 2005 by Steve Vertlieb. 'Untold Horrors of Skull Island' by Paul Mandell, from *Cinemagic* issue 30, 1985. Copyright © 1985 by Paul Mandell. 'Orphan in the Storm: *Son of Kong*' by Gerald Peary, from *Film Heritage*, winter 1973-4.

Copyright © 1973 by Gerald Peary. 'Father of *Kong* Farewell – Willis O'Brien in Memoriam' by Forrest J Ackerman, from *Famous Monsters of Filmland* issue 22, April 1963. Copyright © 1963 by Forrest J Ackerman. '"King Kong Appears in Edo" (A Literal Translation): The Toho Kong Years' by Ken Hollings. Copyright © 2005 by Ken Hollings. 'An Open Letter to Universal and Dino De Laurentiis' by Paul Mandell, from *Cinefantastique*, spring 1976. Revised version copyright © 2005 by Paul Mandell. 'Return of the Urban Gorilla – The Two *Kong*s: A Comparative Review' by Kenneth Thompson, from *Films Illustrated*, volume six, issue six, February 1977. Copyright © 1977 by Kenneth Thompson. 'They Killed *King Kong*' by Robert F. Wilson, Jr., from *American Classic Screen*, volume two, issue one, September/October 1977. Copyright © 1977 by Robert F. Wilson, Jr. 'The Ape Goes East' by Pete Tombs. Copyright © 2005 by Pete Tombs. '*King Kong Lives*: Is It Monkey Sequel, Monkey Do?' by Will Murray, from *Starlog* issue 113, December 1986. Copyright © 1986 by Starlog Communications, Inc./Will Murray. *King Kong Lives* review by Roger Ebert, from *Chicago Sun-Times*, 22 December 1986. Copyright © 1986 by Roger Ebert. 'Racial Imagery in *King Kong*' by Bruce M. Tyler, from *Black Film Review*, volume three, number one, winter 1986-7. Copyright © 1986 by Bruce M. Tyler. 'Kingdom Kong' by Jeff Giles, from *Newsweek*, 5 December 2004. Copyright © 2004 by *Newsweek*. 'Kiwi *Kong* Cometh!' by Paul A. Woods. Copyright © 2005 by Plexus Publishing Limited.

It has not been possible in all cases to trace the copyright sources, and the publishers would be glad to hear from any such copyright holders.

The publishers would like to thank the following individuals and film companies for providing photographs and illustrations: Steve Vertlieb; Kevin Brownlow; Photoplay Productions; Lawrence French; Danny Peary; Paul Mandell; Paul Woods; Pete Tombs; Something Weird Video; Distributors Production Organization; Miramax; Warner Bros.; RKO; Toho; Paramount.